My Random Death

A Memoir

Myra Mossman

My Random Death
by Myra Mossman

Insight Institute Press
1501-H Santa Barbara St.
Santa Barbara, CA 93101
info@myrandomdeath.com
myrandomdeath.com

Copyright © 2019 Myra Mossman.

I have tried to recreate events, locales, dreams, and conversations from my memories of them. In order to maintain their anonymity, in some instances I have given people nicknames.

All rights reserved. No part of this book may be reproduced, transmitted, or stored in an information retrieval system in any form or by any means, graphic, electronic, or mechanical, including photocopying, taping, and recording, without prior permission in writing from the publisher.

Holy Bible, New International Version®, NIV® Copyright ©1973, 1978, 1984, 2011 by Biblica, Inc.® Used by permission. All rights reserved worldwide.

Three newspaper articles reproduced by permission: Vineyard Gazette © 1978, 1979, 2019. All rights reserved worldwide.

Library of Congress Control Number: 2018912590
ISBN: 978-1-7329275-0-6

Publisher's Cataloging-In-Publication Data
(Prepared by The Donohue Group, Inc.)

Names: Mossman, Myra, author.
Title: My random death : a memoir / Myra Mossman.
Description: Santa Barbara, CA : Insight Institute Press, [2019]
Identifiers: ISBN 9781732927506 | ISBN 9781732927513 (ebook)
Subjects: LCSH: Mossman, Myra. | Victims of crimes--United States--Biography. | Women--Crimes against--Psychological aspects. | Near-death experiences. | Courage. | Intuition. | LCGFT: True crime stories. | Autobiographies.
Classification: LCC HV6250.4.W65 M67 2019 (print) | LCC HV6250.4.W65 (ebook) | DDC 362.88082092--dc23

Edited by Barbara Ardinger
Book and cover design by Deborah Perdue, Illumination Graphics
Book production coordinated by To Press & Beyond
Author's cover photo by Doug Ellis Photography

Printed in the USA

For my mother and father,
Phyllis and Teddy Mossman

Part 1

Chapter 1

MY SECOND-YEAR AT UNIVERSITY includes a couple of anthropology courses with Professor Silverman. I once asked him if there is such a thing as mankind. He paused a moment, then told me he's not sure.

Professor Silverman is a brilliant, cultural anthropologist. Maybe five feet, seven inches tall, he is a true hunchback with thick lips, a large bulbous nose, and a Beatles mop of jet-black hair. The way he teaches his students to analyze and conceptualize captivates me.

From the time I was a baby (I was born in 1955), I've known a few things about myself. I have an identical twin sister named Marla and a younger brother named Jamie. I am Jewish. I have to graduate from a university. I have to have a career. I have to find a husband and get married. These notions were embedded in my childhood psyche by my parents as the principal definition of myself.

A muffled sound interrupts my ruminations about my upbringing when a fellow classmate collides with a column. He careens off it and stumbles to the bar, which was set up for the student-faculty party in the basement of the social science building. Although my inclination is toward introversion, especially in crowds, curiosity moves me out of the shadows. I think the drunk will know what I want to find out.

"Hey." I nod toward the dance floor and point with my chin at the odd couple. "Who is she?" I can't believe she's dancing with Silverman.

Watery eyes follow my gesture. "His wife."

His boozy breath and his answer hit me at the same time. I half expected the former, but the latter surprises me. Silverman's wife is a stunner with exotic red lips and long, straight hair. I watch the affectionate way she touches his face and how her hips press against him during the slow songs. From where I'm standing on the sidelines of the low-lit, makeshift dance hall, she looks Polynesian. He did fieldwork over there.

It is the spring of 1975. My current pursuit is a bachelor's degree at the University of Western Ontario in London, Ontario. Which brings me to the essay due for Silverman and the reason why I have to leave the party early. I came to just check who was here. I planned on drafting the outline of the paper tonight, but most of the research and writing will have to wait. My presence at a wedding more than 120 miles away takes priority. The soon-to-be husband isn't mine. He belongs to a third cousin on my mother's side.

The next morning, I dig a suitcase out of the front closet. In go enough underwear, blue jeans, and everyday clothes for the weekend trip home. A little black dress gets folded up, along with a sweater and a pair of black, high-heeled shoes, pantyhose, and a small purse. This is my fancy wedding attire. My sister packed her stuff last night. Frankly, a lot of the clothes I wear were commandeered from her.

Although Marla and I started out at the same place, somewhere along the way I lost my fashion sense. When we were infants, our mother took us clothes shopping and thought it was cute to dress her twins in identical clothing. As toddlers, we hardly noticed, but by the time we were eleven or twelve years old, we decided it was dorky to dress alike, although exceptions were made for our younger but wiser brother Jamie's bar mitzvah and our sweet sixteen birthday party.

Marla and I figured out that buying two of the same thing limited our options. Then the issue of sharing arose. On any given day, we would inevitably argue about who could wear what. As far as Jamie, who is three and three-quarter years younger, was concerned, our arguments over clothes happened far too often. It was probably the main reason he became a practical joker at the age of ten or eleven.

Once, when I was about to open my closet, I heard a light tap, tap. Fingers appeared at the bottom of the door. I jumped a foot, only to find my brother hiding in the closet. Another time, while my twin and I were sunbathing in our bikinis, a large, hairy spider dropped from out of nowhere and landed on Marla's belly. She screamed and tried to brush it off as I rushed over to help. Then we heard giggles and looked up. It was Jamie, of course. He'd tied a plastic spider on a string and was dangling it out of the open window above us. And then there were a few nights when a bodiless voice haunted my bedroom and called out, "Mmmyyyrrraaa. Mmmyyyrrraaa. Mmmyyyrrraaa." I was in bed, petrified, with the covers pulled up to my nose. As it turned out, Jamie had jury-rigged a microphone, so it would travel from one side of the two-story house, where he was, all the way across the roof to my side, where it hung outside my window.

Jamie's pranks always scared us, though afterwards, my sister and I laughed. We loved him even more because his tricks were successful. However, the verbal fights our parents got into, usually about the lack of money, upset all three of us kids. More often than not, our mother provoked the arguments because our father was not much of a yeller. He was more the passive-aggressive type and hid problems from her until it was too late to really do anything about them. So there was lots of shouting around our house. Over time, my sister and I mostly grew out of yelling. Not our mother. She developed into a full-blown rager and could erupt over anything.

As a result of my mother's raging, I became confused about my style. Marla was not, so I began to defer to her sense of fashion, her taste, her finely tuned artistic eye. This resulted in my often borrowing her clothes. My favorite item was a pale pink version of the white dress that Marilyn Monroe wore in the movie *The Seven Year Itch,* in the scene where she stood over the subway grate and the skirt flew up to reveal her panties.

❈

Because of our third cousin's upcoming wedding, Marla and I have luggage. Our plan is to take the train rather than hitchhike to Windsor, Ontario, where our parents and brother live and where we grew up. We catch a city bus at the corner near our apartment building and arrive at London's downtown Canadian National Railways (CNR) station. We purchase our tickets, then race onto the wide-open platform, currently bare of people, just as the whistle screeches and the conductor yells out, "All aboard!"

Red-capped CNR porters help us store our baggage, and then, almost out of breath, Marla and I settle into our seats, facing each other, our knees about a foot apart. The train rumbles up to speed and comes to a gentle, rocking motion that lulls us into silence. Looking out the big windows, we watch the cityscape whiz past. Then wild woods outside of town give way to an occasional, colorful billboard that advertises a hotel or an eatery in a small town. We pass forests and lush orchards and the farmers' fields that give southwestern Ontario its nickname, The Fruit and Vegetable Basket of Canada.

Luckily, our car is almost empty. About half an hour into the ride, we begin talking about the upcoming wedding, which leads to reminiscing about our extended family.

"There is Mom's uncle, the fine artist, who paints huge,

modern-abstract pieces," Marla says. She is currently taking art history courses and fine painting classes at the university. "Mom is fairly deep into Freud and Jung," she goes on, "and good with numbers too. In her family we have a ballerina, an inventor, and some intellectuals, including a Fulbright scholar."

"Our brother takes after the smart ones," I reply, "and you have street-smarts." I point a finger at her. "There are a few gamblers on Mom's side too, eh?" This last group of relatives consists of the playful and the petty, and the high wagers with serious problems. I have learned from my relatives to admire both the creative and the cerebral and to have compassion for the confused.

Except when it concerns myself, I am ruthless.

My sister's face looks pensive. "It's kind of lonely in here, eh? Reminds me of your poem, Myra, the one about trains. I think it ended up printed in the school yearbook." She seems to know my thoughts. We can do that.

"Yeah, that's right," I say. "It was in eighth grade, and we were on a school trip from Windsor to Ottawa. The train car was packed with students, teachers, and adult chaperones. I memorized it."

On a train,
From one dead world to the next.
They say be happy.
There is a smile.
But in the inner Soul,
Nothing.
I turn around.
In the prisons of ourselves,
We cast nothing but shadows.
A line is drawn to divide
And here we sit,
With virgin bodies,
Untouched.

"Geez," Marla says, "those were morbid, dark thoughts

for such a young person. How old were we? About twelve? About the time those schoolkids we thought were our friends abandoned us in the schoolyard and walked away, the whole group of them, if we got close."

"Yep. They liked us in the morning, but when we went back to school after lunch, they fled like a flock of fevered sheep. Their rejection scarred my soul. It affected me more than you," I confess. "The same ones were on that train in my poem. Kids can be mean. Calling us names, us being Jewish, the odd ones out."

My sister flips her hair back and away from her pretty face, a gesture to dismiss the subject. "Do you want to get something to eat?"

Purses in hand, we weave down the aisle toward the bar car, an institution among those university students who travel between Toronto and Windsor and the towns in between. It is not fancy. The last car on the train, it sways more than the other cars and has big windowpanes and vinyl-upholstered seats that wrap around the walls. The atmosphere is usually festive.

We order Cokes and egg salad sandwiches at the foodservice counter, then find a spot where we can sit together and make small talk with our companions in the car. When the train pulls into the Windsor station, we say goodbye and head back to our seats. The earlier tinge of moodiness is all gone.

A couple of days later, my family and I attend our third cousin's wedding in a suburb of Detroit. A Reform rabbi performs the traditional ceremony under the *huppah*, or canopy. After the blessings are said, the sound of shattered glass fills the room. Most know the groom just stepped on a wineglass wrapped in a napkin. In response, we all shout out, "Mazel tov."

Why smash the glass? Some rabbinic scholars say the breaking is an act of remembrance, so Jews will not forget the destruction of the Holy Temple in Jerusalem. Others say it signifies the fragility of marriage and the commitment to care for each other. Most understand it as the end of the marriage ritual and the beginning of the partying.

My family and the other guests spill into the reception room. We talk, drink, and eat appetizers passed around by waiters, and then we search for our name cards at one of the many round tables. As usual, these are set with fine china and silverware and colorful flowers that adorn the centers of the white tablecloths.

As Mom sits next to me and leans over, her favorite Joy perfume wafts by me. "Look over there," she says. "Look how your cousin walks around the room." Her voice is soft. "She is so gorgeous."

There is no need to look. I know who she means. My mother admires her whenever our families are together. It's a third cousin of mine, but not the one who just got married. My mother's words are not malicious, yet their effect on me is like a punch to the stomach. A sense of smallness overcomes me. I hunch my shoulders and shrink into the chair. Mom does not intend to hurt me, but her words upset me. Marla can feel the same way. Our mother's unrestrained adulation of beautiful women, coupled with a sometimes-biting tongue, makes us feel less attractive, less desirable, more worthless. With my propensity for introversion, every day is a fight to overcome my shyness and not withdraw from the world. My mother's unconscious and inconsiderate words make it harder. Her direct, vicious attacks with a spiteful remark or sometimes a coat hanger make it almost impossible.

But despite the blows or the words, I love Mom and continue to see her wonderful side and the gifts she gave me. So instead of saying something and risking a scene, I get up from the table and walk over to my bubbe's (grandmother) table. I stoop down to give her a kiss on the cheek.

"Love your shift dress," I murmur. "Stylish. The pastel yellow looks wonderful on you." Bubbe is a petite woman, and her wedding attire is a change from her usual drab daytime outfit. Now that Grandpa Herman has passed away, she often wears just a bra and a full slip, removes her false teeth, and lets a cigarette dangle from the side of her droopy mouth. It can get humid in the suburbs.

"Thank you, sweetheart." Bubbe's eyebrows crunch together. "And which one are you?"

"Myra."

It wouldn't matter. She can never tell the difference between my sister and me. She's never really tried. Most of her days are spent playing penny poker with her girlfriends. When I was a kid, my grandmother's lack of interest caused me to question my mother. It was before Dad got sick and went bankrupt. It was before Mother's anger started. It was when I still adored her.

"Bubbe hardly pays attention to me," my mother said, rolling her eyes, "and I'm her daughter. You can imagine what it was like growing up. She favored my sister."

When I asked my Aunt Gladys about this, she said, "As the oldest child, I had to take care of all the kids and Bubbe too. She didn't favor me, she just needed me."

❂

Now, from across the wedding reception room, Gorgeous Third Cousin, the one my mother just admired, catches my eye. She saunters over, her body lithe, bringing along a man she introduces as her boyfriend. As a couple, they display the same beauty and the beast qualities as Professor Silverman and his Polynesian wife.

Gorgeous Third Cousin has the cute nose and high cheekbones of our Austrian–Russian forebears, set off by her long, straight, blonde hair. (My hair is dark and naturally curly and has a life of its own.) Her boyfriend is a troll with long, straggly, dark hair, a beard, and a huge, round stomach above spindly legs. It makes him look almost like a Chanukah dreidel.

A few minutes into our conversation, Gorgeous Third Cousin whispers in my ear, "My boyfriend has some stuff to smoke. Just go ask him if you want any."

I trot over to talk to the Troll, who had found his way to the well-stocked bar, set up for this evening's celebration. Before I can say anything, he gulps down the rest of the scotch in his glass and smacks his lips together. "Yeah," he says. "I've got some doobies rolled. Let's go to my car. It's just out back."

He leads the way through a maze of hallways and finally pushes a door that opens onto a parking lot. We are now behind the synagogue. The cool, night air feels fresh on my face, and I take in deep breaths as we walk a few yards to his car. Once inside, the Troll reaches into the glove compartment and pulls out a gold cigarette case. He opens it to reveal a dozen perfectly rolled joints.

My eyes pop wide open. "Wow!"

"What do you want? Something super high? Or mellow for this evening?" He sounds like a connoisseur. "I have other choices, but let's start with these."

"That is an impressive collection," I say. "I'd like the hallucinogenic kind, with some aroma, if you have, please."

He hands me a fat joint and lights it. I take a toke and another puff, and then a sniff of the pungent smell that fills the car.

"Great smoke." I pass it to him.

He takes a toke, holds it in for a few seconds, and lets out a huge cloud of smoke, then passes the joint back to me.

I take a puff and let it out. "What do you do for a living?"

The car leather squeaks when he shifts his weight and settles into the driver's seat. He turns to look at me. "I make handmade jewelry. I use liquid silver and gold, heshi stones, precious and semi-precious gems. Trendy stuff." He takes another toke and out comes another cloud.

"Where do you sell them?"

"In high-rise office buildings. I pick a tall one, somewhere in the Greater Detroit suburban area, start at the top, and knock on doors all the way down to the ground floor, selling my jewelry to the ladies in the offices."

We continue to toke and talk. The Troll fascinates me.

9

A short while later, we walk back into the synagogue, where the reception is in full swing. Many guests are on the dance floor, moving to the live band and lead singer's cool covers of Motown songs. I join Gorgeous Third Cousin at her table, just as her younger sister walks over and sits down next to me and says, "I am pregnant, not married, and have no money." Her voice is quiet, and there are tears in her eyes.

Her opening statement almost knocks me out of my chair. "Can your parents help?"

"They don't know." Her face has the worried look of one who has lost hope.

"Have you tried Jewish Family Services?"

Pregnant Cousin shakes her head. "No. Because then everyone in the community will know." Her belly will soon show, but it is no use to talk about the obvious.

"You're not the only one with unusual circumstances in our families," I tell her. "Our grandparents' generation immigrated to America from several northern European countries. It was a big family. My bubbe and her group settled in Detroit, but she met Grandpa when she visited his family, also her relatives, in Manhattan. You see, she fell in love with her first cousin." I place my hand over Pregnant Cousin's hand and put my anthropological understanding of kinship relations to use. "Their kind of marriage was legal throughout the United States before the Civil War. By the 1880s, it was forbidden in thirteen states. New York considered it a form of incest. Not in Michigan, though. That's where they got married. They moved back to New York City and lived in an illegal marital status for more than fourteen years. To have her babies, Bubbe would go back to Michigan, where her mother, my great-grandmother, lived. She did this three times, and her children were not considered illegitimate. Those kids were illegally raised in New York until their teens, when the family moved to Detroit and my other uncle was born."

While I'm talking, Pregnant Cousin starts to glow. Her spirits lift. "Gosh! Incest. I didn't know that. So I'm not the only bad one." She lets out a little laugh.

"Yes," I say, "there is secret, strange stuff going on."

"Thanks." She squeezes my hand.

A server places a dessert plate holding a piece from the three-tier wedding cake and a large scoop of ice cream in front of each of us. I must have missed the cake-cutting ceremony when the Troll and I went outside for the tokes. Between bites, I remain silent and mentally absorb my pregnant cousin's news, coupled with the Troll's anecdotes about his livelihood.

Suddenly a realization comes to me about the coincidence of this moment.

Chapter 2

THAT ESSAY FOR SILVERMAN'S CULTURAL anthropology class is due in a couple of weeks. The required reading list includes Karl Marx and Friedrich Engels. Simply speaking, anthropology is the study of humanity. Through the professor's deft instruction, Marx's unique language concerning the faults of capitalism, class struggle, and the strengths of communism becomes a socioscientific tool we can use to understand different cultures. What interests me as a twin is to study a people's sense of self through Marx's concepts of "alienation" and "species being." For this assignment, we are to consider Marx's notions of reproduction and production from the perspective of a present-day society.

While eating cake at the wedding reception, I contemplate my conversations with a jewelry maker and a pregnant, unmarried woman. Our talks have taken place within the last hour or so, and both fit the essence of the assigned essay. Marx's concepts concern bringing something into manifestation, be it a baby or a necklace. Amazed by the coincidence of this apparent opportunity, the budding anthropologist in me wants to learn more.

Arrangements are soon made for me to stay for a couple of days at Gorgeous Third Cousin's house, which she shares with the Troll and her pregnant sister. To do the Silverman paper justice, it's essential that I do actual fieldwork to capture the middle-class, Midwestern, Jewish–American cultural perspective of my participants. They offer the points of view of a hippie turned entrepreneur and a young girl facing a life-changing dilemma. There is a one crucial problem. A meaningful interview cannot be conducted without a tape recorder; I am informed there is no tape recorder in the house.

Early next morning, I talk to the Troll. He dismisses my concerns. "No problem. Come with me." He starts to walk away, but turns back, a serious look on his face. "Now remember, you are my secretary. Let me do all the talking. I mean all the talking." His last words are punctuated by the wave of a finger.

I nod and grab my purse, which holds my wallet and the most important item—my pink lipstick—and follow him out the door to his car. He drives a few blocks to a small strip mall with plenty of signage and parks in front of an office supply shop.

Inside, he introduces me to a man with a badge. Then I stand quietly and watch him finagle the store manager into loaning us a tape recorder so that I, the secretary, can test it before he makes a final purchase. We pay for a couple of cassette tapes and leave the man with a promise to return the machine tomorrow.

The Troll does return it after I have conducted the two interviews. Although more research and writing are needed for the essay, when the Troll appears at the doorway of the guest room later in the day and asks me to come along with him to sell jewelry, Silverman's paper gets tossed aside.

We drive a short distance along the expressway, then veer onto an off ramp that leads to a road that takes us into an office complex of four buildings. He parks near one of the skyscrapers. We get out, and the Troll goes to the back of his vehicle. He grunts a bit as he lifts what looks like a large briefcase out of the trunk. Then we enter the glass-and-steel building, and I watch the Troll schmooze the security man, who is sitting at the lobby desk.

We get past the guard and ride the elevator to the top floor. The Troll stops at the first office door, opens it, and sticks his head, plus one foot, inside. "I was just at a meeting down the hallway," he says to the receptionist. "I'm on my way out. Are you and the other ladies in the office interested in seeing my exquisite jewelry pieces? I'm offering discounts."

She's tempted. "Ooh. What kind?" Her question sounds promising.

"I use gems and gold and silver," he tells her. "There are handmade necklaces, bracelets, and earrings. This is the last of my inventory for today. If you buy right now, I'll give you a great price."

"Yes. Yes. Wonderful! Come on in." She waves her hands as we walk into the room. "Hello! Both of you sit. One minute. I'll call the other girls."

I find a seat at the far end of this ordinary-looking office and watch things unfold. The Troll opens his briefcase to reveal a large, portable, jewelry display case. His eyes dart back and forth as he arranges the display case on a side table and next to it sets a handheld mirror.

Soon there is a flurry of activity as the secretaries and clerks pour into the room. They ooh and aah, try things on, look in the mirror, and purchase the jewelry. The Troll seems to dance in the middle of them. He looks almost handsome. His eyes aglow, he helps a lady put on a bracelet and then he helps someone else clasp a necklace. He passes out his business card to the lookers.

When the buying frenzy is over, we say goodbye and walk down the hall to knock on the next office door.

"Not today, sir."

Ignoring this dismissal, the Troll puts his case on the floor, scurries into the room, and leaves a stack of his cards on the corner of the receptionist's desk. "Get the other ladies in the office together," he tells her, "and your friends too, and call me. We'll arrange a private trunk show. I'll have more stuff."

After about two hours, he's had a few misses but a lot more hits than I initially suspected. "It's impressive how you do your shtick with the ladies," I say in a sincere tone. "But knocking on doors and hawking jewelry from the top to the bottom of a building is not my thing."

The Troll shrugs his shoulders and rocks back on his heels, like he's itching to move. "That's okay, Myra. You'll just have to come up with some other business model. I'm going to hit the rest of the floors. Do you want to come with me, or should I drive you home?"

"I'm done." The guilty feeling started a few floors ago. I need to get back to Silverman's essay.

The Troll drives me back to Gorgeous Third Cousin's house. He lets me out at the curb and Pregnant Cousin lets me inside. We chat for a bit, and then I excuse myself to go to the guest room. Once inside, I futz around with the Marxist essay. It goes slowly . . . and then it never happens.

My intuition has been aroused.

The prospect of a handmade jewelry business consumes me. To execute my plan, certain things and people must be in place. There are three people whose help I will most definitely need. One is Jamie.

He came into my life on November 13, 1958. It was the day my father went to pick up my mother, after she had been discharged from the hospital and recuperated at Bubbe's house in Oak Park, a suburb of Detroit. My parents brought home my new baby brother, who was born eight days earlier.

The atmosphere in the living room in our South Windsor house was highly charged as relatives and friends waited in eager anticipation for the arrivals and the bris to begin. A traditional, Jewish ceremony performed by a mohel, a man skilled in Jewish law and surgical procedure, the bris originated in the Torah and is the circumcision of the male infant eight days after his birth.

The front door opened, and we could hear the voices of Mom and Dad. The guests lunged forward, along with the sounds of their "oohs" and "aahs" and "so cutes." The baby was inside the house.

At this precise moment, I had the misfortune to be at the opposite end of the long room.

At that time, I was only three and three-quarters years old, and before me stood a sea of knees. Unlike Moses, I could not command them to part. But I could behave like a football player, shoulders down, and plow through the crowd just like the running backs did when my father and I watched football on TV. I began to shout and weave through the maze of shoes, legs dressed in pants, and others with hemlines. "Let me see. Let me in!"

Just when I was ready to grip the top of the baby basket, the only open spot left, my dad barked, "Don't stand behind him, Myra. Your brother is going to follow you with his eyes. They could roll back inside his head and he'll hurt himself."

Then my father got down on his knees and made a space for me at the foot of the baby basket. This offered me my first peek at my new brother. He glowed. A ring of white light emanated from him. He had a fluff of curly blondish hair, sparkly green eyes with long, dark eyelashes, and a beautiful, happy face. Right away, I knew he was special. For the first time in my short life, I felt safe.

"Say hello to your baby brother," Dad said. "James."

"Hello, James." But from then on, we all called him Jamie.

A few days after the bris, a nightmare woke me. Usually, when I listened to the sound of my sister's breathing, I felt calm. But on that night, I took my pillow, grabbed two big towels from the bathroom, and padded, barefooted, over to Jamie's room.

As quietly as I could, I lay down on my makeshift towel bed next to his crib and fell fast asleep. When Jamie graduated to a kiddy bed, it was, luckily, in a corner, and I curled up at the end, my back against the wall, one foot on the floor and as far away from him as possible, because I didn't want to wake him up. Any movement or twitch would send me scurrying catlike out of the room.

That was way back then. Now Jamie is in high school and everyone knows he is special and brilliant. At seven years old, he received a letter from the government of Canada. Because he was so smart, the specialists wanted to parade him around or do research on him . . . or something like that. What I remember is that he said no, which made me proud. I admired how well he knew himself. I still do.

When I was about ten years old, I was confused about myself. As a twin, I didn't even know if I was a self. Looking at our reflections in a mirror, I was not sure which one was me. In photos of Marla and me, it's impossible to tell who is who unless the shot is a close-up. Then you can see the difference, because my eyes are slightly more almond shaped. Meanwhile, Jamie grew into a tall, handsome fellow with a headful of dark, wavy hair. Before he was thirteen and had his bar mitzvah, he showed a genius flare for making money using his unique collection of dimes.

❃

Now, when I telephone my brother to meet up with the Troll, he agrees to my request to talk about the jewelry business. The next evening, Jamie sits down at Gorgeous Third Cousin's table for a chicken dinner. As we eat, he discusses bead counts to finished pieces and profit margins with the Troll.

I just listen. It gets decided. Jamie goes home, and my task is to stay at our cousin's house for two more nights and learn how to actually make the various pieces of jewelry. Logistics are discussed, and I spend the whole next day stringing beads and squishing certain metallic ones to close the ends off.

The morning after that, I wash my face and brush my teeth and hair, then follow the noise coming from the other end of the house. Gorgeous Third Cousin hears my footsteps and yells out to me, "I'm in the kitchen. Do you want anything to eat?"

"I don't know," I call back. In the kitchen now, I ask, "Where is everyone? What are you having?"

"I'm not hungry," she says. "I'm just making coffee. We're the only ones here." She is also in a housecoat, her blonde hair tied back into a ponytail.

"You hardly ate anything last night," I say. "How can you not be hungry?"

She looks straight at me, a serious look on her face, "Well, do you want to hear the truth?"

"Of course. Are you okay?"

"I took a pill. A Quaalude. I love them. But my boyfriend doesn't want the stuff around. So when he's gone . . . well . . . have you ever done Quaaludes, Myra?"

"Nope. Never. I just smoke pot."

"Want to try it? You'll feel dreamy. And feminine. Do you want one? Here. Just one. Take just one." She hands me a pill and fills a glass with water. "Drink this. You'll feel it in about half an hour."

I swallow the pill.

Someone kisses me on my mouth. Soft hands slowly glide over my body. Fingers try to arouse me. I open my eyes . . . and Gorgeous Third Cousin is lying in the bed next to me. Surrounded by white pillows, on a white duvet, I am naked and so is she. My mind is fuzzy. I cannot remember how we got here. Instead of feeling angry, I am astonished. There is no resistance on my part. Curiosity, like that of an anthropologist in a vast sexual world, overcomes me.

Suddenly a loud intake of breath fills the room. The sleepy sensuality of the moment is shattered.

It is the Troll.

He's leaning against the open bedroom door, panting like a winded dog. Fumbling to get his clothes off, he gets down to his boxers, then runs to the bed and jumps in. Gorgeous Third Cousin and I scramble off.

"Get out! Get out." She shoos him away like he's a pesky fly.

I dash into the bathroom, close the door, and look at myself in the mirror. "Wow. What just happened?" Confusion is staring back at me.

I study my reflection. If I'm ruthlessly honest, it exposes a lost soul outside of God's grace and yearning to be included. That's always been a struggle of mine. Even though my preference is men, my anger is not about being in bed with a woman. No, the guilt, the self-loathing, is about the Quaalude. Marijuana is cool. It doesn't take over my body or leave me feeling out of control.

In the shower, the hot steam seeps into my skin and purifies me from the inside out. The water washes away the self-disgust. The aromatherapy of the fragrant soap refreshes my spirit. When I go back to bed, however, sleep eludes me. Memories surface and keep me wide awake.

From my crib, I knew I was Jewish. I heard about Judaism, God, the Nazis, and the Holocaust. Stories were told about Jack and Jill going up the hill to fetch a bucket of water. Other stories were about Anne Frank, who hid in an attic in Amsterdam with her family. Sunday school and learning Hebrew were mandatory for my sister and me and, of course, our brother.

My father's father established the first Conservative-Orthodox Jewish synagogue, the Shaar Hashomayim, in Windsor, Ontario. He was its first president. Still situated on the corner of Giles Boulevard and Goyeau Avenue, it is mere coincidence that the Yiddish term goy ("a Jewish name for a non-Jew") occurs in the French name of the street.

I remember the main entrance and its long stairway. Inside, the shul was elegant, with wooden pews and stained-glass windows. On a raised platform in the front of the room stood the Holy Ark, the decorative, closet-like structure that houses the Torah scroll, hidden behind long, dark-blue curtains. Toward the back end of the platform a few chairs were built into the wall for the rabbis and the current president during services. My grandfather sat up there. The seating arrangements for the congregation were, of course, divided by gender, although there were no screens to conceal the women. Only in the balcony could the men and women sit together.

As a female child, I felt insignificant. Barely noticed and left out in this holy palace. The shul's kings—the rabbis—seemed remote, formal, and unwelcoming. My own grandfather never spoke to me except on the Sabbath and high holidays when he either said, "Gut Shabbos" or "Gut yom tov." The Hebrew schoolteachers likewise favored the young boys who would soon come here to celebrate their bar mitzvahs. I always felt excluded, especially because some of the boys were bullies and picked on my sister and me. They wanted us to feel stupid. It was hurtful. Even though my younger brother was declared a genius by the government of Canada and would get a bar mitzvah, he never made me feel stupid. It was my mother who called me a dummy. Just once. Nevertheless, her words kept burning inside me and contributed to my sense of inadequacy. As I grew, my self-esteem dwindled.

The men in the shul's congregation wore yarmulkes, or skullcaps. At the services, many also wore the tallit, or shawl-like cloth with elaborate edges and fringes that hung over their shoulders and sometimes covered their heads. Some male members also wore the odd-looking tefillin, or phylacteries. This leather amulet consists of two small boxes with long straps and contains written passages from the Torah. One box is affixed to the center of the forehead between the eyes. The other is placed on the left arm, near the heart, and the straps are wrapped around the forearm and the hand.

When I was a child, these unique outfits, strange objects, and formal customs overwhelmed me. I was the kind of kid who clung to her father's pant legs and mother's dress, too shy to speak to anyone. Although my femaleness proclaimed me an outcast, the sense of God, the spirituality of the shul, and the presence of the Torah, left me caught in amazement.

Even though I understood none of the rituals, the awe of God entered me at a young age.

In my mind's eye, the Torah and the biblical passages came alive. It happened on the High Holy Days, at Sabbath services, or during the Passover Seder or Sunday school classes. I sensed the stories had a personal and historical significance. Despite the negative feelings the bullying boys and the rabbis aroused in me, the tales from the Torah and the Bible, the Hebrew letters, the prayers, and their melodies all appealed to me.

Even as a child, I often thought about God and persecution. I heard about Anne Frank's diary and saw the 1959 Hollywood movie. Taunts of being a "dirty Jew" made it personal. At the time, more than eighty different cultural and religious groups resided in the Windsor, Ontario, area. While I got pleasure and delight in the differences, some people had problems.

I remember taking walks and holding the hand of our first nanny, Innes, a large Jamaican woman with dark skin. My family loved her. On some of our strolls through the neighborhood, groups formed around us. Some yelled "kike" at me, while others screamed "nigger" at her. Less than a decade later, the Detroit riots burned and scorched the city's soul.

Distant cousins on my mother's side sometimes visited our family's home. A man and a woman, they were small, meek people dressed in black who sank into the furniture. They always bought toys for us kids. They also showed us the numbers crudely tattooed by the Nazis on the insides of their arms.

When I was seven or eight years old, my family left the Shaar Hashomayim synagogue to join the new Reformed temple, where keeping kosher was not required. (Although my father was raised in the Orthodox way, my mother never kept kosher.) The young boys at this temple were still bullies, but I found the Reform rabbi elegant and captivating. He moved with a sense of grace, and his tone of voice was friendly.

He was also a homosexual. Although I was too young to understand what people were gossiping about, I eventually concluded that no one there really cared that he was gay. The congregation adored him. So did I. A few years later, this rabbi left to form his own temple, based on a more humanistic practice of Judaism and not centered on a divine co-relationship. My parents did not follow him, which also suited my appetite for a more mystical, personal connection to the Divine.

❂

These memories float through my mind as I lie in the guest bed of my Gorgeous Third Cousin's house. After my encounter with the Quaaludes, my bond with God feels broken. I'm too hard on myself to just forgive and forget about dropping the pill. This lost feeling will probably linger for a while.

Luckily, sleep does not evade me.

Chapter 3

THE NEXT MORNING, I CALL A friend to come and get me at Gorgeous Third Cousin's house. A few hours later, after he picks me up, I decide to try to make the best of the day. We get off the expressway near Lafayette Boulevard in downtown Detroit and park the car near the famous Coney Island Restaurant. After we eat a couple of hot dogs, dripping with chili sauce, white onions, and deli mustard, my friend drives us across the international border to Windsor. Decades later, I will learn there were sautéed chicken livers in the sauce, an unusual ingredient in a chili recipe.

From time to time, I still see Gorgeous Third Cousin at family functions. My mother gushes about how beautiful she is. I agree and say nothing more. I know that Quaaludes are the secret to her easy, breezy stroll.

As for the essay for Silverman's class, it never gets finished. Instead, I submit two tape cassettes that contain only the raw data from my interviews with the Troll and Pregnant Cousin. The professor hands me back an F grade, the second F I have ever received in my life.

The first F was the result of a failed high school math exam. Math is not my forte. That summer, I did not go to Miami Beach with my sister and two other girlfriends. Instead, I stayed home, studied hard, and retook the exam. The result this time was an A+. But the teacher accused me of cheating.

Now I don't care too much about the F from Silverman. My mind is set on new directions and big plans. But F or not, I learned a great deal about myself from the assignment. Marx wrote that it is essential for a man or a woman to "appropriate" nature, that is, to make and create something is our nature. I am inspired to do that with the jewelry, to bring an idea into manifestation with my hands.

My business model is different from the Troll's high-rise system. Turns out, my brilliant younger brother is on board too. The second "must have" person in my strategy is my twin sister. Marla agrees to work with Jamie and me. With her artistic eye, I am confident the designs for our necklaces, earrings, and bracelets will be fantastic and fashionable.

My next focus is on getting a booth at the upcoming Art in the Park Festival. This is Windsor's annual art and craft show held on the grounds of Willistead Manor, a Tudor-style house. The booths are set up around its stunning gardens. Willistead Manor is the estate of the son of Hiram Walker, Canada's whiskey tycoon. Situated in the namesake area of Walkerville, it is now a heritage precinct in Windsor.

I'm eager to be in this prestigious show, and my third and last "must get" person is my former boyfriend, Christopher, an attractive, blond-haired guy who was introduced to me at a high school football game. I was fourteen years old. He was sixteen and from the opposing team's school and old enough to drive a car. A few months before our meeting, I had prayed to God for a boyfriend named Christopher, which is an odd name for a nice Jewish girl to request.

I always call him Chris and can rely on him. He is kind, smart, artistic, and athletic. We went steady for about three-and-a-half years, and during our time together, he helped me with two projects for my English class. Instead of handing in essays, I made slide shows of images I found in magazines and put to music. My sister and I created the slides using a huge, overhead camera located at the school teachers association building, then Chris helped me set the slides to snippets of songs that established the essays' premises. One had to do with Shakespeare's *Othello* and my interpretation of Desdemona as not so innocent.

Although Chris and I broke up about a year ago, he is still my best friend and has a good connection to the art show. Chris' father is a well-known physician, his mother is active in the community. A few days after leaving Gorgeous Third Cousin's home, I telephone him. "Because your mother runs Windsor's Art and the Park affair," I say, "do you think you can get me a booth?"

"What are you going to sell there?" he asks.

"Handmade bracelets, necklaces, and earrings. We handstring semi-precious and precious stones and gold and silver beads. Jamie and Marla are involved too. You know her artistic sensibilities. She has an eye for what's in and what's cool. And you know how smart Jamie is. He can tell us how many tiny beads, findings, and finishings we need to make enough pieces to inventory for a two-day art show. And he does all these calculations in his head!"

Chris laughs. "I know full well about both of them. And you. Let me talk to my mom." A few hours later, he calls me back. "She said yes. I'm happy for you guys. Let me know if you need anything else. I'll be at Willistead too."

"Wow. You're fabulous, always there for me."

We spend the next few days buying the supplies. Once Marla completes the designs, Jamie and I string the pieces together. When everything is done, we create our display table.

Marla knows what to do. "We'll lay the jewelry across huge, white, conch shells. I know where we can borrow a few.

We can also buy a couple of yards of violet-colored silk to spread over the folding tables to show off the jewelry. Plus, we'll make the display of differing heights by putting little boxes under the cloth and draping the necklaces to cascade down. Myra and Jamie, see if you can find some old wood."

"We can drive around Essex County," I begin, but Jamie says, "Marla, what is the wood to be used for? I need to know, to figure out how much we will need."

"I want to mount two mirrors on barn boards," she tells us. "Then people can see what our jewelry looks like on them. We need enough boards for two, one-foot mirrors on each mount." Marla demonstrates her idea with hand gestures to show the size and then adds, "Myra, see if Chris' mom can loan us two large easels from the art gallery. We can put the wood frames on them."

"Okay, I'll ask. Chris said he'd help us if he can."

"We'll need quite a few yards of wood," Jamie says. "Let's hope we find a rundown barn."

I wonder if it's possible to find enough old lumber. Before heading out, we eat lunch: salami, cut thin, on rye bread; chips; a green salad; and Cokes. Jamie drives us to the fertile but flat land of Essex County and toward Leamington, which is known as the Tomato Capital of Canada because the Heinz plant is located there.

It is a warm, sunny day. Fields in full bloom greet us. After the harvest, some of the produce stands will serve hot, buttered corn on the cob. We meander down a few country roads, and twenty minutes into our hunt, we get lucky. A few yards from the road, a dilapidated barn sits in an unplowed field, probably left fallow. Hidden by a growth of oak trees, the gray, weatherworn boards lie scattered on the ground, having tumbled off the beaten-down structure.

We park the car and hide it among the trees, then scurry over to get the wood. I grab armfuls of the dry planks, take them back to our car, and shove them in the trunk. Jamie does the same. Probably, no one will even know the boards are gone. Within five minutes, we have the right amount of wood for the frames.

Could this be construed as a theft? Perhaps. But, the barn appears to have been abandoned for years. That is my defense, if I need one.

❋

There are usually big crowds at Art in the Park, a two-day event. Painters and papermakers are draws for shoppers. Today is no exception. It's a hot day, and our booth is in front of a large hedge. We have neither trees nor a tent or canopy to shade us. Marla is dressed in a lacy, white, strapless dress and a short, red print, satin kimono that she wears open as a cool cover. She looks fantastic. I have on jean shorts and a blue tank top and feel dowdy in comparison. Jamie is also in jeans and a T-shirt, but he looks handsome and fine. I put on one of our necklaces and a pair of earrings to match my colors. That perks me up.

Soon a swarm of people is gathering around our table. The air is alive with murmurs and questions. All morning, a steady stream of shoppers, a few lookers, and more buyers stop and look or just flow by. Around the middle of this sunny afternoon, I see Chris crossing the grass lawn and coming our way. With him is an older gentleman I do not recognize, although he looks like the famous Star Trek actor, Leonard Nimoy, and has large eyes. They seem to penetrate me like lasers as he draws nearer.

Chris introduces him to us. "I'd like you to meet Art in the Park's special guest, Jack Pollock, the famous Toronto gallery owner and art dealer. Over the years, he has represented David Hockney, Willem de Kooning, and Ken Danby."

I reach across the table to shake his hand. "Hello, Mr. Pollock. You have a wonderful guide to show you around the park."

"Nice to meet you," he says.

Chris winks and grins. "Myra is the jewelry entrepreneur in the family, Marla is the artist, and this is Jamie, their brother, a bright guy with numbers."

Jack shakes their hands too and picks up a few necklaces. Although he inspects several pieces, he does not buy anything.

A few hours later, I talk to Chris on the telephone. "What did Pollock think of our jewelry?"

"He said it looked good but thought Marla and you were much prettier."

"Really? He said that?"

"Yep. Right after we visited your booth."

Thanks to my sister's ingenuity, our Art in the Park booth at Windsor leads us to another venue. The two-day Toronto Art and Craft Show is held at the famed Nathan Phillips Square, Canada's largest city square. We set up our booth in this urban plaza that sits in front of Toronto's City Hall, which looks like an alien spaceship positioned between two tall, half-moon shaped, government office buildings.

Thanks to my sister's continuing research, the Mossman siblings venture into the Arts and Craft Show summer circuit that leads us to other towns and cities throughout southwestern Ontario.

These events are a fun way to meet people and to hang with my sister and brother. But something is amiss. Something gnaws at my psyche. When I'm being ruthlessly honest with myself, I feel unenthusiastic about making and selling jewelry. This feeling perplexes me. As objects, jewelry has no profound meaning for me. My desire is to bring something more important, more meaningful, into manifestation. Purposefulness seems to come from my search of self and my relationship to the Divine.

Deep within me, my soul begins to stir. I feel an inexplicable inner call to go west.

Many people are drawn to the western provinces of Alberta and British Columbia. Schoolchildren across Canada are raised on photographs of the majestic, snowcapped Rocky Mountains. The four contiguous national parks—Yoho, Kootenay, Banff, and Jasper—are the country's natural treasures. Students head to them in the summer to work at the resorts and the surrounding areas. In 1984, eight years after my call to go west, these four Rocky Mountain parks became a UNESCO World Heritage Site.

A few days after my internal stirrings about going west, I talk to Marla, though I couch my travel plans differently. "Our university friend, Gabby, has my best, white blouse," I tell her. "She needed to wear it on a date last semester. I am going out of town to get it back from her." This excuse kind of makes sense, because only a few pieces of my clothing would be considered precious. The shirt was.

"Well, how long are you going to be?" Marla asks. "Is she in London or Toronto?"

"No, she's got a summer job in Kelowna, British Columbia."

My sister takes a step backward, her eyes open wide. "That's halfway across the country! You're not going that far, are you? It'll take forever. You know you're supposed to work during the summer to help pay for the fall semester?"

"I'll get a job in Calgary," I reply.

After this pronouncement, my sister's eyes become small slits, "It's 1976, and so far, you've never flown anywhere or gone anywhere by yourself."

"So what? I plan to fly to Alberta." Although I say this with conviction, I have no idea how it will actually happen. "And then I'll go to Kelowna. Did you know it's the only area in Canada that qualifies as a desert?"

"Who cares? It is still too far away." Marla tosses her hair back. "Okay," she admits, "the thing about the desert is interesting."

After that, I speak to Jamie. I don't remember if I mentioned my plans to my parents. They were lost in the torment of their marriage. A flurry of divorces in Windsor's Jewish community has shaken my mother and father's resolve to stay together until Jamie goes away to university in the fall.

A week later, I board an Air Canada passenger jet and begin my first airborne adventure. Flying above the clouds allows me to view their odd, delicate formations that rise toward the heavens. The images become a theatre for my mind. I see the different shapes as creatures or symbols and contemplate my relationship with God and where it now stands. I am over the misadventure with Quaaludes and not burdened by heavy thoughts.

These musings occupy my attention for the first part of the flight. I don't notice my seatmate, a clean-cut young man, until he interrupts my imaginings to introduce himself. We chat for a while, and he politely asks, "Where are you going?"

"Alberta. I hope to work at the Stampede." My answer is short. Almost everyone in Canada has heard about the Calgary Stampede, Alberta's famous rodeo, festival, and competition, which is held every July.

The young man's face lights up. "I know someone who works in the Stampede's personnel department. Here is her name. Tell her you know me." He writes down his name and the information about his friend, then adds, "By the way, do you need a ride into town from the airport? My family is picking me up. We can give you a lift."

Now a big smile spreads across my face. "Thank you. This is very kind of you." My plan was to take a taxi (which would be expensive) to a friend's place. Before leaving Windsor, Chris arranged for me to stay with Buddy, one of his high school pals who is now an architect. Buddy moved to Alberta to design structures for a huge oil conglomerate.

During the ride from the airport, I gaze at the big skies of Calgary, a city in love with buildings. The area has hardly any trees and only a few parks to entertain the eye or soothe the soul. Some say this is due to the frigid Arctic air in a battle with the warmer chinook winds that occur a couple of times a year. A city almost devoid of foliage unnerves me.

Chapter 4

I KNOW BUDDY FROM HIS school days with Chris. He is tall, thin, red-headed, and straightforward, and we get on well because neither of us is the nosy type. However, my nose for scoring marijuana is a plus. Everyone has his or her own way to find a pot source. Mine shifts, depending on the circumstances.

Here in Calgary, it starts with reggae music. Raised on Motown, I became learned on the soulful beat of the Jamaican sound. Yvonne, who was from Jamaica and was my first-year dorm roommate at the university, introduced reggae to me. Her brother was in a band and a Rastafarian. This is an Abrahamic religion based on the monotheistic God, whom they call Jah. Rastas wear dreadlocks, make reggae music, and smoke a lot of "ganja," their word for marijuana.

Now my tactic for finding pot is to ask anyone I meet on the street who looks like they might know where a tourist can go to hear some reggae. A few people suggest a local bar. I get directions and head over there late one afternoon.

For a dive, the place has a lot of windows. Inside, the posters on the walls harmonize with the odors of stale beer and cigarettes.

Jimmy Cliff, my least favorite singer but a popular reggae artist, blares, along with other tunes, from a loudspeaker parked on a stage that is bare save for a drum set and mic stands. A few fellows in cowboy hats and blue jeans lounge around. Minus the hat, I am dressed the same as them. No one has the telltale dreads or wears the green, yellow, and red beanie of a Rasta.

I feel a bit nervous, but I stroll over to the long bar, order a Molson, and sit at a tall table in the back near the windows and away from the tobacco. Then I watch. Like my hero, Sherlock Holmes, who could suss out characters by their mannerisms, I look at the people around me. A few guys try to buy me a drink, but I brush them off. An hour later, the bar has filled up, and I look foolish sitting alone. When the next nice-looking fellow saunters over, I say yes to the drink. He joins me, but I'm keeping my eye on a table in the middle of the room.

Only one guy was sitting there when I first walked into the place. Then a couple of guys joined his table, drinks in hand. He left with one of them. They walked out back, toward the restrooms, only to return a few minutes later. When the new guys finished their drinks, they left the bar.

Throughout the evening, this same scene gets played out as new groups of people come to that fellow's table. Finally, when the original guy walks to the back of the bar with a man, I follow them, a few paces behind. When the guy returns, I ask if he can help me. He says sure.

And that is how I scored pot in Calgary. I give half of what I got to Buddy as payment for sleeping on his couch. He might look conventional and straitlaced, but he is more than happy to receive the weed.

The next morning, I wait in a line at the Stampede grounds, all ready to get hired. As the line inches closer to the door of the Human Resource Department, I survey the large crowd and wonder if I'll get my preference for a placement outside. The Greatest Outdoor Show on Earth includes an agricultural exhibition, market, midway, and rodeo. When it is my turn for an interview, I step into a room that has one window and take a seat in front of a desk piled with paperwork.

Turns out, the guy on the Air Canada plane gave me a good connection. The meeting is short, and I get hired on the spot. However, the personnel lady assigns me to a booth inside the gigantic Stampede marketplace. My job is to sell jars of jewelry cleaner.

Using a site map, I find my way through the maze of blue, yellow, and red tents that house the carnival games and walk around the midway rides until I finally arrive in front of the right building. It looks like a huge airplane hangar. The floor is dirt, and the people who flow though the wide-open doors raise a lot of dust. I join the throng. It is 1976, the first time the Stampede will see over a million visitors since its opening in 1886.

Inside the market, the merchants' booths are situated against the walls, while the center is full of vendors with colorful carts. All kinds of things are for sale under one roof. There are household products, fine art, crafts, and food. The resulting smell is a mixture of humanity, hot dogs, and burnt caramel from the candy-covered apple seller.

And it's loud. In most booths, including mine, the salespeople are expected to act like carnival hawkers. I stand in front of our white workbenches and shout out to the steady stream of potential patrons. "Step right up, folks, and get one ring cleaned for free. Step right up. See before your eyes how your dull jewels turn bright and shiny and look brand new with our amazing gel cleaner."

At first, the spiel feels embarrassing. Then it because effortless to hustle up a customer. I guide a woman over to the high bench and move around to its other side. "I can clean one ring for you," I repeat. She takes it off and hands it to me. I rub the gel on it with a soft, white cloth. "It's like magic, eh? Notice how the sparkles came back."

The woman's mouth drops open. "Oh my goodness! With all those years of soap and gunk in it, I haven't seen my ring look this great since my wedding day."

I hear variations of her response all day. I hawk a prospective buyer in. A ring is cleaned. A happy smile appears. A purchase is made. The owner of the booth, Mr. Jewelry Cleaner, is thrilled. His cleaning gel really works, which makes it easy to sell.

The Stampede's market has a great variety of food. On my breaks, I usually grab lunch from a guy making hoagie sandwiches. When I'm finished eating, I wander outside to walk around the midway grounds and then go see the animal husbandry competitions. The challenge for the largest pig, cow, and horse, or other kind of barnyard animal is fierce. Over at the outdoor rodeo arena, I can see people seated in grandstands, but I never stick around to watch a show.

Other than the Stampede, Calgary is known for its oil and its National Hockey League team, the Cowboys. (Soon they will change their name to the Flames.) The city's downtown area features a large, outdoor, walking mall where locals, students on summer break, and tourists all hang out. I venture over there after work to observe the people.

Then I spot him. He is on the other side of the promenade. What catches my eye is a protuberance that sticks out of his pants. It looks like a sixteenth-century codpiece, like seen in Renaissance paintings. I wonder what it really is. He is an attractive person, and he looks organized too. Everything about him is neat and trim, from his hair to his khaki shirt with its rolled-up sleeves and the tidy, turned-up cuffs on his clean blue jeans.

Some people are standing with him. I watch them talk and laugh. Curiosity inches me forward, and I cross the mall to get nearer to him. On closer inspection, the mysterious bulge turns out to be a dark, brown, leather pouch that is tied to and dangles from his belt. I catch his eye. We smile at each other. This gives me more courage to walk up to him.

Pointing at the pouch, I ask, "What's in there?"

One of the people in his group responds. "It's tobacco. His name is Peter. He's German and speaks only a little English."

Peter reaches into the back pocket of his jeans and pulls out a well-worn book, which he hands to me. It is an English–German dictionary. We translate together. It is slow going. I learn he is in Canada on vacation and is backpacking around the country. While in Calgary, he is staying at the local hostel, but he plans to leave soon. He has a degree in chemistry and is a practitioner of yoga.

The next day, and the day after that, I meet Peter again at the promenade when my Stampede shift ends, and we eat dinner together. The next day after that, he comes to the apartment where, to my surprise, I learn that Buddy speaks fluent German. Those two guys bond, big time. As their bromance develops, they speak German constantly.

"Peter speaks really well in his native language," Buddy tells me, "but he's shy to speak English because of his accent. He is an expert with knives. He thought you would be afraid of him, so he didn't tell you."

Then he turns and talks to Peter in German. Peter walks over to his day sack, which is on the floor, and opens a side pocket, from which he draws out a really, really big knife. And he shows us some sneaky moves.

He stays on at the hostel for a few more days. It's a one-story, brick building with few windows. I went there once but waited outside for him. When we are alone, Peter is mostly quiet. After dinner, we sometimes go to a park and sit under one of the few trees there. He also practices knife throwing and standing on his head, though not at the same time. We seem to communicate in a universal language of immediate friendship. We are instant pals. I trust him.

It is not my practice to pick up guys.

The thing is, I feel a connection with Peter that cannot be rationally explained. Almost a week after we meet, I ask, through Buddy, our translator, "Peter, do you want to hitch-hike to Kelowna in British Columbia with me? I need to find my girlfriend."

Peter thinks about my request for a few seconds, then nods his head. Through Buddy, he replies, "You'll need a warm sleeping bag and some flannel shirts. The mountain air is cold."

Then Buddy says, "Myra, I have a pack, a sleeping bag, and some blankets you can use. You'll be fine." He pulls a box from the closet and we look through the stuff inside it. Peter's exaggerated hands movements and his rapid speech show he is not pleased.

Buddy looks at me. "He thinks you'll freeze."

The next morning, I put some of my clothes in Buddy's washer and dryer, and in the afternoon, Peter and I go to the Canadian Army Surplus store in downtown Calgary. I purchase men's flannel shirts to keep me warm on the cold nights ahead. When I show up at work the next morning wearing one of them, Mr. Jewelry Cleaner looks me up and down. A frown appears on his otherwise happy face.

"Your army shirt is not flattering." He points toward the exit and in an angry tone says, "Go home and change."

The booth next to ours belongs to the seller of a methane-monitoring device. He overhears us and adds his analysis of my outfit. "It's unbecoming and not feminine at all." I hear a hint of disgust in his voice.

But their reaction only evokes my stubbornness. Marla is not here. I cannot rely on her aesthetic sensibilities, but I am learning to rely on my own. My rebuttal to both men is, "I'm staying." I turn to the owner of my booth. "And today is my last day shining rings."

Mr. Jewelry Cleaner drops his head to his chest in defeat. Then he looks up and nods. Despite the "unbecoming" shirt, my sales do not decline. Next morning, I stop by the Stampede's personnel office to pick up my last paycheck, and by early afternoon, Peter and I are hitching a ride to the Trans-Canada Highway that will take us from Alberta to Banff, British Columbia.

For me, hitchhiking as a means of transportation began as a lark. The summer before we started university, a group of us friends hitched from Windsor to London and back. The habit continued while we were at school. Whenever a need to travel out of town arose, I generally hitched a ride. The routine is the same whether I'm alone or with my sister. You stick your thumb out. You can either stay put or walk backward until you get a ride.

My twin sister and I almost never took the train or bus, unless the weather was really terrible, or our bags were too heavy, and we needed a porter to help us. You come to trust your intuition about people, something we developed at a young age while shopping along Woodward Avenue and at the grand J. L. Hudson Department Store in downtown Detroit.

Now Peter and I find it easy to get a lift. A young couple picks us up, and we leave the flat, oil-drenched lands of Alberta and head for British Columbia. After introductions, we are mostly quiet sitting in the back of the car, and we ride with them for a few hours until they let us off near the Rocky Mountain foothills. We pitch Peter's small tent in a wide-open ditch, completely covered with soft, green grass.

Peter makes a roaring fire, and we cook a meal, but later that night I'm freezing anyway, even though the tent is shielded from the wind. He was right. It is too cold for me to sleep in just a blanket and the flimsy sleeping bag. We huddle and kiss to keep warm. It does not feel romantic. Our bodies know we are just friends.

The next morning, Peter takes down the tent and makes another fire. I dig four huge rollers, the size of pop cans, out of my knapsack and curl my hair. It's helpful to look good, though not too dressed up, when hitchhiking. After combing my hair and packing my stuff, I make us some tea and toast with jam. We eat in silence and when we're finished, we kick out the fire.

The whole day is spent hitching rides back to Calgary and the Army Surplus Store, where I purchase a Canadian Army mountain sleeping bag. It comes with its own sack that goes on top of my backpack and gets tied to my new frame, which can handle over fifty pounds. (Peter's gear must be close to a hundred pounds.) These backpack frames extend from our hips to about six inches above our heads.

We spend that night at Buddy's. My new sleeping bag feels soft and cozy. Khaki colored, it is lightweight, made of quilted, parachute-like material and stuffed with goose down. For nights in the mountains, it has a hood I can zip up tight and keep the cold air out.

The next afternoon, Peter and I get a lift to the Trans-Canada Highway. We still intend to go west to Banff, then south to Kelowna. It is a dry, sunny day, and the pebbles on the shoulder of the road crunch beneath my boots, which I also purchased at the Army Surplus, along with some heavy wool socks. Tucked into my dark blue jeans is a long-sleeved, teal blouse. The methane device salesman and Mr. Jewelry Cleaner liked me when I wore this rayon top.

Our thumbs out, Peter and I keep our heavy packs on and walk backward. Every few yards, I turn my head and look at what's ahead. My intent is to avoid a twisted ankle from stepping on an unexpected rock. Peter does the same.

After an hour, we reach a grassy area, and I sit under some bushes for shade. I keep both knapsacks next to me while Peter thumbs a few yards away. We are at busy intersection and watch cars whizzing past. No one stops for us. This nothingness goes on for several hours.

At sunset, sprinkles of rain start to fall. About ten minutes later, a pickup truck slows and pulls onto the shoulder of the road. As we grab our knapsacks and head up to the vehicle, the driver rolls down his passenger window.

"Where are you two going?"

"British Columbia."

"Well, it's going to rain hard. You can come with me as far as the Stoney Reserve. It's an Indian reservation."

"Okay," I say and cock my head at Peter, and he climbs in

after me. The truck has a big front seat, but I lean against my friend and keep my hands in my lap to give the driver space. He appears to be a little older than us. He's wearing boots, jeans, and a faded, tie-dyed T-shirt under a faded, jean jacket. His long hair, graying around the temples, is pulled back into a ponytail, and his teeth are in need of some attention. But his attitude is easy and really cool.

"I live on the res in an A-frame house," says Mr. Ponytail. "Built it myself."

"I'm a student of anthropology," I say. "What tribe are you with?"

He glances at me, shakes his head, then looks back at the road. "Not a native," he says a minute later. "I work and live on the reserve, home to the First Nation, known as the Nakoda people. I tell ya, it is going to be chilly and rainy this evening. You're welcome to stay the night at my place."

Peter and I exchange looks. He understands the offer, and we agree to take it.

A couple of hours later, we arrive at a tract of land. The glare of the truck lights shows we are in a forest of tall cottonwoods. The A-frame is close by. I climb down out of the truck and take in a deep breath of the woodsy smell.

"Now it's midsummer," Mr. Ponytail says, "but in the early spring a sweet scent fills the air."

I nod and take another deep breath. "Hmm. Nice."

The sound of water running over rocks suggests a creek is close by. It is too dark to see only a few feet away, and yet a billion stars and the Milky Way are clear in the pitch-black sky.

The A-frame is homey and rustic inside, with the raw wood beams overhead and colorful handmade throw rugs on the wood floor. Peter and I lay out our sleeping gear in Mr. Ponytail's front room. Then we say good night to our host and fall fast asleep.

The next morning, Peter asks permission to use one of the fishing rods propped against the back wall of the tiny kitchen.

He heads outside to the creek to catch something for our breakfast. I choose to stay inside the A-frame, along with Mr. Ponytail. Seated in a comfy chair, I take a sip of tea. He sits on one side of the living room, a few yards away, and we begin to talk about the plight of the Canadian and American Indians.

"I never can get over the official treatment these two so-called evolved countries gave the indigenous people," I tell him. My serious tone conveys my anthropological knowledge. "In particular, the inhumanness of President Andrew Jackson's death march—the Trail of Tears—uprooted people from their native regions. We pulled the rug out from under them and put their cultural artifacts in museums for their conquerors' viewing. Pathetic."

Mr. Ponytail nods his head in agreement and takes a mouthful of steaming tea. "Now the general public can come to ooh and aah over other people's sacred objects," he says. "It frightens me to think of their lost culture on display. I am here to learn their ways." He holds his mug clutched in both hands to gather the warmth.

"Gosh," I say. "That's noble of you. You have the same passion as my anthropology professors."

Mr. Ponytail sets his drink down on a side table. "Do you want to look at my photos?"

"Sure!"

He ambles over to a wooden bookshelf and pulls down a stack of albums. I've seen hundreds of pictures of our First Nation peoples and expect Mr. Ponytail's are shots of the way of life on the Stoney Reserve. So far, I have not seen it and am eager to look at his images. He takes a few strides across the room and places three, heavy, family-style, photograph albums on my lap, then sits back down in his chair.

He watches me turn the first page and the next and then flip through more pages. He must see the astonishment spreading across my face because I suddenly feel quite flushed.

Chapter 5

"OH. MY. GOSH." I POINT to the other albums on my lap. "Are all these the same?"

"Yes. The same kind of pictures in all of them."

The albums are filled with four-by-five photographs of women who appear to be about my age. But these are not your normal headshots from photo shoots of would-be models. Some women are totally nude, while others are partially undressed, or undressing, all in *Playboy* or *Hustler* poses. Some stare straight into the camera, others are more demure. They seem happy to be photographed by this guy.

"Who are these women?"

"They are students and hitchhikers. Just like you, Myra."

Mr. Ponytail seems cool, but a nervous heat floods my entire body. I jump out of my seat, and the three photo albums tumble onto the floor. I wave my finger at him. "Hold on, now. You wait a minute." I'm almost shouting. "Those girls are not just like me." I'm talking fast. "Don't expect me to pose for you naked or even half naked. I'm not like that."

My voice sounds strong, but my legs feel weak. They move me, inch by inch, toward Peter's backpack on the floor about a yard away. Maybe the knife in the side pocket will scare Mr. Ponytail off.

Still sitting on the other side of the room, he has a white-knuckle grip on the arms of his chair. He begins to breath heavier, his nostrils open wide, like an animal. He takes in a few short sniffs and starts to grin. When he stands up, I push my hands, open wide, out in front of me. "Do not take my photograph. I am not going to pose for you." My heart races as I move an inch closer to Peter's backpack, "I'm not interested in sex. So don't get any big ideas about you and me."

My rant momentarily distracts him. His mouth drops open maybe over my assertion of celibacy. To my surprise, he sits back down in his seat.

A loud screech comes from the hallway. A rush of cool morning air hits me. It seems the hinges on the front door need oiling.

Peter enters the room. In one hand, he holds the fishing rod, in the other, two medium-sized fish dangling from a string. He looks at me and a crease appears between his eyes. He senses something is wrong and quickly hands the fish to Mr. Ponytail.

"For you. A gift. Thank you." Peter turns and looks at me. "We go now."

He nods at the door, strides over and lifts both our backpacks. They are heavy, but he is determined. I gather up some stray things and quickly follow him outside.

The early morning sky is bright, and the warbling of the birds fills the silence between Peter and me. I take my pack, tuck a few things inside it, then he helps me get it on my back. I grab his hand and begin walking down the dirt road we came in on last night.

There is nothing to see of the Nakoda reservation except for shrubs and trees. No buildings, no people. All we hear is that muffled whooshing sound that cars and trucks make when they speed by. As we get closer to the freeway, the noise gets louder. A few minutes later, we put our thumbs up and start to hitch.

Luckily, a ride comes really quick. We tell the driver of a semitruck we want to eventually get to Kelowna but are headed to Lake Louise. He nods his head, and we get into his vehicle. We travel through the Rockies all day. In the evening, we turn off the freeway onto a flat area, the trees all clear-cut. It is set up as a small campground area.

Mr. Semitruck Driver stays snug in his vehicle, while Peter and I grab our stuff and head a few yards away, closer to the Douglas firs. The air smells piney and clean. Although it is summer and still daylight, it is already chilly.

We pitch the tent and then comb the immediate area for fist-sized rocks. We find some near the edge of the forest and carry them a couple of yards to where we are set up. Peter places the rocks in a ring and uses dry pinecones and needles to start a fire in the middle. Blue and yellow sparks dance across the dry matter. When he lays on dead branches, yellow, orange, and red flames begin to crackle and pop. Sparks spit up into the evening sky. Soon the air is filled with the sweet smell of burning wood.

When the fire quiets down and is sufficiently hot, Peter lays a small barbeque grate that he carries with him across the rocks. Before we left Calgary, we bought food at the grocery store. Now water is boiling in a little pot, and we drink tea out of two tin mugs. Meanwhile, a stew of onions, garlic, carrots, green peppers, and celery simmers in a small frying pan. The potatoes are laid directly on the now hot stones.

After we eat our meal, we sip tea and Peter takes out the German–English dictionary. With its help, we talk about this morning's incident at the A-frame.

"Something wrong. I sense it," Peter says. He has a look of concern and puts his arm around me.

"It's the most sexually dangerous thing to happen in all my hitchhiking adventures." I squirm out of his hug. "I was a little worried, but I remembered the knife in your backpack—I could scare the man with it. And you were outside."

Peter puts his hand on my knee, "Yell for me. Next time."

I nod and pat his hand. "I hope there's no next time. Today was nothing compared to some of the stories you hear from the Detroit news media."

"Yeah, we heard about the Detroit riots in Germany."

As we talk, the beauty of the Rocky Mountains captivates me. It is almost dark out and the silhouettes of the mountains beyond the forest are haunting. Even after Mr. Ponytail's photo album escapade, I feel comfortable and close to the Divine.

Thoughts of God occupy me as I go to bed. They are part of the process of accessing my stupidity—my good girl–bad girl, good daughter–bad daughter, wrong behavior—and I chastise myself. It usually ends by me asking for guidance and hoping for God's forgiveness. This routine of mine feels more desperate and therapeutic than mere prayer.

Tonight, as I'm near sleep in the woods of British Columbia, I wonder why the girls in Mr. Ponytail's photographs seemed happy. Hmm. Then my memories settle on Father Nolan. He was the head of the Roman Catholic church on Roselawn Drive in my neighborhood when I was a child.

Sunday school classes came to an abrupt end for my sister and me about the age of ten or eleven. We were not allowed to continue with the boys in our class as they prepared for their upcoming bar mitzvahs, when they would read a portion of the Torah. My Hebrew studies thus came to an end.

My soul began to wander. Not from spite. It was a matter of convenience. During that time, we had a Roman Catholic live-in housekeeper named Frances, whom we loved like a family member. Father Nolan would ride his motorcycle to our house to talk with her. About what, I never knew and never asked. But I liked him.

A holy man is a holy man. Although I'm Jewish, I recognized that a Roman Catholic priest is as holy as a rabbi. Sometimes when Frances went to church, I accompanied her to hear the father's sermons. When she was not available, I attended Sunday services with Roxanne, a girl my age who lived a few doors down from our house on Virginia Park Avenue in South Windsor.

It was about this time that I felt my greatest connection with the Divine. This was due to something fairly insignificant: a lost, colored pencil. After I rummaged through the house in search of it, I prayed to God. Then a thought came to me: investigate the liquor bar in the recreation room in our refurbished basement. This was not a logical place for a child to look for a pencil. But I did. Lo and behold—inside one of the built-in cupboards was a pencil case. I had never seen it before. It felt heavy. Once I'd unzipped and opened it, I found the lost pencil, plus all kinds of other colored pencils.

I took this to be an unexpected gift. It made me feel close to God. I became a bit smug about my divine relationship.

A short time later, when Father Nolan asked Roxanne to serve the fathers' and brothers' lunches at the church, she asked me to help her. Actually, we helped an older woman who took care of the needs of the clergy and did the housekeeping. The kitchen was well equipped, with a long dining table in the center of the room.

"Can we help make the sandwiches?" Roxanne asked the woman.

"Yes. Please. Maybe one of you would set the table. The dishes are in the far cupboard."

I jumped at the opportunity to get the plates and the forks and knives and set the table. The younger clergymen sat down to wait for their lunches, Father Nolan started to talk about God. At first, I was nervous, but then I felt comfortable enough to speak.

"I think Jesus was a rabbi," I said, "because he taught in the temple. What do you think?"

Father Nolan considered my statement. "Perhaps, early on in the beginning. But what about his baptism by John? I think that made him different from other rabbis."

"I agree. From my Sunday school classes," I said, "I don't remember hearing about baptisms, but we do have the *mikvah*, or ritual bathing, especially for Orthodox Jewish married women."

Over the next few months, I helped prepare lunch and talked about God with Father in this chitchatty way. But I never told my family about these luncheon gatherings or the discussions.

Then one day I heard Father Nolan's motorcycle pull into our driveway. My dad and I were home, but the priest wanted to talk with Frances. After their conversations, he came into the living room and sat in a big chair and began exchanging pleasantries with my dad. A question was burning inside me. "Is our everyday life, and all of us, like a dream in God's mind?" I asked at the first opportunity.

But before the priest could answer, my dad let out a gasp and yelled, "Myra!" Then he slapped me, hard, across the face.

I was totally embarrassed and surprised. My father was hardly ever angry or hit me. Usually, we were close and hung out together and watched sports on television. The one or two other times he spanked or slapped me were just like this time. I never understood why he did it.

"Oh, dear!" Father Nolan leaned forward in the chair and reached between us. He wanted to separate and keep my dad and me apart. "It's okay," he said. "It's okay."

The priest then told my dad about the lunches I helped serve. He explained an older nun was always present and said we talked openly about God. He knew my question was in earnest and was not meant to be disrespectful. And yet he never gave me a satisfactory answer. He just told me God loves us and Jesus helps us find the right way to live on earth.

Mind you, I didn't always get along with the nuns. When Marla and I were eight or nine years old, we were sent to St. Mary's Academy to learn to play the piano. It was a Roman Catholic school for girls and a nunnery where anyone could go for art and piano lessons. It was a huge, four-story, brick structure surrounded by manicured lawns, with a stone front gate, a grotto with religious figures in it, and vegetable gardens in the back. A ring of fruit trees and a ten-foot fence enclosed it all.

My sister and I were scared the nuns would find out we were Jewish. Convinced they would then hang us from the belfry, we walked meekly up the large, stone stairway and down the hall with its dark, wooden wainscoting and high windows. The building had many rooms and corridors and was impressive. Except for the nice, young lady who was our piano teacher and not a nun, I always hoped no one saw us coming in.

But our piano teacher did not save us from our fears. Marla and I were put in separate rooms that were modestly furnished with a wooden chair, a bench, and a piano that faced a wall. Instead of learning scales, Marla and I created coded notes and tones to communicate to each other through the connecting wall. So preoccupied were we with "talking" in this manner instead of doing our music exercises, I think we were the only kids who failed their first-year piano classes.

The fence on the east side of St. Mary's Academy separated it from a big recreational area known as Central Park. Many kids from the nearby neighborhoods had both adventures and misadventures there. In addition to large patches of grass, there were two swing sets, a merry-go-round, and a seesaw. In the summer, kids attended the YMCA day camp held in the park. We had matches on the tennis courts and swam around and dived into the deep end of the Olympic-sized, outdoor, public swimming pool. Once, after a rainy day, Marla and I got stuck in the wet muck of one of the three baseball diamonds. Only six or seven years old, we had made the unwise decision to cross the infield. We were totally embarrassed when the men from the Fire Department had to come and pull us out of the deep mud. Almost everyone from our street came to watch them do it. Most of the time we laughed and played in Central Park, whereas St. Mary's was the foreboding site that inspired nightmares.

Now, decades later, lying in a small pup tent pitched high in the Rocky Mountains, I am untroubled and sense an inner lightness. I feel connected to divine grace. My memories of Father Nolan, Central Park, and St. Mary's fade into the night as I snuggle close to Peter, who is wrapped in his own sleeping bag. We sleep peacefully, as the wind whispers lullabies through the tall evergreens.

Early the next morning, Peter builds a fire while I wash my face and brush my teeth. Before we went to sleep, Peter filled the kettle with some water from a nearby stream. While he starts to take down the tent, I dig my red, plaid, flannel shirt and jean shorts out of my knapsack, get dressed, and then make tea and toast on the grill. We also have packets of strawberry preserves and hard, yellow cheddar cheese that can last a long time without refrigeration.

We don't say too much to each other.

Our silence is broken by a loud sound, like metal grinding against more metal. Of course. It's the semitruck. Last night, the driver told us that when the engine starts, it is the signal that in ten to fifteen minutes he'll hit the road.

We are ready to go south with him. Peter walks over and leans his knapsack against the back wheel of the semi, then attends to putting out the fire. I continue to clean our campsite of any trash.

A few minutes later, the silence is broken with another loud noise: squeaky gears.

"*Nein. Nein. Nein!*" Peter barks. Then there's a huge crunch. Peter races toward the truck. I race after him. Part of his knapsack is now stuck under the huge back wheels. My stomach starts to hurt.

Mr. Semitruck Driver is jumping out of the cab. "Why did you put your knapsack there, on the passenger side? Geez! I backed up and never saw it." He sounds angry, as he grasps his head with both hands and spins around in the dirt. "Oh, geez. I heard and felt something crunching and tried to stop the truck from rolling backward."

Peter says nothing. He squats down near the wheel and shakes his knapsack free. The frame is badly bent. He grasps it with both hands and twists it somewhat back into shape. Next, he opens the pack, looks through the stuff inside, and draws out a crushed camera. He turns it this way and that, then just laughs, shakes his head, and walks over to a trash bin and tosses the camera in. Nothing else is broken, and nothing is said about the damaged camera. Peter is able to salvage some negatives though.

Lucky for us, the teakettle, pot, pan, and mugs are not tied to the bottom of his pack. They are drying near the embers of the dying fire. When attached to his pack, they dangle and clang like a noisy shaman's cloak.

The rest of the day is uneventful. Which is good. We ride with Mr. Semitruck Driver to Vernon, British Columbia, which is situated at the top of the long Okanagan Valley. Known as Canada's desert, the area is dry with a moderate climate. At the bottom of the valley is the town of Osoyoos, and Kelowna is in the middle of the region. Just east is the Myra Canyon, the home of Myra, an old mining rail station, and the Myra-Bellevue Provincial Park. The Okanagan area is precious, not because it shares my name, but because of the orchards that are full of apricot, cherry, peach, and tangerine trees. In later years, it will become a world-class, wine-producing region.

In Vernon, the first thing we do is find a Laundromat. We strip down to what is on the edge of modest and pull out all our dirty clothes. Once we're cleaned up, we seek out a restaurant. After eating at a diner, we hitch a ride out of the town.

It's a short trip. We are let out at the entrance to the highway, a road surrounded by thick forests. The air is so still, I can hear both the mosquito buzzing around my ears and the sound of a jet airplane flying high above us. The whole expanse of sky is painted in the colors of dusk, hues of dark blue, grays, oranges, and reds. In the fading light, the trees are dark brown and green. The moment feels mystical in its clearness and simplicity and sustains my sense of closeness to God.

It is nighttime when our next ride pulls into Kelowna. The city has a cowboy-town feel derived from the dress and the laid-back attitude of the folks we meet on the street. We track down the place where my university friend, Gabby, works. Before leaving Windsor, I wrote to her about my plans and then again in Calgary, I told her about Peter.

Now she greets us in a hotel lounge that looks more like a saloon. Dark wood and gaudy pictures are everywhere, along with a few mirrors. I give Gabby a hug and introduce her to Peter. She takes us behind the bar and points to where we can leave our backpacks, and then she draws him a beer from the tap.

"Take a seat, Peter. I just want to talk to Myra." That said, she pushes me toward the ladies' room, opens the door, and pulls me inside. Her mischievous smile exaggerates a slight harelip that makes her look exotic, a bit like the classic movie actress Ava Gardner. "I couldn't wait until you got here," she tells me. "I want to fix you up with the town's heartthrob. I figured one of the twins would be able to handle him." Her long, luscious, black hair is tied in a ponytail, which she coyly twirls in her fingers.

My eyebrows almost lift off my forehead. "Never mind about Peter, eh?"

"Ohhhh. Your letter from Calgary said you're just good friends." A furrow appears between her eyes and then relaxes as she comes up with an idea. "I can get someone to take him trout fishing on Okanagan Lake."

"Perfect!" I almost shout. "He'll love that. So, Mr. Heartthrob has an ego problem? I'm surprised you thought Marla or me could put him in his place."

My friend nods her head. "You guys are so strong."

"Because we can hitch rides, eh?"

"Yep, And other stuff."

I let out a laugh, "Well, I'm glad you see us that way. I'll wear that white blouse you borrowed."

❉

The next afternoon, I adjust my reclaimed top to lie a bit off my shoulder and pair it with a pink, flowered skirt and beige sandals I purchased in Calgary. I've only worn them once before, a few weeks ago on a date with a man visiting the Stampede from Calcutta, India. He took me to dinner at a Tiki Gardens and complained that I ate too fast. He instructed me on how to chew food while leaning back to relax.

Cleaned up for just this occasion, I feel feminine. Twenty minutes into my Kelowna dinner date, however, and I am done with Mr. Heartthrob. He has nothing important or interesting to say, and the waitress hasn't even brought our meal. The guy babbles on while my head nods to mime listening.

I am really reflecting on my new friendship with my German-speaking traveling companion. With his deep eyes, high cheekbones, and pouty mouth, he is cute enough. Although there are no romantic feelings between us, something drew me to travel to western Canada and meet up with Peter. It is not a habit of mine to pick up men. Nor is it my habit to hitchhike or camp out with strangers. He is special.

For the next few days, Peter and I stick around town. Then we travel back and forth to Calgary, using a more direct route. I decide to hitchhike by myself one bright sunny morning. The ride takes me just past Kelowna's city limits, where a two-lane county highway winds through forests of stately pines. Some of the trees are over a hundred feet tall. They keep me company. I start to walk backward on the grass rather than the gravel shoulder and hold a handmade sign that says, "To Alberta."

It is curious. My introversion seems to reveal itself indoors where there are people. I seem to sense their thoughts and feel insecure. When I'm out on the road and here with nature, I feel carefree.

This is not due to any naïveté. My awareness of evil people and what they can do to one another started in my childhood. The stories my parents told me about the Holocaust. Name callers and tattooed numbers I saw on arms. Even my own research. Perhaps my low self-esteem was inherited, passed down from generation to generation of persecuted Jews. I identified too much with them, probably a weakness.

It's funny that Gabby thinks I am so strong. So focused am I on my insecurities, I am surprised she sees my strengths. I cannot really relate to that part of me. Life is full of challenges. My mother taught me to look deep inside myself to overcome my negative aspects. At the same time, she said, I should try to enjoy just being alive.

About twenty minutes into my thoughts, I see a station wagon slowing and pulling off the road. I remember this car. The same family picked Peter and me up when we hitched here from Calgary a few days ago.

"Hi, Myra. Come on in."

"Hello! Thank you so much for stopping. Oh, my gosh. I am so impressed you remember my name."

While I sit in the back seat and watch nature whizzing by, I think about this trip out west and what I've learned so far. For sure, it's been stripping my ego bare, much like the anthropology courses tore up the fabric of my worldview. And yet ideas I gleaned from Professor Silverman's failed essay about Karl Marx's notions of reproduction and production still play on my mind. As we drive toward Alberta, the mountainous landscape becomes the backdrop for my thoughts.

If I were to bring an idea into manifestation, what would it be?

Not object fixated, and knowing jewelry is not the answer, I still seek a better and more meaningful answer. The quest to find my authenticity is a constant in my life. Being an identical twin, by definition, presents an existential crisis. Sometimes I wonder . . . am I even a self?

Certainly, this trip is helping me to regain my fashion sense and, more important, to become openhearted and learn to follow my intuition.

❋

I know it is time to go home.

Peter and I agree to hitch east across the Prairie Provinces to Ontario, where we'll head south to Windsor. We buy some groceries, empty Buddy's place of our stuff, load our backpacks, and then say goodbye to our friend. The guys commit to stay in touch. I give Buddy a big hug and a bigger bag of marijuana as a thank-you for his friendship and hospitality.

Our return home is tedious from the get-go, as we spend long hours waiting for a ride. The sun is hot, and the road shines in the heat. Finally, an eighteen-wheeler stops. Great.

Not much is said after we climb into the modern cab with its big windows and introduce ourselves. A couple of hours later, the driver pulls off the road near a roadside diner and stops. A few trees surround a long structure, but the gem of the place is the small lake situated in back, half a football field of grass away.

We get out of the truck, and the guys talk about a quick swim while I head for the long building, which has screen doors on both ends. I open the closest one and enter a narrow room. My carefree mood changes.

It's some kind of museum. Dull yellow walls and a low ceiling make me feel cramped. The chipped and cracked display cases are full of old ladies' knickknacks. Set nicely on doilies are hand-painted teacups and saucers and old-style jewelry. Sitting beside these common curios are a few oddities, like funny skeletons made out of mixed-up animals' bones. A small rodent's skull paired with the bones from a bird's wings.

These remains might be from road kill, carcasses left to rot and dry out. I'm sure the highway delivers these dead art supplies free of charge.

Feeling ill at ease because of the morbid artifacts, I scurry out the door and jog a few feet to the diner. Thankfully, the décor is typical. There is the familiar smell of fresh, brewed coffee. It's nearly empty of people, and I look for a waitress. She apparently finds it hard to smile as she slinks over to my booth.

"Whaddya want?"

What I always eat in a diner. "Eggs over, not runny, a side of crispy bacon, buttered toast, and coffee. And bring me some extra packets of strawberry jam. Friends will be joining me in few minutes, but you can bring me my order now."

"Coffee first? Cream?"

"No. Bring it with the meal, and yes to cream."

She writes nothing down and shuffles off to the kitchen. The guys join me. Not sure when we'll get another chance to have a hot meal without lighting a fire, I eat too much.

For the next couple of days, Peter and I hitch more rides and camp close to the freeway. The landscape is always the same, flat and full of wheat fields. At first, the tall, golden stalks of grain, which look like caterpillars with long feelers that dance in the warm breeze, charm me. Then the dullness sets in. Hours and hours of their unchanging color and form fatigue me.

So far, my luck is holding. None of the people who pick us up are cigarette smokers. My mother is a smoker, and being in a car with her makes me feel like I have the flu. Nausea, headaches, and clammy skin.

After a few days of the monotony of the Prairie Provinces, Peter and I reach Winnipeg, Manitoba. In the gateway city to western Canada, our first inclination is to ask around for a Laundromat. Once everything is clean, we get a quick bite to eat and then wander around the city. An old bookstore near the train station captures our attention.

While thumbing through a hardback book on West Coast Indians, I come to a realization. I turn to Peter. "I am tired of our hitchin' and campin' ways."

He looks up from the picture book of antique knives he's studying and looks at me. "What do you want to do?"

"I want to take the train to Windsor. I'm done."

He pauses for a moment, then nods his head. "I meet you at your home. I thumb rides."

We walk across the street to the station, where I purchase a cheap ticket on a milk-train run. This means we stop everywhere and have to sleep in our seats because there are no separate compartments with beds. I give Peter my address and directions and wish him luck. Then we hug, and he watches me get aboard with my gear in tow.

The slow train rambles from village to town to city. The mix of girls and guys in my car and I become instant friends. Most of them are about my age or younger. We play cards. I listen to their stories about how great they are and eat ham-and-cheese sandwiches from the CNR food-service counter, or warm meals at diners during the many thirty-minute stops.

My arrival in Windsor finds my parents still wound up in their own misery. My father meets me at the train. We hug, and my mother welcomes me home with a sour face. They both ask questions about how my trip went.

When we are alone, Mom says, "I'm thinking of leaving your father once Jamie goes to university."

"Geez," I say. "I understand and am not surprised, considering all the years of bickering and yelling."

She looks sad and a bit heavier than she did a few weeks ago. The key with her is to try to stay calm. Now is not the time to mention the fights that were instigated by her inability to cope with my father's laid-back personality, his bankruptcy, his bout of Bell's palsy, and then his heart attack. These financial and physical ups and downs have worn her out.

Decades later, I come to realize only an angel would have done better than her.

At times, my mother was an angry, self-involved woman. By the age of seven, I unwittingly became her confidant and psychoanalyst. It was a tough role, and I was either a good therapist or a bad daughter. Decades later, she apologized for taking advantage of my empathic qualities. Even when I was young, my mother helped me to see life from a deep and meaningful place. She introduced me to the thinking of Sigmund Freud and the benefits of self-analysis. In turn, we freely talked about everything.

And I do so now. We talk about my time out west. I tell her that Peter is hitchhiking to Windsor and will be here in a few days.

Excited to catch up with Marla and my brother, I ask them, "How did the arts and crafts circuit go while I was away?"

"We did the Tecumseh Corn Festival," Marla says, "and met an interesting artist named Cec, who made cloisonné jewelry. They loved my designs at London, Ontario, Freedom Festival. It was a cash cow." Her eyes open wide. "Jamie and I made over a thousand dollars in two days there. Our pockets, purses, and wallets were stuffed with money."

"You're a really good artist," I say. "What do you mean stuffed?"

"No checks. Only cash, and many people had small bills."

Jamie laughs. "I didn't know where to put it all after a while."

Chapter 6

THE FALL SEASON FINDS THE LEAVES of the maple trees turning from green to gorgeous colors. I watch an orange and red leaf float gently in the breeze and land a few feet in front of me. Except for the evergreens, the foliage around London, Ontario, will soon be barren. I'm somewhat underdressed for the weather, and the cold wind mocks me on my walk home from the university,

I'm still a seeker, still trying to find that one meaningful idea to bring into manifestation. My third-year anthropology courses include one with Professor Silverman. My focus is on the cross-cultural notions of self. I'm also taking an elective course in Eastern philosophy, plus required sociology and statistics courses.

For the rest of this weekend, however, I can forget about my studies. It is November 15, 1975. In a few hours, I'll be at the Bob Dylan and his Rolling Thunder Revue concert. Of all his albums, the songs on *Desire* are my favorites, by far.

When I dated Chris, we often went to Cobo Hall in downtown Detroit to see the big bands play. He was into rock, so we also went to a Rod Stewart concert and saw the Rolling Stones and David Bowie on two of their tours. We caught the performances of Stevie Wonder, B.B. King, Ike and Tina Turner, Led Zeppelin, the Moody Blues, Aerosmith, on and on and on. I went with Marla and my best friend Laurie to see The Who perform their modern-day, rock opera, *Tommy*.

Paul, a friend from my high school days, got the tickets for Dylan. Tall and thin, he was the standout basketball player in Windsor. Now he's a musician, and so is his friend, Craig, someone I kind of know from the Jewish community. Both are cool guys, and a few years older than me.

The morning of the concert, Craig and I sit on Paul's couch while we wait for him to get ready. Our drive to Niagara Falls, New York, will take a couple of hours. We are eager to start. Then there is a knock on the door. Before anyone can answer it, a young woman walks into the room.

Craig leans over and whispers in my ear, "Paul's girlfriend."

She is a petite, nuts-and-berries-looking kind of person, with long, ash-blonde hair and a flowing skirt. What sparks my curiosity is the small object in her hand. When she sits down next to me, I ask her, "What is that?"

"It's a book. I made it myself."

"How?"

"I used cardboard and paper, with dental floss to hold it all together."

"Kind of like a pamphlet, eh?"

"Yes. The floss is sewed through the paper." She opens the book to its middle section and the pages fall neatly to each side, which reveals the waxy thread sewed in and out down the center of the fold. "I used a thin board and covered it with wallpaper and wallpaper glue."

"That sounds easy. I never thought about making a book by hand."

As we talk, I sense a change in my body. It is a kind of quickening of heat that flows through me. A clear thought pops into my head. This is it! This is what I want to bring into manifestation. A book.

Some call it an epiphany, or that aha! moment. I just had one. Yes, a book. Something so seemingly ordinary is really so special to me. And yet I've never thought about how books are made, either by hand or machine.

Memories flood through my mind about how books came into my life. When I was five or six years old and bored one day, I said to my father, "There is nothing to do. What can we do?"

Dad was often great fun to play with. One day back then, he took my hand and led me down the stairs of our home to the back room of our basement. Along the rear wall were long, built-in bookshelves. My dad took one book off the shelf and handed it to me.

"Here, read this. You will love reading it on your own."

That instant was a rite of passage. From then on, I was always reading. It could be in bed. Sometimes, it was under the covers with a flashlight, so as not to disturb my sister, if she was not reading too and was already asleep in the other bed. Or I read in the bathtub, with a pillow and a big towel to cover me. Libraries became another kind of candy store. My father took all us kids there to browse around, borrow books, and delight in them at home. Other little girls found comfort with dolls; I found the same physical sensation when holding a book.

During that same time period, I used to go to the Woolco Department Store on Dougall Avenue. My mother and father drove, or I walked with a group of friends. Once there, my first destination was always the stationery section. Transfixed with longing, I gazed at the blank notebooks, diaries, and journals, and imagined them filled with my thoughts and my memories.

I remember a hobby of mine. In grade school, the blank exercise books were fair game, so I stole a few every so often from the supply room. This theft was the result of my ambition to be a club president, which meant notebooks are needed to keep club records and workbooks for the members. I had a private club, with two other members, but only for a couple of weeks. In the seventh or eighth grade, the class voted me to be the president of the school's science club.

These thoughts accompany me on the drive to Niagara Falls. At the Dylan concert, we find our seats on the convention floor, but we rarely sit in them. The crowd sings along to Dylan's hit song, "Hurricane." It's about the one-time, world-champion boxer who was doing time for a crime he didn't commit. Dylan and his band play the whole *Desire* album. They sound fantastic. Emmylou Harris is on stage too.

❉

Now it is the spring semester of my third year at the university and four months after Dylan's concert. It is a gorgeous day outside. The morning light shines in through the windows of the apartment I share with Marla in downtown London. I'm thinking about the day of the concert and meeting Paul's girlfriend. Still in bed, I say out loud to no one but myself, "Oh, Myra, what's taken you so long? Get up and go get some cardboard, paper, and dental floss to make a book."

When my self-chastisement ends, I get myself up, dress, and jog over to the campus to buy the materials at the university bookstore. Only a few students are there, so it's as quiet as a library. At the checkout counter, the silhouette of a man walking across an aisle catches my eye. He seems to be in search of a book. I hope he doesn't see me.

About six feet and a couple of inches tall, with beautiful, honey-colored skin and a slight moustache, he was a fellow classmate in my first-year, classical studies class. He told us he was Jamaican and seemed to be twice as old as most of the students. His comments had a touch of sexual innuendo. He intimidated me. The professor played up to the man's raunchiness when Catullus, the late Roman poet, and passages from Aristophanes' *Lysistrata* were added to our reading list.

Now, in line at the bookstore, I hope to buy the stuff needed and get out of here before the Jamaican comes over and says something that embarrasses me. To avoid this possibility, I lift the piece of cardboard up to cover my face and try to hide behind it.

Then I hear a baritone voice with a refined British accent (acquired when he studied in London). "What are you doing with that cardboard, my dear?"

Oh, God, he recognizes me! I lower the cardboard. "Hi," I say. "Making a blank book with it."

He looks me straight in the eye, smiles, nods his head, and leaves the bookstore. For once, he has nothing to say. After paying the cashier, I walk out of the store only to find this same man waiting in the hall. His eyes fix onto mine like lasers, which compels me to approach him.

He puts out his hand and says, "My name is Vernon. I am a professional hand bookbinder. You know, there are only five of us in all of Canada."

I had no idea there was such a profession. "Hi, I'm Myra. Can you teach me how to make a book?"

"Yes, I can." His face beams. "I recognized you from class. How were you going to make books with that cardboard you bought?"

"I recognized you too," I say. Pointing to the door of the university craft room opposite the bookstore, I explain, "Well, my plan was to cut down the cardboard in there and sew the pages together with dental floss and then giftwrap each cover with wallpaper."

He throws back his head and roars with laughter. "Oh, my dear. I never heard of such a thing! Please, come to the bindery tomorrow afternoon."

"What do you mean 'bindery'? Where is it?"

"I make and restore real books there," he says. "It is in the School of Library and Informational Sciences. Go down the hill, or you can go a bit underground through the music school tunnel.

"I'll figure it out. See you tomorrow then, Vernon. Thank you for the opportunity."

Awestruck by this coincidence, I watch him walk away. Despite the failing grade, my work on Professor Silverman's essay about Marx's concepts of production and reproduction led me to ponder the notion of bringing an idea into manifestation. In pursuit of this idea, I began to create and sell jewelry, traveled out west, and (most important) began to look deep into my soul. The essay was the engine that brought me to this moment. Now, my inner desire to make a book has connected me to a bookbinder. Our serendipitous meeting seems like a window into fate.

❀

Underground tunnels lace the campus. Used mostly in the winter because of London's location in the snowbelt of Canada, where fierce winds can cause mighty blizzards, they also are useful on rainy days. Although the region is flat—prehistorically once an ocean floor—the city lies in a valley. Windsor, Ontario, gives proof of this large, prehistoric ocean with the salt that is mined nearby and internationally exported.

Because it is early spring with no rain in sight, I don't take the tunnel, but stride across the campus in the direction of the School of Library and Informational Sciences. My thoughts are still on the notion of fate. Yesterday's meeting with Vernon seems like a miracle, considering that there are only five bookbinders in all of Canada. In my Eastern philosophy course, we discussed the *I Ching*, or *Book of Changes*. I'm thinking it might help me to understand this phenomenon. Perhaps, the used bookstore has a copy of this ancient Chinese text on divination and transformations.

Dressed in a sweatshirt and jeans, I walk past the music school. Its stone foundations, ivy-covered walls, and array of chimney stacks signal an older era. A turn to the left and a short trot down the grassy hill brings me to the front of the library school, a modern-looking building. A quick glance at the directory at the entrance tells me the correct hallway to take to find Vernon. I head past offices and classrooms, a few in session and some empty, to the back of the building, where the bindery is.

Inside, I see a room full of equipment. Something that looks like a long, heavy vice is bolted to the floor. A small table, holding a one-handed guillotine. A large, two-handed machine sitting on the other side of the room. Both have bright silver blades, just like the ones I've seen in the craft room up the hill. Stacks of large book boards, bolts of multicolored book cloth, and rolls of paper are stacked in the corners. A faint, sweet smell mingles with the odor of a tuna salad. Perhaps that is Vernon's lunch. A few, narrow windows are open and let in natural light and air. Workbenches line two of the four walls.

The pictures tacked on the walls stop me cold. Three, oversized, travel posters of Jamaica show voluptuous women wearing skimpy, two-piece bathing suits about to take a dip in turquoise waters. These pictures adorn the bare spaces between built-in shelves, full of handmade and exotic tissue paper. The loud, obvious display of sexuality makes me nervous.

Vernon, who looks like a National Football League (NFL) tight end, although he sees himself as Shakespeare's Othello, stands in the middle of it all. A huge grin on his round, golden face makes him glow. "Forget about the ladies," he tells me. "Don't be timid. I'm glad you are here. Come in. Come in."

"Hi, Vernon." I step into the room.

He shakes his head. "Dental floss. Oh, my dear Myra. Let me explain how you really make a book." Vernon's formal English is now laced with a Jamaican lilt.

Hesitant at first, I walk with him around the room as he explains how the various tools and machines are used. Book parts are similar to the human anatomy, he says, and he points out the different tools used to sew the body of the book, to make the curve of its spine, and smooth out the cloth or leather on the head, the front, and the back. He giggles and makes risqué hints. I make furtive glances at the almost naked women on the walls.

Next, he leads me over to one of the workbenches, where the sweet, candy smell that greeted me gets stronger. It emanates from a pot sitting on top of an electric burner at one end of the table. I look more closely and see thick, bubbling syrup.

"What is this used for?" The mystery of one odor is solved, but I cannot figure out where Vernon keeps the tuna salad sandwiches.

He follows me over to the pot, and hands me a stick to stir the molasses-like substance. "This is animal glue made from horses' hooves and used for binding with leather." He lets out a chuckle. "Hot and sticky, eh, my dear?"

Now Vernon explains his responsibilities for the university's collection. "The work in the bindery is to conserve and restore the school's main libraries and rare book collections. Come over here." We walk to a tall chest, and he opens a drawer that reveals movable lead type in a number of different fonts. "With our letterpress and the gold, silver, and bronze leaf, we can imprint the titles and authors' names on the newly bound spines and fronts of the books."

The university's head bookbinder and conservator sounds professorial now. He directs me to the second workbench, on which sits an odd-looking contraption. This device is about two feet high. Two vertical posts attached to the bottom of its frame hold a horizontal bar. The first pages of a book lie on the platform.

"This is used to hand-sew the signatures, or the folded pages, of books." Vernon lightly taps down the papers of the partially sewn book with his fingers. "Everything is archival quality. We use strong linen thread and linen cords for the raised bands on the spine. They will help to keep the signatures joined too. The spine is then protected with linen, paper, and polyvinyl emulsion glue, or we sometimes use rice flour paste." He laughs and winks. "You need to protect your spine, right, my dear?"

He takes a seat in front of the frame and tells me to do the same. "I will show you how the sewing is done, Myra. Special knots must be made at the ends of the paper signatures to secure them together. Tight knots." His eyebrows lift, his grin reappears.

To observe Vernon's handiwork, I pull a stool next to him. My leg touches his. The movement of his large hands is delicate as he pushes the sewing needle in and out, making small stitches down the center of the signature. He ends with a tiny knot and a loop to start the next signature. Other types of knots extend the linen thread.

My leg touches Vernon's. Again. Under my blue jeans, my skin feels hot. I shift on my stool. After his sexual innuendos and the almost naked women on the walls, this closeness is all too much for me. Within a few minutes, I jump off the stool and mumble a quick, "Thank you." And then I race out of the bindery at record speed.

Forget about my desire to bring a book into manifestation. Vernon is way too sexual for me.

Chapter 7

AW, GEEZ. THERE HE IS AGAIN. I sure hope he doesn't see me. Before he gets any closer, I run and hide around the corner of the medical school building. Head held high, he looks straight ahead and saunters right past me. Sometimes I hide behind a tree trunk, a pillar, or a bush or duck into a doorway. These maneuvers and avoidance tactics have been going on for the past three months.

But for some reason, today I muster up enough courage to approach him. "Vernon, can you teach me how to make a book, again?" My voice is meek, and my knees are trembling.

"Yes, Myra." His eyes are intense. They look straight into mine. "Yes, and I can even pay you. You're in luck. The library school just budgeted for me to have a part-time assistant. So I can offer you ten hours per week."

"Great! Thank you. My job shelving books at the medical school library ends next week. I can start then."

Vernon shifts his feet, about ready to leave. "Oh. You work over there? So that's why I keep seeing you hanging around the corner of the medical school." He winks and walks away.

A few months into my bookbinding apprenticeship, I have learned the procedures for hand sewing; making a curved spine; making a basic, library-style binding in buckram book cloth; and the technique for paring down pieces of leather. The goal is to get the skin thin enough to fold around the corners of the archival book boards. All these steps must be perfected to make a proper book.

At the start of the summer of 1977, I graduate from the university with a three-year general bachelor's degree, but I do not attend the ceremony. About the same time, Vernon lets me use the bindery to make my own blank books. Multicolored papers are sewn together and bound with colorful felt fabric. He helps me, and the results are perfectly made books. But they look odd. The rainbow colors are fine, but I'm not sure of the furry effect of the felt.

My siblings and I are scheduled do a number of jewelry shows in southwestern Ontario's arts and crafts circuit. It's our second summer. This time, alongside our jewelry, I want to sell my handmade, blank books. At the Carlisle Bluegrass Festival, Canada's three-day version of a mini-Woodstock, a fellow crafter and I set up our display tent in a special artisans' area. Although bluegrass is not really my kind of music, the event is lots of fun and one person buys a book.

By early September, my part-time bookbinding assistantship turns into a full-time position, and I continue my apprenticeship with Vernon. It is not common in the British Commonwealth for women to be taught hand bookbinding skills. Mostly, they stick to tasks that involve sewing the pages or signatures together.

From time to time, usually on a Friday, Vernon and I catch a bus and eat a late lunch together at a Chinese restaurant in downtown London. Along with huge egg rolls and a scrumptious Cantonese buffet, the place boasts a well-stocked jukebox. Vernon is a regular. Somehow, he gets me to dance when a fast Motown song is played. Then a slow song follows.

When he grabs me with both hands just above my hips and pulls me closer, the electricity is undeniable.

"Vernon, I want to meet your wife."

He cooks all the food. Tonight, it is his specialty, curried goat. I am the guest of honor at the family dinner. It is a few weeks after I made my request at the Chinese restaurant. Over the delicious and, thankfully, not too spicy meal, we discuss my feelings about the bindery. And Vernon. I mention another housemate, who interests me.

This causes Vernon's wife to burst out, "She does not want you. She likes this other guy. Victor."

A dancer and mother, Vernon's wife is one of the strongest women I know. She understands he could have an affair, though not with me. With her hands on her hips, she often tells him, "Not in my kitchen. It stops at the door. If you blow smoke in my face, don't bring your girlfriends into my house."

As for Victor and me, we first met a few months ago, when he came to the house where I rented a room. He wanted to know if another room was available. The spare bedroom across from mine was empty, and so he moved in. Years later, Victor told me he had heard one of the twins had rented a room in that house, which is why he'd come to inquire that day.

I like him. Almost six feet tall, he has sandy hair, a beautiful smile, a somewhat large nose and a thin, but athletic body. He walks with a slight limp, thanks to a high school soccer injury.

At first, we chatted about history and philosophy and world affairs. Now we talk in an easy way about emotions and feelings and can share from a deep place. Originally from the United States, Victor is also a twin. This is probably the reason we communicate so well with each other. Whereas Marla and I are identical twins, Victor and his sister are fraternal twins. He tells me she is a model for catalogs and print advertisements.

Then one day it happens. The morning starts off innocently enough. We have a philosophical discussion about something.

Victor has to go to work. Instead of cutting our talk short, as would be usual, I follow him to the communal bathroom. Leaving the door open so we can keep talking, he takes off his shirt and starts to shave. His shaving cream has a masculine smell to it. Maybe it's mint.

I watch the twists and contortions of his handsome face and notice how his muscles tighten in his chest and arms. And I fall in love. Although nothing physically happens between us, the sensuality of this moment is undeniable.

Later, we kiss. We become a couple. Then we decide to rent our own apartment.

He chooses the location, gives me the address, and tells me to meet him there. I arrive to find it is the attic of an old mansion. Victor, broom in hand, stands in the middle of a dump. The dirt is everywhere, on the floor and the furniture, and cobwebs seem to hang between everything.

"I'm not sure this will work," I say as I head toward the door. "I'm going to buy a postage stamp. I'll be back."

Instead of going to the post office, I walk to the corner store and buy a local newspaper. In the classifieds, I find an apartment to rent and catch a bus to take a look at it. It is a furnished, two-bedroom apartment in the basement of a small house. The unique aspect is the built-in workbench that spans an entire wall of the spare room. It's an ideal place to do my hand bookbinding.

That evening, we somehow get out of the rental agreement for the attic dump, and Victor and I move into the new place. That night, and for many nights, I experience incredible, lucid dreams. When I mention this to the owner of the house, who occupies the ground floor, with her bedroom directly above us, she tells me about her interest in psychic phenomena. She associates my dreams with material in Jane Roberts' books about Seth, an energy personality Roberts claimed to channel.

I fly in my dreams. The sensation of taking off into flight feels real. Soaring high above the city streets with a bird's-eye view is vivid.

The homeowner tells me that Seth believes I actually am flying. He associates the dream to the death state, where the time-space dimension of our physical world is absent. Here we have an opportunity to develop, meet people and "extend the limits of our consciousness." The phenomenon of flying intrigues me more than reading the Jane Roberts' books that the homeowner suggests.

Besides the sensations of being airborne in my dreams, I find it easy to live with Victor in real life. As for being sexual, we hang out around third base and don't go "all the way." Although I'm adventurous, my intention is to be a good Jewish girl.

A few weeks after we move in together, news comes that Victor's stepmother and father will be in London. They live on the West Coast of the United States and will be in town for a medical conference. Thanks to my former job, shelving books at the library, I know the university's medical school has a first-class reputation. My boyfriend tells me his father is a world-renowned doctor.

Because it is not too hot outside, I decide to walk to work instead of waiting for the bus. It will take about forty-five minutes to get to the campus gates, then to the library school's bindery. On my crosstown hike, I can't seem to shake off thoughts of meeting Victor's dad. Like a Buddhist or Hebrew chant, my internal dialogue keeps repeating his father's name, over and over again. My pace becomes measured to its beat. The probabilities of encountering the man are slim, as I'm not sure where the conference is held or what his father looks like. My vague memory of his image comes from an old, worn photograph.

Once on campus, I make an unusual decision to take the underground route and enter the tunnel that connects the music school at the top of the hill to the library school and the bindery at the base. On such a sunny, summer day, one would ordinarily choose the outdoors route. But something compels me to go underground.

I enter the building, proceed down the stairs to the basement lobby, and stride across a long floor toward the entrance of the underground passageway. To my left is a bank of telephones. The place looks empty.

I become more alert, therefore, when a man comes into view at the opposite end. Either he entered from the outside stairway or he is coming from the tunnel. He is middle-aged, dressed casually, and looks like a professor. He walks straight toward me, and we look at each other. When he is about twenty feet away from me, I hear a light, jingling sound. Then the loose change in my pocket falls out from the bottom of one of my pant legs. About four dollars' worth of Canadian coins clink onto the tile.

The stranger is still approaching. I come to a dead stop, embarrassed. One hand comes up to cover my mouth. There's a hole in my pocket. Why now? Time seems to stand still. The man looks at me. We both are quiet until the echo from the stream of coins goes silent. Then the man stoops down, scoops up a handful of coins, and gives them to me.

"Here you go." His manner is mild.

I'm scurrying around to pick up the rest of the money. "So sorry. Thank you."

My coins in my hand now, I hurry to get away but look back just in time to see the man heading in the direction of telephones at the far end of the hall. He turns and waves with a big smile on his face.

My feet propel me toward the library school, and I arrive in a state of exhaustion. It is not from the walk, which I've done plenty of times before.

After listening to my story, Vernon says, "Go home, Myra. You need rest. Your psychic energy is depleted. Feeling drained stems from your psychical thoughts coupled with coming across a man you believe is Victor's father."

I leave the bindery and catch the next bus to my apartment, and then go straight to bed, even though it not even noontime. Later that night, Victor hears about the coins and the chance encounter.

"Well," he says, "you'll meet my father and stepmother tomorrow night. They've invited us to dinner."

"Great. Where?"

"The race track. With a bunch of doctors and their wives."

"What should I wear?"

"Wear a dress or a skirt. The women always get dressed up for these conference occasions."

But I am way overdressed when we arrive. This leaves me feeling timid and reserved. This fancy, cream-colored, linen suit of mine is pretty with its scalloped, tailored jacket and below-the-knee full skirt. It is a bad choice. The doctors' wives wear slacks and nice tops, as does Victor's stepmother, who is an attractive, blonde, Norwegian woman with an inner sense of calm that gives her a stately manner.

With my confidence at a low, I am not sure now it was Victor's father at the incident with the coins. He looks thinner and younger than the man I saw in the tunnel. After dinner, I gather my courage and speak to him. "Yesterday, were you in the basement of the music building when all of a sudden my money fell out of my pocket? Was that you, Doctor?"

"Yes, yes, Myra that was me. That was you!" The renowned surgeon slaps the table and waves his hand to get everyone's attention. "Hey, you guys. Listen. Myra, tell them how we met yesterday. Go ahead. I wish Victor's twin sister was here. She loves this psychic stuff."

From then on, the dinner and my bets on the horses go well. I loosen up and laugh at many of the doctors' jokes. When they say good night, Victor's parents invite me to visit them at their West Coast home. Later, my boyfriend tells me they were quite taken with me. "My father told me not to let you go."

Chapter 8

VICTOR AND I CAN ENDURE ONLY a few of months of living underground. We move into a studio apartment in a high-rise with large windows and an outdoor balcony. Still in London, we are closer to the university and my job at the bindery.

My twin sister Marla lives in Toronto, where she has a trendy job selling advertising space to restaurants for a top-notch magazine. Meanwhile, my younger but smarter brother attends the university in the same city, where he takes a double major in finance and actuarial science. Our mother and father, now empty nesters, have separated, though they both live in Windsor.

It is September 1978, almost a year after the start of my full-time apprenticeship with Vernon.

Standing in the doorway, I scan the room and engrave it in my memory. On the wood sewing frame is the beginning of a book. Its half-made spine is naked, unbound to reveal the intricate patterns of linen threads, linen cords, and the tiny knots I precisely tied to ensure the stitches stay secure. Making or repairing a book comes with unique sounds. The thud of the hammer makes a curved spine, and the whoosh of the blade cuts paper and cloth.

In the bindery, all my senses are alive. The sweet, candy fragrance of the amber-colored animal glue informs me it is ready to bind with animal skin. I finally figured out that strong odor of tuna salad: it's not a stash of sandwiches but polyvinyl acetate. Similar to Elmer's glue, polyvinyl acetate is used to bind book cloth and fancy-colored endpapers. I dip my nose closer and smell the delicate, starchy aroma coming from the clear, rice-flour paste. It's perfect to use on the fragile Japanese tissue used to repair holes and tears in the pages of the rare book that lie open on what used to be my worktable.

I look again at the personal touches Vernon added, the large, multicolored travel posters showing barely dressed women ready to take a dip in the waters of his beloved Jamaica. Often, I have teased Vernon. "This is a bookbindery, not a bordello."

I do not make any jokes today. Today is different. Today is my last day here. The university has released a new budget and cut the funds for a bookbinder's assistant job. We knew this day was coming, and because of the pending funding cuts, I planned ahead. A job prospect arose at the New England Documentation Center in Lawrence, Massachusetts. My dual citizenship with the United States will come in handy if I emigrate.

Victor and I had planned for this day too. When he learned about my interview, set for the end of September, he offered a suggestion. "Let's leave earlier than the meeting date in Lawrence." His eyes sparkled with excitement. "My folks have a place on Martha's Vineyard. We can stay there a week and then go to Lawrence."

For some reason, I did not answer right away, though I'm not sure why. Finally I leaned over and gave him a kiss. "I'd love to see your family's place."

Then we gave a month's notice to end our rental apartment agreement.

And now it is my last day at the bindery. I watch Vernon glide across the room and stop beside me. For a large man, he is quite graceful. In addition to being a bookbinder and conservator, he is an award-winning stage actor and director, which accounts for his big personality and presence.

A huge grin spreads across his face as he places a large, gift-wrapped box in my hands. I immediately unwrap it and find a set of moveable, metal type. Also in the box is a single-line type holder. And sheets of gold and silver leaf used to imprint titles and names onto books. And a couple of animal bone folders and two fancy glue brushes. Then I pull out the hardware for a backing vise to make the curved spine of a book. This completes his thoughtful present.

Tears flow down my face as Vernon pulls me close and we hug. Through my sniffles, I say, "Thank you. You promise, and I'll promise, to stay in touch."

"Yes, my dear."

By some coincidence, an opportunity arose for Victor and me to purchase a used Toyota mini-pickup a week before we plan to leave the city. We bought the used vehicle from the university's maintenance department. Functionality prevailed over beauty, and now we begin filling the back of it with clothes, books, and a few mementos. After a big black tarp gets thrown over all the stuff and is secured with heavy rope, Victor drives us out of town toward the Canadian–American border. Luckily, we breeze through customs and head toward the Cape Cod area.

We assume the job in Massachusetts is mine.

❇

On the ferry ride over to the island, the skies are an unexpected gray, and a slight breeze of melancholy seems to drift onboard with the sea air. My sadness deepens when we near Martha's Vineyard. This confuses me. I expected to be happy.

When we reach Oak Bluffs, which is on the island, my spirits lift. It is a picturesque town. Holding hands, we walk down streets lined with multicolored, gingerbread cottages. Their unique style and bright colors make them look all dressed up. Some are homes, whereas others are storefronts whose windows are full of art, clothes, and touristy items with a nautical, New England theme.

When we first entered the Martha's Vineyard harbor, the dark clouds cast a dull shade on the periwinkle blue, shingled houses that dot the island's edge. The darkness got to me. But here in Oak Bluffs, a basic blue structure enchants me with its bubblegum pink eaves, lime green wooden railings, and purple trim around the windows.

After the colorful detour, Victor heads our pickup toward the tip of the island and chats about its past as he drives. "It was incorporated in 1668, along with Chappaquiddick. You know, in 1969, the place of Ted Kennedy's tragic car accident that killed Mary Jo Kopechne."

I look over at Victor. "It's sad about the girl"

"Yes, sad for her family and sad for Ted Kennedy. Some say it's why he never ran for president. And the—"

"Hey!" I interrupt him with a smile, "Let's talk about something more palatable. Where are the good places to eat on the island?"

He changes the subject with ease. "Edgartown is the historic hub, where you find the better restaurants. The Terrace at the Charlotte Inn is one of them."

I almost lick my lips in excitement, but the seafood will have to wait until we get settled. A short while later, we turn onto a narrow, county lane called Lobsterville Road. On both sides are forests filled with oaks, beeches, and pitch pines. The woods are so thick, we cannot see any houses.

"Menemsha Bight bay is just up ahead." Victor points with his chin. "The beach is around the bend in the road. It's hidden by all the trees."

"How far is it from your family's place?"

"About a ten-minute walk."

Soon, we turn in to an even narrower, dirt track that cuts through the woods. We continue at a slow pace, deep into the forest. A few minutes later, we come to a clearing of trampled-down earth that forms a large, circular area in front of the two structures that are Victor's family's compound. Our modest, copper-colored pickup, the back filled to the brim, fits in perfectly with the dark wood, two-story, main house. The lighter colored A-frame cottage sits a few yards away. Other than the surrounding forest, there is no landscaping to enhance the buildings.

This East Coast home and cottage have been in the family since Victor was a child. My expectation was to find distinguished-looking dwellings reflective of his father's reputation. He resides on the West Coast and is a world-renowned surgeon, head of the Department of Orthopedics and Sports Medicine at the University of Washington, and head physician to a professional sports team. Instead, their architectural style reminds me of Victor, who favors denim jackets, denim shirts, and denim pants, an outfit known as the "Canadian tuxedo." While studying at the university, he gets by in life as a basic line cook, albeit in notable restaurants. It was Victor's natural elegance and charm that won me over; the exteriors of the main house and the A-frame are neither elegant nor charming.

Victor pulls a key from his pants pocket and opens the front door of the main house. Dry, stuffy air rushes out. Along with it, I catch a faint whiff of melancholy. A scan of the rooms reveals nice, teak furniture, but a rather austere décor. The big windows provide views of the lush trees outside, and the large sundeck on the second level makes up for the emptiness inside.

A few days later, we wake up to Indian summer weather and sunshine. The subtle, unhappy smells are all gone too. Out and about on the island, I finally indulge my desire to eat fresh-caught lobster tails with drawn butter. I also try chunky clam chowder and locally caught fish. At the supermarket, Victor has the eye of a seasoned chef and spots packages of filet mignon.

"They're fresh." He points at the date stamp. "Let's take two back and cook them on the deck over charcoal."

"Great. I love almost anything grilled."

Back at the main house, I prepare a simple salad while Victor attends to the barbecue. We divide our chores evenly, which is why we've lived so well together for the past year. Under a canopy of a billion stars, made brighter by the dark forest that encircles us, we enjoy our meal.

"You said your father was in the produce business?" Victor asks me as he scoops up some baked potato with sour cream and chives.

"Yes," I reply. "Fruits and vegetables are in my blood. After emigrating from Northern Europe, my father's father and his six brothers started selling fresh produce from horse-drawn wagons in the Windsor/Detroit area. Eventually, they owned markets and sold wholesale to hospitals and hotels, like the famous Elmwood Casino. Frank Sinatra played there. Do you know what's interesting?"

"What?"

"Turns out, my father married a carnivore. No, really." I giggle. "My mother doesn't like anything fresh."

There is a curious look on my boyfriend's handsome face. "She cooks for you, right?"

"Yes, all the time, and she always did, except when we went for Chinese food. At least once a week. Anyway, she's an excellent cook with meats and poultry. She only eats chicken, beef, or pork and a bit of fish and not a lot of vegetables."

I take a bite of the filet mignon and then another. So does Victor. We're eating in silence, too busy chewing to talk.

"This is delicious!" I squeal with delight. "It's done perfectly. With a bit of char. Forget about the seafood. You've cooked the best thing I've eaten since we've been here. I'm surprised. I had no idea there are slaughterhouses on Martha's Vineyard."

Victor grins. "It's a well-kept secret." Then he winks and takes a sip of dry red wine.

After the heavy meal, we share in the cleanup and spend the remainder of the evening outside on the deck, talking until we're exhausted, and then we head to bed. The next morning, over a simple breakfast of toast and jam, we make some plans.

"Let me teach you how to drive the manual pickup," Victor says. "Don't worry. You'll be in an area no one goes to."

I butter a piece of toast and shrug my shoulders. "Not sure about the clutch. Tried it before and didn't get it. But okay. Let's go."

We change into jeans and T-shirts, and I grab my purse and a sweatshirt. A few minutes later, we are in front of a vacant office complex surrounded by fields of shrubs and weeds. Beyond them lie the ocean and the sky. In the driver's seat now, I am briefed on the proper technique for using the car's manual transmission.

Although my intention is to perform well, the result is a bumpy ride around the empty parking lot. Part of the problem is my thinking while I'm trying to drive. I wonder if there is a hospital on Martha's Vineyard. Does it have an ambulance? How long will it take to get to the main house? I don't understand my thoughts. Why is my focus at the main house and not here, where I am driving?

"Work the clutch, Myra. You don't want to grind the gears."

"Sorry. Can't concentrate. I'm not used to the stick shift."

Victor drives us home. Exhausted, I remain quiet. He would probably want to tell me about the history of hospitals in the Cape Cod area. I'm not sure why I'm worried, but I am sure about these feelings of foreboding.

Chapter 9

AS I'M HIKING UP THE hill, I notice a white van parked at the crest, its front end hanging over the edge of Gay Head Cliffs. It glows in the sunlight, and I mentally compare it to the mini-pickup we recently bought on the cheap. Automotive vehicles do not often mesmerize me, even though I was born in the Motor City and raised across the border in Windsor, the tool and die capital of Canada. Cars and trucks were everywhere, in whole or in parts.

Victor and I reach the top of the hill where it levels off at an open lot. As we walk closer to the van, it appears empty. There are no letters or logos on the door panel that faces us. But standing on the other side of the van we see a man.

He is leaning against the vehicle and gazing out over the Atlantic. Below him, at the base of the cliff, is the infamous Jungle Beach, where Victor and I were strolling a few moments ago. Nude sunbathers are usually lying there. But not today. It is too cold.

The man leaning against the van is at least six feet tall. He is wearing a jet-black hat, a bomber jacket, pants, and boots.

Only his back is visible to us. An ice-cold shudder flows through me as we walk past him. "That is an evil man," I whisper to my boyfriend. "An evil man." There is nothing obviously unusual about his appearance, yet I sense his malevolence.

Victor wraps his arm around my shoulders and pulls me closer, then guides me to our pickup, parked a few yards away. Once inside, I sit huddled against the passenger door, drained by that brief glimpse of evil. Victor does not question me, and I welcome the silence. It gives me an opportunity to reflect on the mythos of the Cape Cod region.

An idyllic, sunny, vacation spot, Martha's Vineyard (off the east coast of Massachusetts) is known as an island retreat for the wealthy and the prestigious, including presidents of the United States. It seems counterintuitive to realize that it's a place where crimes are committed, especially the hard-boiled kind.

As Victor drives us away from the white van and the Evil Man, my cheek rests against the cool glass of my window, but I am oblivious to the view. In all my years of hitchhiking, I never came across a stranger like that man. Back at the main house, I am still physically and psychically exhausted and do not share my thoughts with Victor. Maybe I'll do it later. Or maybe tomorrow.

The next morning starts out well. Sunshine greets us when we wake. We make plans for the day ahead and eat a light breakfast. I say nothing about the man we saw yesterday.

"This afternoon," Victor breaks the silence, "James Taylor and Carly Simon are giving a free No Nukes Concert to protest the use of nuclear weapons. Do you want to go? As it's late September," he adds, "it's just for the islanders, 'cause most of the tourists are gone by now."

"Not really," I say. "Folk rock isn't my style of music. Motown and reggae are my favorites. Something deep and soulful. And good vocals too."

"That's my style too. I guess it's one reason we get along." Victor gets up from the table to give me a light kiss, then takes our dirty dishes to the sink. "Let's get our chores done.

I already told you some friends of my family are due to arrive later today. They'll stay in the main house, so we need to move our stuff over to the A-frame."

"Okay. It's only for one night, anyway. We can pack most of our things into the pickup and be ready to leave for Lawrence tomorrow."

He nods. "Yep, that's the plan. Are you nervous about your interview? It's for paper restorer and bookbinder, right?"

"Yes. Not really nervous. I'm sure the meeting will be fine. I'm excited to see what the people at the New England Documentation Center are working on, because this is an old part of the United States, as you well know."

We move our belongings to the smaller cottage, some to the pickup, then we make sure the big house is spick and span for the new guests. An hour later, when the tasks are done, we sit on the deck and exchange ideas about what to do next.

Victor offers the first suggestion. "Let's make love," he says. "It's been awhile."

I shake my head, but he walks over and puts his arms around me. "Lighten up, will you? Think of it as just adult play." A big smile stretches across his handsome face. "Let's fool around like we're kids. Myra, imagine we're naked in a playpen. Let's just have some fun."

We've lived together for almost a year, and I have not gone all the way to fourth base with Victor. He is a gentleman, not a pushy kind of guy. But I do not have the heart to tell him that he feels more like a brother than a boyfriend.

Instead, I stand and say, "I need to go for a walk. By myself." I pull out of his arms. To take the sting out of my rejection, I add, "I love you, but I need a break from our constant togetherness. It's been our routine for the past few weeks. Maybe it's why I don't feel so romantic."

"Okay. Okay." Victor throws his hands in the air, as if to show he's lost an imaginary fight. "I love you too. So where are you going all by yourself?"

"To that beach you mentioned, the one up the road. And I am going alone."

Dressed in a hooded sweatshirt and jogging pants, I set out toward the path through the woods, then I turn onto Lobsterville Road. Although I'm concerned about my safety, I am comforted by the thought that Victor and his twin sister played here when they were little kids.

A short walk up the road takes me around the bend to where I can see the water and hear the waves. This road runs parallel to a wide-open expanse of beach. A few yards up ahead, three guys are fishing, but except for them, the area is empty. It's late afternoon now, and most of the people on the island must be at the No Nukes Concert.

I kick off my sandals and carry them as I walk across the stretch of sand, which feels warm and good between my toes. At no particular spot, I plop down and sit cross-legged to watch the waves rubbing up against the shore and losing themselves among the shells, pebbles, and bits of things discarded along the water's edge. On any other day, I might rummage around the stuff and look for pretty colors and odd shapes.

Not today. Instead, my gaze is drawn toward Menemsha Bight bay off the Vineyard Sound. The effects of the weirdness from the last few days begin to fall away and soon I feel relaxed. Nature can do that to me.

This calm state continues, and now my mind is clear. In this quiet space, my inner voice whispers, *You are here for a reason. You are here to learn something. You are here for a reason. You are here to learn something. You are here for a reason. You are here to learn something.*

These sentences are repeated over and over, and the inner chant mesmerizes me. *You are here for a reason. You are here to learn something.* On and on it goes. Then the chant stops. For a while, there is only silence in my head, which I take as a signal to leave the beach. I pick myself up, shake the sand off my sweatpants, and walk back to Lobsterville Road, where I put my sandals on and walk back to Victor's house.

But just a couple of minutes later, a white van appears on the road. It passes me on its way to the beach. It's going too fast for me to see the driver, yet my intuition tells me it's the same van we saw yesterday at the Gay Head Cliffs, the same one the Evil Man was leaning against.

The van speeds past me again. Now it's going away from the beach. I watch it take the curve in the road and disappear from view past the forest of birch and pitch pines.

When I'm past the bend in the road, however, I see the van again. Now it's parked up ahead on the opposite side of the road. Its front end faces the beach, the hood is up, and the driver is leaning into the engine area. His face is hidden. I think at first that he might be a neighbor, but as I get closer, my body gets tense and my heart seems to be thumping out of my chest. Something is wrong. It has nothing to do with the white van.

I pick up my pace and jog past the van. My sandals barely touch the road. Tap. Tap. The sound is slight. I hope the man doesn't notice me.

The entrance to the mud track that will take me through the woods to Victor's place is on the other side of the road. But before I can take another step, the driver crosses the road and is now on my side.

Even though he is looking up at the trees, my stomach knots up. We're about fifteen yards apart. I know he is the Evil Man I saw yesterday. Rugged, fit, and probably in his thirties, he turns and looks straight at me. This is the first time I see his face. He's handsome, but his strong features are almost erased by his blank expression.

The Evil Man suddenly takes a step toward me. I take off, but I cannot outrun him. He catches up with me and grips both of my shoulders with his strong hands. He twirls me around and looks at me with his dull, dead eyes. I try to shake loose, but he grabs me by the wrists and swings me around again, then he tries to tug me into the woods.

I manage to keep my balance. This is what the spiritual message at the beach was about, I think. This is it. It is happening. In an effort to free myself, I pull back and yell, "No, no, no!"

The Evil Man does not say a word.

I yell again.

There's no one else around. No one can hear me. Victor's house is too deep in the woods and too far away. Most of the people on the island are at the No Nukes Concert. Twisting and turning, I finally break free. But the Evil Man is too big, too strong, too aggressive. He seizes hold of both of my arms and yanks me with him into the forest.

The chirping of the birds and the buzzing of the insects mingle with the thudding of his footsteps as he pulls me deeper into the forest. As I struggle to get free, my feet give way and I fall onto my back. The man drags my body along the rough ground. Somehow my sweatshirt and bra come off. Twigs and sticks snap and scrape my bare skin.

I feel no pain. My mind is focused on the man's movements. When he stops and lets go of my arms, I try to get up. He pushes me back down, then sits on top of me, his thick legs straddling my body. Pinned down, I squirm and try to dislodge him, but cannot move him off me.

Still not speaking, he stares down at me with his cold eyes. His hands wrap around my neck. I can't pry those hands off. A faint, oily odor wafts into my face as his grip tightens. He calmly keeps up the pressure on my throat.

I try to fight, but my punches are useless. I can't knock him off. I now sense the Evil Man's intention. This is not about rape. This is about murder.

My inner voice whispers again. *You are here for a reason. You are here to learn something. You are here for a reason. You are here to learn something.* All the weird premonitions that occurred over the last few days flash before my mind's eye.

My mind races to comprehend this extraordinary moment. I think, *How can Victor find me dead? What is death? Is death being snuffed out like the flame of a candle? Is death a form of consciousness contained in a coffin? Is death nothingness?*

My inner voice calls to all the gods for help. But I'm alone in the forest. There are no heroes. There is no God. There is no Moses. There is no Jesus. There is no Buddha. There is no Allah. There is only death. There is only nothingness. No thing.

There is no escape. I'm exhausted, and my only choice is to let go. My body stops squirming. I feel it relax. My arms stop fighting and flop, weightless, to the ground.

I accept death.

Chapter 10

BEFORE MY EYES CLOSE, I manage to focus on nature, on the environment around me. Not on the face of my murderer. I do not see him anymore.

The leaves of the trees and plants seem to have crystallized. The forest shines. I sense the Divine presence, which emanates from a large, sparkling, diamond-shaped crystal that seems to be floating in midair a few feet away.

It is a portal. I know I am going there, to a holy place. An incredible sensation of peacefulness comes over me. No more fear. No more doubt. No more worry.

The angel of death enfolds me in smoky-black wings.

Chapter 11

NOTHINGNESS IS SHATTERED.

The sound of my inner voice penetrates the void. *Murderer. You are not going to get away with this. You are not going to get away with this.*

In stillness and darkness, this small inner voice speaks from my soul. It is taunting my murderer.

I feel no other physical sensation beyond the fury of my killer. My inner voice is measured, direct, assured. *Murderer!* My killer can try to flee. My killer can think he is free, but my inner voice says, *You are not going to get away with this. You are not going to get away with this.* The chant repeats itself. Over and over, it rings out inside me.

My mind's eye opens.

The darkness begins to organize itself. It transforms itself into dynamic squares of white fire on black fire. The squares begin to coalesce. Although there seems to be fewer of them now, they become larger and fill my mind's eye.

Murderer. You are not going to get away with this. You are not going to get away with this. The squares decrease in number to the rhythm of that inner chant. *Murderer. You are not going to get away with this.* The sentences repeat until there is only the outline of a single square of white fire on black fire in my inner vision.

My inner voice screams one word. *Now.*

It is a signal. My arms push up against the darkness. It is as if they sense it is time for me to come back to everyday consciousness. My breath is labored. I feel a sharp pain in my throat. My eyes open. Sunlight floods them.

I am alive.

Incredible.

Trees and plants, the soil and the grass all come into sharp focus, along with all the scents of the forest. Twigs snap under the crush of my elbows and hands as I raise my head and shoulders off the ground.

But now fear enters and worry and doubt begin to consume me. My body starts shaking. Where is he? What if he finds me? This time he will surely kill me, and I will not come back to life. I want to live.

I look around, but I cannot see or hear the Evil Man. My sweatshirt and bra are gone. Never mind them. I have to get away from here. I have to find the path to Victor's family's house. I have to find the path that will take me to safety. I stand on wobbly legs and start to move. Instead of panic, stupid jokes begin popping into my head, like the one about the farmer's daughter who runs half-naked out of the haystack . . . but I can't remember the punchline.

I feel like that girl. Exposed.

While I'm moving to get away, the spiny bushes sway in the breeze. It's like they're laughing at me. The police could laugh at me too. But I must be believed. Will they think I am a seductress, that I "asked for it"? Will they blame me?

Fatigued, I'm stumbling along. Despite the attack, my navigational senses are still acute. Once I'm on the mud track,

I try to yell, "Victor! Victor!" but my throat hurts, and my voice sounds feeble. I'm able to raise one hand to cover and protect my throat.

Suddenly I see my boyfriend up ahead! He's running down the dirt path toward me. I fall into his arms.

"Myra, Myra. I was in the cottage and I heard this . . . this sound. I didn't know if it was animal or human. I ran to find out what it was."

"That Evil Man from yesterday," I manage to say in a raspy voice, "he tried to kill me. He did kill me."

Victor somehow remains calm as he picks me up and carries me to the main house, where he lays me down, still half-naked, on the sofa. Then he calls an ambulance and the police. The soft fabric of the couch feels warm and comfortable to the scrapes and scratches on my back and arms. I feel safe. My body relaxes.

And now I think back on the Evil Man. He was so calm, his killing me was so calculated. He never said a word. The odd, oily smell drifted by when his hands were around my throat. It must have come from his fingers, perhaps from something he touched when working under the hood of his van.

I remember scenes from the weird premonitions that flashed before my inner vision and then were gone in an instant: our moody arrival on Martha's Vineyard, the delicious meal of grilled filet mignon and not the area's famous seafood, my concern about an ambulance going to Victor's place when I was learning to drive somewhere else, and sensing the malevolence in the Evil Man the first time I saw only the back of him at Gay Head Cliffs.

But in the moment of death, there was nothing. I don't know how long the nothingness lasted. Then my inner chant started. *Murderer! You are not going to get away with this.*

In death, I saw squares of white fire on black fire squares. Perhaps there were as many as a hundred small squares. I witnessed a sacred geometry acting when the squares started to reduce in number. A hundred became ninety-six and then ninety-two, and so on. The reduction came in geometric regression, just the opposite of how the cells of a fertilized egg unfold in arithmetic progression. Although the outlines of the squares of white on black fire increased in size, they occupied the same expanse in my mind's eye. This kept me in the constant embrace of a protective, energetic net that completely covered my visual field. My soul knew to wait and be still while the squares of white fire on black fire decreased in number. When there was only one giant square in my mind's eye, my soul knew it was the right time to break back into life.

Perhaps the Evil Man was still around while the squares were acting, and my soul knew to wait. When I did regain consciousness, I was not sure of his whereabouts. I became afraid. He could kill me again.

The process of coming back to life was hard, like lifting heavy chains. I could hardly breathe and had to push up against a great force. Perhaps this is how a baby bird cracks through a hard shell.

As for us human beings, doctors claim that infants have an innate drive to meet their mothers. This urge creates the cervical push and supports the fetus' movement toward life. If there is any sense of evil or harm outside the womb, a newborn has no choice but to face it. There is no way to crawl back in.

My re-emergence into life was decidedly different from my actual, physical birth. That happened in January 1955. Though the Detroit weather forecast had called for a bitterly cold day, my mother was snug behind the thick walls of Women's Hospital. When first built in 1910, it was the only medical facility in Michigan devoted to women and children. Renowned for its pioneering treatments, it possessed the area's first incubators for newborns.

I was born in the maternity ward at 4:15 in the morning, five minutes after my identical twin sister. For me, the problem was not the cold weather but my size at birth. Health rules in the 1950s required a hospital to not release a baby if it weighed less than five pounds. My sister made the cut. She could leave. But a nurse parked me in the famous incubation chamber.

To most people, a five-minute age difference might seem incidental, a small increment of time. Not to a twin. There is a hierarchical birth order based on who is born first. Although the American and Canadian perspective sees the second born as the younger twin, other cultures consider her the older, stronger, and wiser of the two. For example, the belief system in Nigeria, the Ivory Coast, and China considers the second born as older, the one who kicked the firstborn twin out of the womb to test the world for her.

Behavioral geneticists maintain that my sister and I have the physical and psychological characteristics of a single egg that split into two about seven to twelve days after conception. Generally, the second-born twin of a late-splitting egg is a half-inch taller, slightly thinner, longer waisted, and noticeably shyer than the firstborn. This is true in my case.

Concern over the transmission of infectious diseases created another hospital protocol that restricts the touching of incubator babies. Before birth, I shared close quarters with my sister. After birth, I lay in solitary confinement in the incubator. I don't fit the concept of a tough, take-charge-in-the-womb, second-born twin those other cultures talk about.

❀

Decades later, when Victor and I moved into the basement apartment of the Seth lady's house, I had a dream. Perhaps, it gave me a clue about my birth.

In the dream, it's storming outside and a house teeters on the edge of a big cliff. Marla and I are asleep in a totally dark room in that teetering house. All of a sudden, I wake up and look over at her. She is fast asleep. I see a faint light seeping in through the crack under the door. I have the impression that my mother is on the other side of the door and is about to leave with a strange man. I want to say goodbye to her, but Marla blocks my way. I can't climb over her for fear that I might topple the whole house over the cliff. I must wait until my twin sister gets up. She has to leave first. The dream ends there.

❊

My actual, physical birth was not a happy launch into reality. The first days of my life were spent stuck in a glass box, in a kind of prenatal holding pattern. Alone. An incubator is surely a place where negativity can thrive. Either the baby has the will to survive or it dies. Perhaps this is where the determination to stay alive was germinated within me.

Growing up, I always felt abandoned. Perhaps this feeling was born by the nurses who were not able to hold me while I was banished to that glass house. Or maybe it arose from some of my mother's words and actions. When I was still young, I asked her, "How long did I have to stay alone in the hospital?"

"Your sister and you were born a little earlier than expected," she told me. "Your birth was easy, so easy. I thought I just had to go to the bathroom. But it was just you two wanting to come out." She giggled and then got serious. "We were able to take your sister back to Bubbe's house, but not you. When we did take you home, you still looked like a bird."

"Why a bird?"

"When the doctors released you from the hospital, you were still so small and fragile. Your throat was sore from crying. The nurses said you cried all the time. To keep you quiet, they stuck your thumb in your mouth. And you could barely eat. We had to feed you through an eyedropper, like a little bird."

Now, older and wiser, I understand. To the nurses, my thumb was an earplug for them. But to me, it was salvation. Sucking my thumb enabled my internal circuits to stay in balance and allowed me to get quiet and listen to myself.

Although I'm a twin and I adore my sister, I became fascinated with aloneness early on. From an early age, I associated it with personal power. Yet being alone also intimidated me. Perhaps this belief stems from my doing time in the incubator.

I never did get a straight answer about the length of my confinement, which I think of as "The Myth of Days." Of course, the actual number can be found in the records of Women's Hospital, now Hutzel Women's Hospital. And there are clues. Some came together decades later. About 2002 or 2003, my sister and I were talking on the telephone about the problematic relationship my mother had with our bubbe, her mother.

"I bet no one even visited you while you were in the incubator," Marla said.

This non sequitur made me ask, "What do you mean?"

"Look at the setup. After giving birth to us, Mom goes to stay at Bubbe's house, in Oak Park, Michigan, which is about half an hour away from downtown Detroit where the hospital is. I am released right away, so Mom already has one kid with her. So she does not need you there to give her a sense of her own family."

I was nonplussed. "I never thought about it that way. What makes you so sure no one came?"

"Mom is recuperating," Marla said. "Bubbe and Grandpa Herman don't drive. So who is going to visit you?" Before I could speak, she answered her own question. "No one."

"Okay, okay," I said. "But maybe Dad did come to see me? I imagine him looking through the glass window into the maternity ward. I'm lying in the incubator. He sees me and waves at the me."

"I'm not so sure he did," my twin sister said in a tone more logical than emotional. "Let's look at it from his perspective. Dad worked all day at the produce market. He was exhausted from schlepping cartons of fresh fruits and vegetables around. I bet he was too tired, and either he went straight home to South Windsor or he crossed the border and took the freeway straight to Bubbe's house. His family was there. Who needed you?"

"Yeah. I see what you mean. Why would he stop in downtown Detroit just to look at me through glass?"

"It doesn't make sense for him to stop when he's all tired and worn out. No one visited you while you were in hospital, Myra." My twin sister concluded her summation in a tone of absolute conviction. "I am sure of it."

To appreciate Marla's version of "The Myth of Days," knowledge of the area's geography is necessary. The main boundary is the Detroit River, French for the river of the narrows. It cuts an almost mile-wide gash that cleaves Canada from the United States. The Detroit River is an international border. The boundary line runs down its center. The area's vehicular tunnel runs under the river with border customs at both ends. At the time of my birth, the tunnel connected the smaller, provincial downtown of Windsor, Ontario, to the busy, cosmopolitan city center of Detroit, Michigan. On the American side, tentacles of expressways linked the metro-hub to its outer-city suburbs. Big transport trucks and motorists can also take the suspension Ambassador Bridge a couple of miles away. It spans the river and skirts the inner cities of both countries.

A third tunnel exists exclusively for trains. My only experience with it was in my childhood nightmares. I am alone, curled up in the corner of a small train car. It has no roof. The ceiling of the tunnel is wet, and I am scared it will cave in on me.

We were almost two months old when Mother left Bubbe's house and returned to Windsor with her two baby girls. She had acquired landed American immigrant status when she married my father, a Canadian. At that time, Canada also allowed people who intend to live in the country to become citizens at their first port of entry. Therefore, my twin sister and I were declared Canadian citizens on March 15, 1955. Due to our young age, an oath of allegiance to the Queen of England, the head of the Commonwealth, was not required.

Chapter 12

"GOD SAID, "LET THERE BE light." Following this divine fiat, a point, a mere dot, penetrates the darkness. It is the first day of creation. But I did not see a point or a dot. What I saw were squares that created my second birth, as they helped me emerge from death and fully come out of the darkness. Squares have a symbolic association to the notion of mind, or rationality.

While I'm still lying on the couch in the living room of Victor's family's main house on Martha's Vineyard, footsteps intrude on my contemplations. A policeman strides in with an air of determined confidence. He is tall and gorgeous, built like a rugby player, with dark hair and a chiseled face that looks like Rod Taylor in the Alfred Hitchcock movie, *The Birds*. He introduces himself as Sergeant Marshall.

Despite my exhaustion, I perk up. Sexual sensations flood my body. This is most inconvenient and surprises and confuses me. Perhaps my newly returned life force wants to rinse away the foulness of my murderer with more positive sensations.

Victor's eyes widen as he senses my arousal, probably because he hasn't seen me like this for quite a while. "Officer," he says, "she is much prettier without all the bruises and scratches."

Sergeant Marshall removes his uniform jacket, walks over to me, and drapes it across my naked upper body. Then he pulls a wooden chair next to the sofa, sits down, and tells us that Chief Kenneth Belain of the Gay Head Police Department had driven along Lobsterville Road, a few minutes before Victor's emergency call came in. But he hadn't seen anything suspicious.

"Why are you so calm now?" Sergeant Marshall leans closer to me. "Most women are in such a state of shock after an incident like you had that they won't let a male officer near enough to interview them. They don't want any men near them."

He's in my face. From the tone of his voice, he sounds suspicious of me. Maybe it's just his job. But this is the exact reaction I expected from a man, especially one in law enforcement. Somehow their knee-jerk reaction is to assume the entire fault must be the victim's. Mine. Perhaps this is why most women do not speak up about sexual assault.

Now my credibility is at stake. Will he believe me? I need to think carefully about how I should respond. I immediately dismiss the desire to yell, "I'm happy to be alive, you idiot!" I remain silent about the psychic premonitions and the spiritual message I received on Menemsha Beach. Used to hiding the intuitive part of myself, I'm worried that the omens might confuse the officer and bring into question the trustworthiness of my account. Then justice will never get done.

"It's because of him." I nod my head toward Victor, who is standing next to the officer's chair. "He is with me now. He is my fiancé."

A huge smile spreads across Victor's face. We both know what I just said is an incredible statement. Before the strangulation, my feeling toward him was more like that of a sister. Now I've just proposed to him. Well, it's partly true. Being with Victor feels like "home" to me, no matter where we are. But we lack the passion necessary for a successful marriage.

To the police officer, my response appears plausible. His demeanor changes, the muscles around his jaw relax, his shoulders slump, and he leans back in the chair. Tension that comes from a suspicious mind visibly leaves his body. "Have you ever seen this man who attacked you, Myra?"

Another decision to make. Quickly. My choice is to not tell the policeman about seeing my killer the day before. After all, I only saw his back. The officer might not understand my sensing the evil in the man. He might become skeptical. I cannot put the investigation at risk. He might label me as one of those "crazy psychic people."

"No," I say quietly. "He is a stranger to me."

"What color are his eyes?"

"Dark and evil."

The questions continue. I give a succinct description of my murderer and the vehicle he drove. The officer repeats this information into the microphone of his citizens band radio, which he clicks on and off during the interview. The broadcast goes out to all the police on Martha's Vineyard to be on the lookout for the Evil Man.

Timing is everything. It is still daylight. The Evil Man can easily catch the ferry and get off the island and soon be long gone.

There are more questions. My throat still feels rough, and now it's getting too hard to talk. Sergeant Marshall halts the interview when the ambulance arrives. I'm too weak to walk, so the medics bring in a stretcher. As my fiancé, Victor is now deemed a family member. He can ride in the ambulance with me.

As the ambulance departs the house, I look out the side window and see the new guests of Victor's family drive into the compound. They haven't expected to see an ambulance and look aghast, some with their mouths wide open and their noses pressed against the windows of their station wagon. A little dog paces back and forth in the rear of it.

What a way to end a vacation. Mine. What a way to start. Theirs.

It is still daylight as we speed across Martha's Vineyard to the island's only hospital.

I'm consumed by the full measure of the moment. Then a revelation occurs. I am born anew. Metaphorically speaking, I now carry a bit of the diamond-shaped crystal that appeared in the forest just before my death. It's in my back pocket. Symbolically, it becomes a prism for me to view the world through. This refraction of godly light can help me better understand both my life's circumstances and myself. A clear moment of realization overcomes me. My destiny is revealed as an emphatic sense of knowing. I am an initiate. I am a novice.

A new direction unfolds, a fivefold pathway. (1) I must move to the other side of the continent. (2) I must learn a martial art. (3) I must learn to meditate. (4) I must learn a mystical form of metaphysics. (5) I must learn more about meaningful coincidences. These five paths make up my divine directives.

People who have near-death experiences often find their whole world changing. I too died and came back to a life that has now completely changed. I no longer identify as just being a twin. In my newfound individuality, these five divine directives serve as my guideposts, even though the pathways are not yet clearly defined.

About that last directive, I already know something on the subject of coincidences. The used bookstore in London, Ontario, had a copy of the *I Ching*. For the past few months, I've been studying this ancient practice and throwing the sticks to come up with a hexagram and gain insight into my circumstances.

My internal musings stop when the ambulance arrives at the hospital. My first task is to heal. I must be well enough to aid law enforcement's investigative efforts and help arrest and convict the Evil Man. My soul's desire is to see my murderer get the justice he deserves. He is not going to get away with leaving me like a pile of dirt.

The paramedics put me on a gurney and push it through the emergency entrance. Once I'm placed in a private room, it takes a nurse almost a half hour to draw my blood.

"I can't find a vein in your arm." Her frustration is palpable. "I'm so sorry. It seems yours are the size of a newborn."

I feel the need to reassure her. "Don't worry. You're not hurting me."

"You seem so relaxed for someone who was just attacked and strangled almost to death."

"I'm really glad to be alive," I say quietly. I do not correct her "almost to death." I'm also intrigued by her reference to my baby-sized veins. No other medical professional had ever said that to me. This physical fact seems to confirm the sensation that I'm being reborn.

After X-rays are taken, the doctors conclude that my hyoid bone is broken. This is the bone in the front of the neck that serves as a base to the tongue. This is one reason why it's so hard for me to talk. They are concerned that if my neck swells, they will have to perform a tracheotomy on me. Then they decide their hospital is insufficient for my medical needs. They invite Victor into my room to hear the news too.

Then a nurse says to us, "The United States Coast Guard will take you across the waters of Vineyard Sound to Falmouth Hospital on Cape Cod. We've arranged for an ambulance to take you to the dock at Tisbury harbor."

"You're sure they can help me there?" I manage to ask.

"About a year ago, the Falmouth Hospital expanded its emergency, X-ray, and laboratory departments. The Intensive Care Unit can monitor your status during the night and perform a tracheotomy," she looks directly at me, "if necessary."

In no time at all, the orderlies lift me off the bed, put me on a gurney, and wheel me to an ambulance, which then whisks Victor and me to the dock, where the air is thick with the smells of the sea, the wet wharf, and fish and men. I'm surrounded by men whose earnest looks are all focused on me.

The paramedics and the doctors are all men. The police officers and the Coast Guard personnel are men. And everywhere are the everyday men who hang around the pier.

A couple of the men lift me onto the Coast Guard boat. I lie on the stretcher, flushed from all this silent attention. In this moment, I feel special.

The feeling is short-lived, however, as I reflect on the divine directives and all the new things I'll have to learn, do, and master.

Chapter 13

THE CURTAIN IS PUSHED ASIDE, and two nurses enter my cubicle in the Intensive Care Unit at the Falmouth Hospital. They set an oxygen regulator beside my bed and position the plastic tubing to blow across my nose. Victor relaxes in a chair and keeps me company for about half an hour, then he is escorted to a room where he can get some rest.

Throughout the evening, one after another, nurses stick their heads into my little cocoon and ask, "Do you need anything? Are you comfortable? Do you want to talk to a social worker?"

"No, thanks," I reply each time. "I'm fine."

Later that night, I do have a request. "Nurse, can you shut off the bells and whistles coming from the cubicle next to mine? The sounds are keeping me awake."

"No, honey, we can't do that." The nurse leans closer and whispers to me, "You see, it's a man who tried to kill himself. He used a shotgun and missed. I mean, he didn't die. He blew off half his face. Those bells and whistles you hear, they're keeping him alive, honey. That's why he's in the ICU."

The contradiction is uncanny. That man desired death, while I had to accept it. Unwillingly.

After the nurse leaves, I start to jury-rig the oxygen tubes to get the sound of the blower to muffle the noises coming from the machines in the next cubicle. I tinker with it and finally get it just right. No more bells and whistles. A deep, delicious sleep swallows me up.

The next morning finds me lying in the fetal position, one ear buried in the pillow, the other lulled by the gentle flow of oxygen puffing along two and a half inches above my head. The only thing different from the night before is that I can see two sets of fidgety fingers at the level of my eyeballs.

I wonder. Maybe it's Tweedledum and Tweedledee. Maybe I'm still in a hypnopompic, semi-dream state. I look past the hands and become wide awake.

The fingers belong to two men in white coats with stethoscopes around their necks and worried looks on their faces. They both seem uneasy. One takes a small step closer to my hospital bed.

"Hello, Myra," he begins. "We are your doctors and we have been monitoring your situation since yesterday. A small bone in your throat is broken. This is a rare type of injury. In your case, it occurred by strangulation. What is remarkable about the hyoid bone is that with five to six weeks of rest and relaxation it can heal itself. From the experience you had, you are lucky you did not go into a state of shock, which would have tightened your neck and made it difficult for you to breathe. Last night, we had a chance to talk on the telephone with your twin sister. She told us, and I quote, 'We bruise but we do not swell.' This is good." He looks at me and smiles.

I smile back at him. "I like how my twin sister phrased that."

The silent doctor nods his head and the first doctor continues. "We understand your fiancé has been with you. We talked to his father too. He's a well-known doctor and is checking up on us." A nervous chuckle escapes as he smiles again. "Our major concern now is if you start feeling anxious. Labored, anxious breathing could be dangerous in your situation."

"I understand."

Both doctors look uncomfortable and shuffle around a bit, and then the talkier one says, "Well, we hope so. That is why we are here. Last night, we also spoke to your mother. For no apparent reason, she started to scream, and yell at us."

"I'm sorry. My mother can be that way."

The doctors look nervously at each other, then the first one squares his shoulders. "She and your twin sister got on a plane and will arrive here later this afternoon. It is our medical opinion that it would be best if you did not see your mother today. If she upsets you, it can cause serious injury. We understand this is most unfortunate news. We can only offer our professional advice. The decision whether to see her is yours to make."

With that, the doctors leave the room and leave me in the depths of a dark deliberation. My mother comes from a long line of women who rage. It's like the biblical Sarah, whose wrath led to the ouster of the concubine Hagar. We can only imagine what might have happened if Abraham had told Sarah to shut up. If only my father had told my mother to shut up! Instead, he buried his feelings in a bankruptcy, a heart attack, and a passive-aggressive way of coping with her.

But I thank God Marla will be here. She can help with mother. The doctors do not quite realize my circumstances. Forbidding my mother to see me would not get the anticipated results. She would redirect her anger upon my sister, and I'd feel horrible.

It's always been ring-around-the-rosie, coping with Mother's resentments. One way or another, she'll get to everyone. Everyone, that is, except Jamie, who is currently at the prestigious University of Toronto pursuing a double major in math and actuarial sciences. My sister and I always felt a need to protect him from our mother's wrath. And I certainly do not expect either him or my father to visit me in hospital.

My thoughts are put on hold when two orderlies come in and lift me onto another gurney and wheel me to a private room with a beautiful view of trees. A nurse's aide brings me breakfast, something that looks like baby pablum and smells like oatmeal. Actually, the Falmouth Hospital food tastes rather good.

After breakfast, a woman dressed in the uniform of the Massachusetts State Police enters my hospital room. She's a rather large person, and the vinyl upholstery squeaks in protest as she squeezes herself into the chair and scoots it closer to my bed. She sits there with her feet sticking straight out. This is Trooper Leroy, who conducts an informal discussion rather than an official interview, with her doing most of the talking.

"The suspect is in custody," she begins. "He is married, with one child. His wife has red hair. He's at Martha's Vineyard for a fishing vacation with his brother. Now he's been charged with attempted murder, attempted rape, and assault and battery."

"A wife?" I say. "I can't believe someone could love him or marry him. Anyway, it was not a sexual assault." My voice is emphatic. "The man never tried to rape me. He wanted to—and did—kill me. Yes, I was dead. I don't know why he did it."

The trooper ignores my assertion that I was dead. "Well, Myra, it was an uncontested touching, so the attempted rape charge fits. The man we have in custody has a prior conviction for attempted rape while he was in the Army."

"Just an attempted rape, eh? He never tried that with me."

Trooper Leroy nods her head. "Now, in your case, he was on his way to pick up his brother, who was fishing at Menemsha Bight bay. He saw you walking and turned around and tried to kill you."

Her honest, straightforward approach puts me at ease. I correct her again. "Not tried," I say. "He succeeded. He did kill me." Out of fear of not being believed and judged as a "looney psychic," however, I do not speak about the premonitions and the transcendental aspects of my violent death.

Trooper Leroy again ignores my assertion that I was actually killed. "It seems none of you people went to hear the James Taylor and Carly Simon concert that day?" she asks.

"Nope. I wasn't interested. Not my kinda music. I like Motown, soul, and reggae music. No, no concert. I just wanted to be alone."

"Okay. Your information was immediately broadcast to island law enforcement. One of the officers was stopped at a red light. He looked into his rearview mirror, saw the van you described right behind him. He pulled the suspect over and got his identification and where he was staying. But the man was wearing a baseball cap. You did not mention a hat. So the officer let him go."

"Because he wasn't wearing a hat when he killed me," I say. "The officer was stupid—"

"Hold on now," she says. "Four hours later, the Gay Head police realized he was their man."

"Four hours! Geez. He could have left the island."

She nods. "They realized their mistake and located the house at the address given by the suspect. The suspect's younger brother answered the door. The police explained that his older brother was wanted for questioning. If he did not tell them where he was, they said, the brother would be charged as an accessory after the fact."

Trooper Leroy shifts her position, gets more comfortable in the chair, and continues. "From what law enforcement can tell, the suspect attacked you and then proceeded to pick up his brother at Menemsha Beach and drop him off at their cottage. Then he went to a bar. That's where he was arrested."

I am astonished. "You mean, he was drinking. Some bartender! He had no clue and served a murderer beer. The murderer could have caught a ferry and left the island, but instead he went drinking."

Trooper Leroy perks up. "He thought he was being arrested for murder. He thought he'd left you for dead."

"Yes. He did leave me for dead." I study her face for a reaction, but the trooper doesn't bite, so I move on, "If he had left the island, what would the police have done?"

"To start," she explains, "we would have taken measurements of the tire tracks he left on the side of Lobsterville Road. Identified the make and model and tried to track down his vehicle. But the guy went to a bar and now he's in police custody. If he is the guy, a court of law is going to determine if he is fit to stand trial."

"What do you mean, 'fit'?"

"If he understands what's going on in the proceedings."

"He can't be too cuckoo, can he?"

The trooper rolls her eyes. "Tomorrow, two detectives will come here and show you pictures so you can ID the suspect. It's called a photo array. They will hand you a photo album to look through." She shakes a finger at me. "You just have to point out the right guy."

The interview now concluded, Trooper Leroy leaves me in a slightly anxious state. I wonder if I'll be able to pick him out. The pursuit of justice surely hangs on my ability to do so, but it's all too nervous making. And the doctors said I am supposed to stay calm.

After a liquidy lunch—a soft egg with vanilla ice cream on the side—a nurse's aide helps me walk to the bathroom. I'm too weak to stand by myself.

❊

It is late afternoon when the door of my hospital room opens again.

My twin sister Marla enters, our mother trailing behind her. Marla sees me and gasps, "Myra, you look like a tiny bird! You look so frail. And your face is all scratched. It's bright red. I can't believe it!"

At the same time, Mom comes closer, leans down, and gives me a kiss on the cheek. When she straightens up, her face looks pinched. "Your son-of-a-bitch father wouldn't come with us. Now there's no one here for me."

This is it. This is what the doctors warned me about.

My sister and I roll our eyes and shake our heads, but Mom is too self-absorbed to notice. She stews in her anger and seems ready to serve up a dark dish of misery.

"Mom," I protest, "Marla's here for you. She came with you."

My mother flicks her hand in a dismissive wave and goes to stand next to the window.

This drama cannot escalate into trauma. My hand reaches for my throat and without any thought, I say, "Mom, Victor and I are getting married."

The magic in these words takes effect. My mother's demeanor immediately changes. Her face lights up. She sits on my bed beside my sister. Her abandonment issue seems to have disappeared. We jibber-jabber about the wedding and who to invite.

"I know Aunt Gladys and Aunt Helen will give you a bridal shower," Mom says, referring to her sister and sister-in-law, respectively. "We'll have to see when everyone is available for the wedding."

"I hope it's soon," I say. "Victor and I need to move to the West Coast."

"What are you talking about?" Her mood suddenly turns. "What about the bookbinding interview in Lawrence? I thought that's why you came here."

"I'm not going to the interview. I have to move to the other side of the continent. After I get better, we'll drive to Vancouver, and I'll try to get a job doing bookbinding there once we settle down."

"Okay, okay." She seems to be mollified. "Okay. Until you feel better, you and your fiancé can stay with us in Windsor. Then you can see your father. I can't stand that man for not coming here with me." She still sounds venomous when she speaks about her husband.

"Mom," Marla says, "you know he didn't join us because of the money. The costs of the airplane ticket. He's always worried about money."

"Come on, Mom," I add, "let's try not to get angry. Let's get back to picking wedding dates. Victor's parents, his family, have to come from Seattle, and cousin Bonnie from California. Just to get everyone together, I'll have to wait 'til next summer to move to Vancouver." I say no more and tuck the travel issue away for now. It's a good card to play to get out of the whole marriage thing.

Speaking of availability to attend a wedding, Marla now informs us she is on an emergency leave from her work. She is the representative of an internationally acclaimed photography studio headquartered in Toronto, the home base of the advertising and fashion photographer Frank Anzalone, who is recognized for the stunning qualities of his lighting and of his use of attractive women. A large man, built like an NFL linebacker, he's a real Italian salami who likes his models in heels and lingerie. His famous line to new sales reps seems apropos here. "You're no good to me once you get married." He likes to say that marriage kills a woman's sex drive, business drive, and appeal. Hmm.

Marla fits into Frank's siren category. He also respects her highly evolved sense of aesthetics and trusts her instincts about what to consider good art. To live in art and the artist's way of life is a burning ambition in my sister. Her major inspirations are Gertrude Stein and Peggy Guggenheim.

A few minutes later, my mother, my sister, and my fiancé (who just joined us) are silent, as I give my account of the attack on me. They are mesmerized by it. It feels good to be open and speak to them about the metaphysical side of the story. They listen and do not judge me. Then I tell them about the photo ID session coming tomorrow and explain all the things I need to do. Move to the other side of the county. Learn about metaphysics. Learn martial arts. Learn to meditate. And learn about meaningful coincidences. The five Ms. I refer to them as my divine directives.

By the time I've told them all this, I am worn out. Marla takes my cue and ushers everyone out of the room. Their plan is to get something to eat. After they leave, I realize the afternoon drama and our fun with the wedding plans were mere distractions. The thought of the impending meeting with the detectives and the photo ID session never seriously entered my mind until now.

Chapter 14

THE NEXT MORNING FINDS ME deep in thought again, thinking about chance meetings and the people who came into my life in that special way, like my former boyfriend Chris, Vernon, and Victor's father. Soon after breakfast, I hear Victor coming down the hall. He's beaming with excitement as he enters my room carrying a newspaper.

"Myra, a funny thing happened today. Our houseguests drove onto our Martha's Vineyard property just as the ambulance was taking you to the island hospital. Well, they brought a little dog with them on the trip."

"Yeah, I saw them. I saw it in the back of their station wagon."

"Well," he goes on, "the dog found your brassiere in the woods. He trotted back to the compound holding it in his mouth, the straps dragging on the ground. He acted like he had the greatest toy in the world and wouldn't let go of it. Everyone tried to pull it loose from him."

We both laugh at this vision. "Did the dog find my sweatshirt too? It also came off when I was dragged through the woods. Or maybe the killer took it with him."

"Who knows, but your bra certainly got the dog's attention." Victor leans down and kisses me on the forehead like he is giving me a gold star. "And there's an article about you in the *Vineyard Gazette*."

He hands me the newspaper. It is dated September 26, 1978.

> Syracuse Man is Charged in Assault
> Fast Police Work Ends in Capture;
> John Lasinski Attempted to Kill Canadian Visitor, Police Say
>
> A Canadian woman was seriously injured during an attempted rape in Gay Head Saturday afternoon.
>
> Less than six hours after the incident, police took into custody John S. Lasinski, 30, of Syracuse, NY. In district court yesterday, Mr. Lasinski was charged with attempted murder, assault with intent to rape, and assault and battery.
>
> The victim, Myra Mossman, 22, is now in the Falmouth Hospital recovering from throat injuries.
>
> During the arraignment proceeding, police alleged that Mr. Lasinski attempted to strangle Miss Mossman.
>
> Gay Head police Chief Kenneth Belain said yesterday that the incident occurred about 4:30 p.m. Saturday, when Miss Mossman was walking on the Lobsterville Road not far from a house where she and her fiance have been houseguests.
>
> Mr. Belain said her assailant came upon her while driving on the road. He apparently stopped the car, got out of it, attacked the woman, dragged her into the nearby bushes and departed, leaving Miss Mossman unconscious.
>
> When she recovered, Miss Mossman returned to the house at which she had been staying and the Gay Head Police were notified.
>
> Mr. Belain and Sgt. Michael Marshall received from the victim a description of the assailant's vehicle, and

then a description of the assailant himself. These were immediately broadcast by the communication center.

Within 15 minutes after the broadcast, West Tisbury patrolman David Welch observed a vehicle matching the description traveling up the Old County Road. He followed it into a driveway and questioned the operator.

He was shortly joined by state trooper John W. Giardino, who assisted on the case at the request of the Gay Head and West Tisbury police departments.

The police returned to the West Tisbury house at about 10 p.m. that evening to arrest Mr. Lasinski.

Immediately, after the incident, Miss Mossman was transported to the Martha's Vineyard Hospital by the Tisbury ambulance (The tri-town ambulance was busy on another unrelated case.) From the hospital here she was transferred to the Falmouth Hospital.

Mr. Lasinski was held in lieu of $10,000 bond over the weekend. At the hearing yesterday, he was ordered kept on custody for examination. The case was continued until Friday.

Mr. Belain says Mr. Lasinski has been visiting the Island for a short time. Trooper Lorraine Leroy of the state police headquarters in Boston traveled to Falmouth Sunday to interview the victim of the attack.

Police officers involved in the case all say there was no relation between the attack and the concert in Chilmark, which was just winding down at the time. Police also say Miss Mossman and Mr. Lasinski had never met before the incident.

(Used by permission of the *Vineyard Gazette*.)

As I read this, I feel heat building up in my body. When I finish, I feel like I could explode. "Vic, the newspaper gives my name without my permission. Did the reporter talk to you?"

"Nope."

"Geez." I shake my head, in disbelief. "What if the man in custody is not my assailant? What if he's still at large? He might start looking for me, and this article leads him right to my twin sister and me. My privacy is at stake." I fold the newspaper and toss it back to Victor. "This puts my life in danger, and my twin sister's life is in jeopardy too."

My fiancé takes my hand. "I know. You're under a lot of pressure to pick the guy out in the photo ID. You've already come through the hard stuff though. It's going to be fine."

His voice sounds reassuring, but I am not convinced. "I don't know that Evil Man," I say. "Before this newspaper article, I felt anonymous, an unknown, an anybody to him. He never said a word to me or seemed to know me, he didn't want to know me. He just wanted to kill me. Not rape me. He dragged me into the woods, not into any bushes. The reporter never spoke to me. Or you. Some of the facts are wrong."

"I guess it's like that children's game, telephone," Victor says. "Your story was passed along, and the paper didn't get it all right."

"What the newspaper did manage to do was give the Evil Man my identity and take away my anonymity. My protection. He killed me! I was dead, not unconscious. And I came back! No one was there to see what happened."

"What do you mean?"

"State Trooper Leroy told me when they arrested the suspect at a bar, not at his house, he thought he had killed me. She also told me he had a prior arrest for attempted rape while he was in the Army. And he's married. With a child."

We talk some more until Victor tells me he has errands to do for the houseguests and leaves me deep in thought.

❋

When I'm not studying or doing research, my favorite books to read are mysteries, crime novels, courtroom dramas, private detective stories, Sherlock Holmes, and spy thrillers. Based on my reading, which is mostly fiction, I expect the police will present me with a ledger full of mugshots.

Soon after my fiancé leaves, another group of people enter my hospital room. Two men and a woman, and the men look straight out of *Dragnet*. They're dressed in trench coats and talk just like Detective Joe Friday. "All we want are the facts, ma'am." I'm not sure who the lady is, but I suspect she's a defense attorney, here to assure her client that no undue influence or anything else unlawful happened to help me pick out her guy.

I sure hope I finger the Evil Man.

There is no chitchat. No small talk. The detectives immediately get down to the business of the photo array. One of them hands me a photo album. I'm surprised that it's not a police ledger, but a common photo album. It looks like Mr. Ponytail's albums full of hitchhiker porn. The police album has a pink and green floral cover. I feel apprehensive about opening it. Like the outside cover, there is nothing official about the inside either. Instead of mugshots, pasted on one side of each page are two typical-looking, five-by-four photographs. There are about a dozen pages in the album.

I don't recognize anyone on the first page. Nor on the second or the third. So far, all the men are dressed in casual clothes, have dark hair, and are the same size and build as the man I described to the Gay Head police officer. Some pictures are outdoor shots, others were taken indoors.

My uneasiness increases. I turn page after page and see no familiar face. Then, on the sixth page, my heart starts to beat harder and my body feels flushed. That's him: the Evil Man. He's wearing a plaid, flannel shirt and blue jeans, and his handsome face and dark eyes stare straight into the camera. Straight at me.

"That's him. That's the man who killed me."

Chapter 15

SHERLOCK HOLMES IS ONE OF my heroes. It doesn't matter that he is a fictional character created in 1887 by Sir Arthur Conan Doyle. I admire Holmes' mental aptitude, how he knows himself, his ability to be alone. I admire how he trusts his intuitive capabilities. The first "private consulting detective," Holmes can identify a murderer by a cigar ash, the fleck of mud on the cuff of a pant leg, the ink stain on someone's finger. With his superb faculties of observation and the science of deduction, he conducts his examinations without the use of modern-day forensics.

Still stuck in bed and too weak to be released from Falmouth Hospital, I mentally pit the brilliance of Holmes against the investigative skills of the two Martha's Vineyard police detectives. They had their man and let him go, only to have to go find him again four to six hours later. Favoring Holmes, I need to muster some faith that the detectives got it right this time. With the identification of the Evil Man, my part in their police investigation is over. Although I made the ID with absolute certainty, the detectives left the room without saying I'd picked the right guy. This lack of assurance leaves me with a slight stomachache and a small degree of trepidation.

When Marla and my mother return to the hospital, it is dinnertime. I forget about the man the police have in custody and concentrate on the proposed menu for my wedding. It proves to be a fruitful distraction as we converse about my favorite foods—almost anything grilled or chocolate or from the Cantonese cuisine—and colors—almost all shades of pink.

When visiting time ends and sleep comes to me, so does a dream. It takes place in a room full of pastry display cases. There is a play of light and darkness, as in a Rembrandt painting. Inside the mahogany cases are different kinds of desserts. All are rich and look delicious. In the dream, I stand outside one of the displays, my nose pressed against the glass, peering at all the appetizing cakes and cookies.

The next morning, which is my last day in hospital, begins with a few concerns. Although I'm certain to get a job offer from the New England Documentation Center, I haven't taken up residency in the United States. My hope is that the Ontario Health Insurance Plan (OHIP) will cover some of the costs for the Martha's Vineyard ambulance and my care in the two hospitals. Even though the incident happened in the United States, I am sure the healthcare coverage applies to a Canadian citizen who is traveling abroad.

It is almost dinnertime when my discharge order finally comes. A nurse officially wheels me out of the hospital. My mother and Victor are still here, but Marla took a flight back to Toronto last night. Today, Mom is dressed in a casual pantsuit. I wear a foam rubber ring around my neck to protect my throat. One of my eyes is bright red, due to a blood vessel torn in the struggle. But never mind. I feel fantastic.

We pick an informal place to eat. The restaurant is warm and comfortable. The meal tastes of garlic, with grilled lobster on the side. After that, I order a slice of fluffy, chocolate, butter-cream cake and share it with Mom and Victor.

The police detectives have not contacted me since the photo array in my hospital room. But I'm not sticking around. My intention is to leave the island and ditch the bookbinding and paper restoration interview in Lawrence. As we eat chocolate cake, Mom and Victor and I talk about airline tickets and departure times. Victor will remain here on the island and drive our pickup truck to Windsor in a couple of days.

Once I'm healed, my plan is to drive across country to the West Coast. Moving to the other side of the continent will fulfill the first of my five divine directives. I know Victor will agree to join me on the journey.

Later that night, alone in our hotel room, we sit next to each other on the bed. After Victor hears me out, he says, "Okay. But let's visit my grandmother in Wilmington, Delaware. She's my father's mother. We're very close."

"Sure."

"She's about eighty years old and still teaches the violin to children, using the Suzuki method." He goes on with a brief history of her style and how it differs from other violinists.

"She is quite a character," I say. "I can't wait to meet her."

"By the way, she adores me and always gives me money. My grandmother thinks I'm lacking my father's attention since he married my stepmother."

"Poor you." I give him a kiss.

The next day, my mother and I fly home. Being in Windsor is uneventful, which is good. Vernon plans to visit from London, but then is detained by work in the bindery. Instead, we have deep discussions on the telephone. Friends of my family and me come by the house or call. They all want to say hello and know if I am okay. One of Mother's friends is a psychotherapist. I almost agree to talk to her but hold back. My sense is that she won't comprehend the mystical and psychic aspect of my death experience. It's a judgment call and comes from my innate tendency to hide this side of myself.

Then Victor telephones. He's having truck troubles. It won't start and is currently in the mechanic's shop. He can't leave Martha's Vineyard for a few more days.

And somehow it comes to pass: arrangements are made for my father and me to go to New York City, along with his current business partner and his son. The visit is for a long weekend. My mother, occupied with thoughts of bridal showers and wedding plans, stays home.

While we're in the city, we attend the Broadway play *On the Twentieth Century* starring Imogene Coca and a young Kevin Kline. He is brilliant at slapstick, which is usually not my favorite style of comedy, but he helps an otherwise boring play. My father's business partner falls asleep after the intermission and starts to snore. Luckily, we are seated in the back row of the theatre.

Later that evening, my father is sad. Concern shows in his furrowed forehead and dejection is written on his face. Sitting in a chair in our hotel room, he appears small next to the large window with its partial view of the famous New York City skyline. He tells me his business partner agreed to loan him money for this trip.

"But," Dad adds, "I'm not sure he'll live up to his promise to cover expenses."

My father's business partner is a bulvan, which is a Yiddish term that means a boorish, loud-mouth, know-it-all. I understand my father's anxiety and give him a hug. "I love you, but you didn't have to bring me. Anyway, thanks for the trip. I hope he keeps his promise too."

"Your mother was angry at me, for not flying to Falmouth with her," he says. "She convinced me it was the fatherly thing to do to bring you here."

"Let's just try to have fun."

He's still sad the next day, and not even a lunch of corned-beef sandwiches at the legendary Carnegie Deli can help his disposition. When I have dinner with just my father at the

Waldorf Astoria, however, he is in high spirits as he talks to the woman next to him at the sushi bar.

I nudge him and whisper. "Geez, with this lady, you're all happy."

Usually a gentleman, Dad slams his hands down on the countertop, turns to me and whispers, "You give me the goods on the side. Just like your mother."

"Sorry. I'm sorry."

"Myra, this is what you do at sushi bars. You talk to the people who sit next to you. You decided to sit at the end of the row."

"I guess I just wanted your attention."

Dad calms down and pats my hand. "I understand. It's okay."

Oy vey! By the time we leave the restaurant and get into a cab, I am feeling his sadness. "Sorry for upsetting you," I tell him again. "I felt left out. And I don't like it when you compare me to Mom and her bad side."

"I know."

My father is actually still upset with the bulvan, who was given two baseball tickets to an important game scheduled for tomorrow afternoon. It is between the defending champion New York Yankees and the Los Angeles Dodgers. The bulvan is now being an ass about having the tickets. "He bragged all day long," my father says. "I guess I took it out on you. I'm sorry too." He kisses my cheek, and my happiness returns. In the taxicab, we talk over his misfortune and agree to try to find two tickets before tomorrow's game.

Early in my life, I figured out that properly loving my father meant watching sports with him on television. It started when I was still small enough to curl up on his lap and suck my thumb. Be it football, baseball, or golf, most of the games and their announcers soothed me to sleep. I clearly remember learning both the grammatical structure of sentences and the rules of the games when my father corrected my English and answered my sports questions. "What's a down?" "Why are there four of them?" "Why did the guy walk to first base?" "What's a shank?"

When I was older, we went to Detroit a couple of times to catch Tigers games. Baseball is always more exciting when you're right there in the stadium. Caught up in the atmosphere of the controlled conflict, the crowd can be of one mind and cheer or boo at the same time.

❋

It is Sunday afternoon, October 15, 1978. The bulvan, his son, my father, and I are squashed into an overcrowded subway car. It seems like half of New York City is on their way to Yankee Stadium. My main goal is to stand still, feet firmly planted, a white-knuckle grip on a metal pole, as the car bobs and weaves its way to the Bronx.

Near me, I overhear the bulvan murmuring into my father's ear. "The probability of getting seats is nil. And two together at that? Hah! Impossible." When we arrive at the stadium, he tells us his section, then chuckles and says, "On the remote chance you get in . . ."

His insinuation that my father is a loser makes my father all the more determined to get tickets. We watch the bulvan and his son stride toward their seats, not looking back, and then we set off to find the scalpers around the corner.

Dad yells out, "I need two tickets, two together."

"I got two," one of the scalpers shouts back. "Two over here."

A crowd swarms around the guy. We rush over too. When my father and I finally squeeze up close to him, we find out he was lying. The seats are not next to each other.

This scenario, the shouting back and forth between the scalpers and their potential customers, continues. After a while, the crowd thins out. By now, all those in need have bought tickets and the scalpers have vanished. Darkness fell at least an hour ago. Now my father and I are all alone outside Yankee Stadium.

Smoking a cigar, my father is the image of depression. A Nat King Cole song comes into my mind. "The party's over. It's time to call it a day." I don't want to call it a day. It doesn't matter how long we stay out here. I say a silent prayer to God: *Just let my father be happy. Please, help my father.*

Suddenly a man comes running toward us. In his hand are some tickets he's waving in the air. He's a scalper.

Dad shouts at him, "I need two together."

"Yeah. Two together."

The bidding starts. For what are usually $6.50 seats, my father pays $35 apiece. He examines the tickets and hands one to me. Inside the stadium now, I hear a loud crack when a bat meets a baseball, then loud cheering. Dad still isn't quite convinced our seats are together and mumbles something about the stadium steps maybe splitting us up. Then he stops and declares, "But first things first, Myra."

He leads me away from the section printed on our tickets and we scurry through the inner corridors of Yankee Stadium. Its well-worn smells of ballpark franks, oily vendor foods, and the occasional acrid bathroom odor accompany us. My father heads into the stands and walks down some steps. I follow him. Then I understand. A huge smile spreads across his face. When the bulvan and his son spot us, my father waves his hand at them. A frown appears on their faces, betraying their lost sense of superiority.

When we get to our section, the game is well underway. Then a miracle happens. Our seats are indeed side by side. Mine is at the end of the row, where I usually feel less confined, and next to the stairs. My father looks extremely pleased.

Soon I'm starting to feel cold. All I'm wearing are a jean jacket, a T-shirt, and blue jean shorts. It was a hot day when we started out, but now it's cold, and because my seat is at the end of the row, a breeze runs up the open stairway. My father notices my discomfort, takes off his trench coat, and covers my bare legs.

By now, both of us are also thinking about food. We hail a man selling hot dogs, one hawking potato chips, and another pushing Cokes, make our purchases, and then settle in to watch the game. Yet I am slightly distracted. Maybe it's because our bleacher seats are too far away from the bases, or maybe it's the chill in the air. Or maybe it's because I can't stop thinking about my encounter with death. I just can't get into the game. It's too bad. Tonight is the fifth game of the World Series, with two wins apiece for the teams.

The Yankees won that night. Their next win crowned them the 1978 World Series Champions.

Chapter 16

MY MOTHER GREW UP IN New York and always fed my imagination with tales about her impoverished life in the Bronx during the Great Depression and the elegance and magic of Manhattan. Now my memories of those stories contribute to my feeling at home in the Big Apple. The famous shops and expensive restaurants, the street food and the brownstone stoops, the everyday noise and commotion. They're all worlds away from the woods and the silence of Martha's Vineyard.

I realize something while I'm in the big city. The people who come into contact with me know nothing about my tragic death and return to life, even though it happened only a few weeks ago. Although Sherlock Holmes was unique, I thought everyone had some capacity, even me, to observe and see through people, to sense or intuit things about them. Guess not. Or perhaps it's an underdeveloped talent we all have.

My father and I arrive back in Windsor to find Victor, but not our pickup truck, which is still with the mechanic on Martha's Vineyard. Victor caught a flight to Windsor without telling me and showed up at the house. I hadn't told him I was going to New York City, but, luckily, my mother was home and able to greet him.

Now I give him, then her, a hug. After some chitchat, my mother takes me aside. "There is a problem with the wedding dates," she says. "Victor's twin sister can't make it in June and cousin Bonnie can't make it in May. What should we do?"

Bonnie is my first cousin and like an older sister to me. I very much want to include her in the ceremony, along with another first cousin, Mollie. I hope my aunts and uncles and other family members will be there too.

That's if I do have a wedding.

"Mom," I say, "I need to discuss this with Victor."

Later that night, Victor and I sit together on my bed. He looks pensive while I do most of the talking. "A way out just materialized," I'm telling him. "Let's not do the marriage-wedding thing." I slide closer to him. "Let's just get out of Windsor and move to the other side of the continent. I love you, but the wedding problems will keep piling up. We have a good opportunity to get out before it all starts. Get out easily and harmlessly."

Victor remains quiet for a minute, and then says, "Not get married, eh? You want to leave now?" He shakes his head as he weighs my proposal.

"Yeah. My real need is to get away, as far away from the Atlantic Ocean as possible. I need to get to the Pacific Ocean to fulfill my first divine directive. We could live in Vancouver. Two girlfriends of mine live there."

"Well," he says, "first, we need to go back to Martha's Vineyard and get the truck." He looks up at the ceiling, then straight at me. Then he draws an imaginary map in the air with his finger. "We can drive across the United States to California," he points to the state on his imaginary map, "and then up the coast to Seattle. We can see my parents and my twin sister. From there, we can drive to Canada and then cross the border into Vancouver."

"That sounds like fun. And it's not too expensive. We can stay at cheap motels." Although I'm squeamish about dirty hotel linens, the TV ads I remember always say the motels are clean. "Let's do it," I finally add. "On one condition."

"What's that?"

"Let's not smoke pot. And you can't drink beer on the trip."

He frowns. "What? No fun?" He laughs, grabs me, and playfully wrestles me down on the bed.

"Let's get to Vancouver without an event," I manage to say. "No attacks, no one out to kill me. No events. No trauma-dramas. We'll try it. What do you think?"

"No pot? No beer?" He rolls his eyes and laughs. "The trip doesn't sound too exciting. Okay. Okay. We'll fly to Wilmington first and see my grandmother. Then we'll fly to Cape Cod and get a ferry to Martha's Vineyard and pick up our truck. It should be fixed by then—"

I stand and interrupt him. "And we'll tell our families about calling off the wedding. Then we can make arrangements for our great trip across America."

No one takes the canceled plans too hard. The idea of marriage had served its purpose with the police, the nurses, the hospital staff, and then with my mother. Although the planned wedding was just a Band-Aid for her anger, the strategy actually glued Victor and me closer together.

We're making arrangements to buy airplane tickets to Delaware and the Cape Cod area, when a sudden impression overcomes me. I need to stay in Windsor. Victor should go to Wilmington ahead of me, and I'll follow a few days later. The reason for my delay is not entirely clear to me, but I have to trust my intuition. That's one lesson I learned from hitchhiking. It was reinforced on Martha's Vineyard.

Victor catches a flight that night.

The next morning, a loud knocking on the door awakens my family. I roll out of bed, grab my housecoat, and run downstairs to open the front door. To my surprise, it's my old traveling partner, Peter. His backpack sits on the porch next to him. I haven't seen or heard from him since my call to go to the western provinces a couple of years ago.

Peter has arrived without notice. Except for my unease about leaving Windsor with Victor, I would not be here. What I learn a bit later is that my hitchhiking pal has come to talk to my father about sponsorship for a Canadian work visa. Peter wants to eventually apply for Canadian citizenship.

Dad listens to his story. Then he declines the request. "This is not a personal reflection upon you, Peter," he explains. "It's because you're German. I remember Hitler and the Nazis. I was in the Canadian Air Force during the Second World War. And we're Jewish, so . . ."

"But Peter wasn't even born then," I protest. "He is hardly a Nazi sympathizer."

"Don't pressure me, Myra." Dad appears agitated and rubs the back of his neck. "I've sponsored lots of people before, but never anyone from Germany. These are my principles."

"Well, it seems more like prejudice than principle." But then my voice softens. "I do understand your feelings about the Nazis."

My father and I had had it out a few years ago on the subject of racism and prejudice. Dismissing my parents' misguided "Archie Bunker" feelings, I chose to leave home for a few days. The argument first arose over my dating an African American man named Joe. Never mind that he was a successful model with a graduate degree from a world-famous business school and a high-paying job with great career potential. Although my parents allowed me to go steady with Chris, a wonderful, non-Jewish guy, when I was younger, the color of Joe's skin was pushing it for them. Too bad.

After the talk with my father, Peter feels dejected. This rejection comes on top of his difficulty getting into Canada because his arrival coincided with Germany's troubles with the actions of the infamous Baader-Meinhof Gang. An antigovernment group, they had kidnapped, held for ransom, and killed a German government official. Interpol, the international police network, alerted countries that were the "likely escape routes for this fugitive gang." The possible connection to Peter was his last name, which is, coincidentally, the same as the group's ringleader. Canadian immigration detained and questioned Peter for hours over any possible affiliations. They released him yesterday.

Because my father has turned down Peter's request for sponsorship, it is time for Peter to leave Canada and for me to go to Delaware. We catch a flight from Windsor International Airport to Toronto International Airport and land just in time for him to purchase a ticket and board the only available flight to Germany. We have to say our goodbyes and good lucks quickly before the airline officials pile Peter and his gear into a wheelchair. He is perfectly fine, but the wheelchair facilitates the rush to get him to the plane.

My flight for Wilmington is almost ready to go too. A new adventure and, eventually, a new life in Vancouver will soon begin for my boyfriend and me. This time, my call to go west is propelled by the death experience and the divine directive to move to the other edge of the continent.

The timing of Peter's visit has been an interesting coincidence. Another of my divine directives is to learn more about meaningful coincidences, those seemingly accidental occurrences that can change the direction of our lives. I'm not sure how Peter's visit qualifies as a coincidence, even though he is the man with whom I made my first visit out west. Peter followed me home to Windsor at the end of that trip. Now, as I begin a new important journey to the west, he shows up again. At a minimum, this signals me to be more alert and pay attention.

These thoughts stay with me as I wait to board the plane to Wilmington. I don't like all the hustle and bustle that goes with flying, like the anxiety about being on time and making connecting flights. I'm surveying the waiting room in the hope of seeing a friendly face when a man asks if he can sit in the empty seat beside me.

"Sure."

Chapter 17

THE MAN IS HANDSOME, WITH dark hair, piercing eyes, and even features. He's dressed in a sophisticated businessman's suit. We have a pleasant yet penetrating chat and proceed to board the airplane together. I head to my seat in economy, while he stays in the front compartment. This confirms my impression of him as first-class person.

After the airplane levels off, a flight attendant approaches me. She explains that a gentleman would like me to join him at the front of the plane. Of course, I accept. It must be the man from the airport terminal. I follow her.

Mr. First Class greets me with a smile and tells me he enjoyed our conversation in the waiting area and hopes to continue it. I agree and sit in the empty seat next to him. He tells me he is the CEO of a successful, industrial-chemical-and-manufacturing company.

For some reason, our discussion quickly turns to mystical matters as Mr. First Class says, "I usually feel the need to keep this side of myself under wraps, especially from my fellow board members and professional colleagues."

My thoughts immediately go back to my premonitions on Martha's Vineyard and how I sensed the Evil Man and did not feel comfortable about telling the police detectives about my impressions. "I know exactly what you mean," I say.

"We are on the same page then," he says. "Do you meditate?"

His question touches another of my divine directives. "No, but I want to learn. Do you?"

Mr. First Class nods his head. "I believe in meditation and have practiced it for over a dozen years. During meditation, my mind is calm. I am able to sort out and solve seemingly impossible problems. Some of our business concerns would be in the magnitude of fortunes lost. If not for my meditating in an attempt to find a solution, it would require the company to conduct costly investigations and tests."

This interests me. "Can you give me an example?" I shift in my seat and look straight at my flight companion.

"Well, here is a recent situation that beset the company." The tone of the CEO's voice gets serious. "It involves an incident with a Toronto-based firm. They hired us to manufacture a piece of engineering equipment that must be manufactured to precise specifications. Soon after our company delivered the product, however, the customer started to complain of difficulties. We sent troubleshooters to sort it out, but to no avail. The deadline for my company to solve this customer's problem was coming close. I needed to meditate about this dilemma.

"After an hour or more of sitting quietly in my office," he continues, "the solution came to me. It was like a revelation! I realized something. Although the product seemed to conform to specification, we had overlooked the dimensions of a small screw. It wasn't long enough and was causing pressure on the steel. I immediately called a board meeting and told the directors of my findings. After some discussion, they agreed that this was the answer."

"Did you tell them you found it through meditation?"

"I did not. I feared the directors would not comprehend it and would only ridicule me."

I nod my head. "I understand your reluctance. My preference is to hide my sensibilities too. You know what?"

"No. What?"

"It's interesting to talk to you about this. I have been called to learn to meditate."

"What do you mean?"

I feel comfortable with this man and tell him about my encounter with evil on Martha's Vineyard and my premonitions and intuitions. "I'm only still learning," I say. I pause a moment and decide to explain about the crystalline world of dying, the squares of white fire on black fire in death, and the five divine directives I received upon my return to life. "Like the crystal I keep in my pocket to take out and view the world through," I tell him, "the death experience and these directives are guidelines for my life journey. For me, the call to meditate is a call to get more in touch with the soulful aspects of myself. Through a quiet mind, I can discern different levels of reality and gain knowledge. At least I presume this, because I don't practice yet. But my encounter with you clarifies things."

Our plane is ready to land. I am about to say goodbye to Mr. First Class when he asks for my telephone number and if he can see me while I am in Delaware. I explain my relationship to Victor and say we are staying at his grandmother's house in Wilmington.

He laughs. "Wanting your telephone number comes from my enjoying the freedom of talking to you. I would take pleasure in another exchange of ideas. Also, it would be nice to meet Victor. Will both of you join me for dinner? Of course we will invite Grandma too." A smile spreads across his face as he reaches into his pocket and takes out a small pad and a pen.

I give Mr. First Class the phone number. Then it's off to the ladies' room to get ready to see Victor. The man probably won't call, and I do not plan to tell Victor about Peter or Mr. First Class.

These men are not sexual liaisons, but my boyfriend might think they are. Even though Victor is goodhearted and not subject to suspicions, I don't want to create problems between us.

These coincidental meetings are demonstrations, signs from the universe. I must pay attention to them and learn from them and develop my intuition. I should not judge people and miss the gifts they can give me. From my prior studies of the *I Ching*, I know there might be coincidental aspects to everyday events. When understood, they can be significant and help us move forward in life.

Right now, though, the center of my attention is Victor's grandmother. When we meet, her energy inspires me. Small-boned and wiry, she is not afraid to speak her mind. "When I look into a mirror," she says, "I don't recognize myself. The person staring back is an old, wrinkly woman, but I feel so exceedingly young."

Yet this woman can also repel me, as when she looks over her nose at me and says, "I would never take you as a violin student. You would not be suitable with those double-jointed fingers of yours." Grandma does not consider me a prospective pupil for her Suzuki teaching method. She shuts me out of other things too. Over the next few days, I witness her overprotectiveness of her grandson as she excludes me from some conversations and concentrates only on him when we talk about what occurred on Martha's Vineyard. "Victor is always so level-headed," she declares. "He called the state troopers right away. He is so mature and gallant in how he handled the situation."

I nod in agreement, but I also want to yell at her. *Well, what about me? What about how well I'm handling death by a stranger's hands?* But I remain silent and excuse myself and go into the bedroom and cry.

Lying across the bed, I think about the psychotherapist friend of my mother's, the one who came to the house in Windsor. She was concerned that I needed to talk. But I wasn't ready then. It did not feel right to expose myself.

Now it does.

In this moment, I feel so unimportant, so unloved. It reminds me of when my mother first arrived at my hospital room. I understand that Victor is this woman's favorite grandchild, but when her only comment about the attack on my life, which occurred near or on her son's property, revolves around her grandson, it's a lot to take.

Alone in the bedroom, a realization comes to me. I seem to pick and choose who to open up to and who not to. I seem not to trust the police, the detectives, the doctors and nurses, the therapist, and the grandmother. These are people who, for one reason or another, do not earn my full disclosure. They appear limited and without psychic awareness.

My skepticism is just like Mr. First Class'. It causes us to overjudge, to evaluate everyone's spiritual and psychic capacities. Even before the strangulation experience, my reserved nature made me reluctant to talk about myself. Perhaps it is these inhibitions that trap me in isolation and loneliness. I long for some guidance.

A knock on the bedroom door interrupts my thoughts.

Victor comes in and sits on the edge of the bed. "Myra, don't mind my grandmother. She's old and she dotes on me. I love you. I think you handled the Evil Man way better than I would have."

I'm touched by his concern. "Thanks. A part of me understands her, but a part also feels left out."

Victor curls up next to me and we take a short nap.

A few hours later, when we're awake and the telephone rings, Victor's grandmother passes it to me with a suspicious look on her face. After she leaves the room, I say hello and hear a man's voice. The call surprises me. After a brief conversation, I hang up the telephone and go find Victor and his grandmother.

"My friend from the flight just called to inquire about a possible dinner date. With all of us." I look directly at grandmother. "He is an interesting man, the CEO of a famous company. He is currently in Wilmington to do business. But I politely refused his offer."

So instead of going out, we stay home and eat a light meal that Victor and I prepare. A friend of the family drops in and joins us. He is a lawyer who recently argued before the Supreme Court of the United States. The legal case concerned some complicated challenge to the over-the-counter antacid Tums. The conversation around the dinner table is pleasant and casual, but I am politely ignored by the grandmother and feel somewhat intimidated by the lawyer. My contribution to the discussion is to tell that dumb joke about Tums spelled backward.

Chapter 18

THE STRANGE THING IS THAT for Victor and me to travel west, we first have to go the East Coast.

A couple of days after our dinner with the lawyer, we leave Delaware and fly to Cape Cod and then catch a boat to the island. The last time I came here, it was cloudy. Today I feel the need to leave, even before we arrive at the dock. As we pull closer to Martha's Vineyard, we are greeted by the same Cape Cod architecture. It still appears cold and unwelcoming, with its wood-shingle sidings and roofs, all done in hues of gray-blue, brown, and beige. But the sun is out, which is a good sign.

Before we pick up our truck from the mechanic, we stop by the state troopers' station to find out about my case. We are told to take a seat and to wait until the desk officer gets off the telephone. As we sit there, my eyes wander around the room. A poster of the FBI's Ten Most Wanted Fugitives hangs on the wall just above the fake green leather couch. There is nothing else to read, so I study the info on ten of America's most infamous men. Many are murderers and rapists.

It is strange, but the more I read, the more pleased I feel about the Evil Man. These men not only killed and raped their victims, but they also did other unspeakable things to them. Some of the female victims survived but were maimed, as when the man cut off one woman's arms at the elbows or another sliced off a girl's nipples. Other victims were severely beaten with chains or fists. My heart goes out to these women for the unbelievable suffering they had to endure.

Then the unlikely happens. The more I read, the happier I feel that the Evil Man was just a normal murderer and not like these demented, sadistic men. He did not try to rape or disfigure me. He strangled me to death. That's all. Just an archaic kind of murder. I am grateful.

After reading the most wanted list, I study Mr. State Trooper still on the phone at the desk. The more I watch him, the more he seems like a bumpkin. He's sitting with his feet up on the desk, leaning back in his chair, and his arrogance pervades the room like a stench. He's in his late twenties or early thirties, has red hair, and is tallish and thin. And he speaks in clichés and street slang, "Afro Americoons. Uh-huh. The blacks," he tells the caller. "You're right. Yep, those niggers."

Victor is sitting next to me, calmly looking out the window. I lean over and whisper in his ear. "That police officer, the one who first came out to the cottage . . . I wish he was here. This guy on the telephone? He's a fool and talks like a racist. If all the island's law enforcement were like him, then they couldn't have found the Evil Man without divine intervention. Let's just see how things are progressing. Then let's get out of here." I lift my chin in the direction of the trooper and add, "I'm getting the heebie-jeebies just listening to his bigoted jibber-jabber."

Finally, the phone conversation ends. The trooper removes his feet from the desk and motions for us to come over and take a seat. "What can I do for you two?"

I give him my name. "I want to know about the status of my case."

He nods his head in recognition. "The man we have in custody was charged with attempted murder, attempted rape, and assault and battery."

"But I was not raped, nor did he try to rape me. I am a victim of a murder."

The trooper's eyes seem to pop out of his head and he raises his hands in mock surrender. "Lady, what do you want? You're standing in front of me. So you're not dead. I'm just a desk officer." He rummages around on the desk and comes up with a report. "Your assailant is being held over for an examination to determine if he's fit to stand trial."

"What's that mean?" Victor asks.

"Maybe the guy in custody is crazy and doesn't understand what's happening to him. About the charges and his arrest." The trooper sounds official.

Victor stands up and says, "We are moving to Vancouver, British Columbia. That's in Canada. You can keep us posted using this number." He hands him a piece of paper with my parents' telephone number written on it.

I stand too. "When we get to Vancouver, I promise to phone the station with my new number."

"Uh-huh."

Victor heads for the front door. I follow him but turn back to see the trooper pick up a newspaper and put his feet back on the desk. Outside, we get directions and make our way over to the office of the *Vineyard Gazette*. Now I want to talk to the reporter who did the story about me.

The clerk at the newspaper's front desk is alarmed when I tell him my name. "It is not often victims of violent crimes walk into a reporter's office for a second chance at a news story," he tells me. "That journalist is on assignment. You can hang around if you like. I'm not sure when he'll be back."

Victor and I exchange glances. "Thanks, but we've decided not to wait."

Perhaps the reporter is lucky to be out. Although my anger has subsided, I had planned to give him an earful about my privacy rights. His story put my twin sister and me in harm's way when the paper published my name without my permission. But in all fairness, I suppose the editor was confident the police had the right man in custody.

We leave the *Gazette*'s office and walk over to the mechanic's shop. While Victor pays the guy, I check our belongings in the back of the truck under the tarp. Our stuff seems intact, so we grab a quick lunch and leave Martha's Vineyard that afternoon. On the ferry ride to the mainland, I feel certain I will never to return to the island. It has no draw for me anymore.

Our intention is to drive west. Victor will do all the driving while I do the sightseeing. Our pickup is almost perfect. For a small vehicle, it has the advantage of large windows. The huge transport trucks are the best rides though. When I hitchhiked around southern Ontario and through the Rockies and central Canada, the eighteen-wheelers were the kings of the road.

Because of the Evil Man, of course, it is highly unlikely that I will hitchhike again. There is always a risk when getting into a stranger's vehicle. Now I am too suspicious, too watchful, and too cautious. I would feel confined. The situation would probably overwhelm me. I'd be assessing the driver's every word, movement, and gesture and not be able to relax. I can never again stand alone at the edge of a road with my thumb out, waiting for a ride. The thought of a van stopping, a man jumping out and dragging me inside frightens me. I never thought this way before, but now the idea of being on a road surrounded by woods, like when I was on the outskirts of Kelowna, seems overwhelming.

❁

Although I have driven with my family to Florida, and my dad let me take the wheel when I got my driver's license, I have never traveled clear across the United States. My knowledge of the states comes from reading the *World Book Encyclopedia*. My parents purchased the set when I was about nine or ten years old. The twenty volumes were kept in my brother's room, and I read through every one of them. Another favorite reference was the *National Geographic* magazine, which I found in libraries in Windsor. The back of each volume had the addresses of the tourist bureaus of many cities in the United States. I wrote to a few of them and was excited to receive replies and materials.

Now, as Victor and I drive to the other side of the continent, I am eager to see the things I read about as a child. A necessary first stop is in Washington, DC, to visit the Smithsonian Institution. A big attraction is the NASA exhibit, which features the capsule from the *Apollo 11* command module. It is tiny, smaller than I expected. I'm sure anyone would be uncomfortable inside it. Without a successful reentry and landing, it becomes a cone-shaped coffin. Ugh.

Our next destination is the Library of Congress. As a research facility for congressional members and the home of the US Copyright Office, it houses most of the material published in the US. It looks like a book palace, both inside and out. The stunning marble floor in the Great Hall of the library's Thomas Jefferson Building presents the famous zodiac design. Although we have not joined a tour, I happily scoot around a reading room and we take a peek inside other rooms.

The beauty of the library, plus being surrounded by books, reaffirms my ambition to be a bookbinder. The first gleam of my goal lay in the essay on Marx that I failed to write for Professor Silverman. Now, in this grand, historically important library, it is clear that my love of books comes from the knowledge they contain and how they can take us places we've only dreamed of. A book is a noble physical object to make. My plan is to continue with this endeavor in Vancouver. But I'm not sure how I'll do it.

Victor and I next cruise past the US Supreme Court, an august building. I think about our Delaware dinner guest and visualize him walking out through its large bronze doors and down those famous stairs after his oral argument before the court.

Next, we walk to the Capitol Building, then down the mall to the White House, but we do not go inside either building. After we wander around the city and see other famous landmarks, it's evening, and we stumble upon a great jazz place. The music draws us in. The décor includes black leather-upholstered booths with shiny brass finishings. It is dinnertime, and we have delicious grilled fish smothered in garlic butter.

The next morning, we are on the road again, heading for Memphis, Tennessee, and Graceland. In my early teens, I had a huge crush on Elvis Presley and saw all his movies. But my expectations are deflated by the reality of his palace. It is just a two-story, white, colonial-style house with black shutters and trim and manicured lawns and trees. Okay, it's in the medium-to-large range of mansions. Perhaps the inside is more interesting.

Unfortunately, today Elvis' home is closed to the public. Other tourists are here too and in the same predicament. All we can do is peer at the grounds of Graceland through the enormous black gate. My hands grip the wrought iron like a prisoner, but one who is on the outside. I suddenly think of the Evil Man and his view through his cell bars.

Even though we cannot see how the king lived, our souls are soothed when we find a place to eat Memphis-style barbeque ribs. They do taste good. It is a dry rub that is similar to how ribs are served at Windsor's famous Tunnel Bar-B-Q restaurant. I don't like the wet sauces.

The next day—westward, ho! Victor drives us through middle America, with all the glory of her small towns and some big ones. Along the way, he tells me about historical events that occurred at this place or that one. My boyfriend's chatter keeps me engaged while I view the passing scenery.

We find different places for picnic lunches that we purchase at local grocery stores, an apple or a pear, cheese, bread, a small Italian salami or luncheon meat, two pops (referred to in some places in the US as soda), and chocolate bars. We eat breakfasts and suppers at some of the many highway diners. Except for their weak coffee, the food is generally good. Our only requirement is that the place has to be clean, which includes how it smells.

The same goes for the "$9.99 a night" motel rooms. For 1978, this price is affordable. They must be sanitary, even if the price is cheap. These bare-bones rooms are similar, no matter what city or state we are in, with a bed, a nondescript bedspread, a dresser, a TV, a toilet, a sink, and a prefabricated shower stall.

Cleanliness means us too. The morning we arrive in Gallup, New Mexico, our first stop is at a Laundromat. Victor takes care of washing our clothes. He plans to sit quietly and read a book while the machines do the work. Meanwhile, I wander around the town and buy today's picnic food.

To get to Gallup, we drove on roads that pass through Indian reservations. As history and anthropology majors, Victor and I talked about the plight of those who are forced to live here. Their forlorn, prefabricated houses reflect on the early settlers who occupied Indian lands and the genocide of the indigenous people. It is a despicable part of our past and a wound in the body politic of our current society.

By the time I walk back to the Laundromat in Gallup, Victor has folded and packed our clean clothes. After a picnic lunch, we get on I-40, drive past the town of Defiance, and a couple of hours later cross the state line into Arizona. Now our travels take us along Arizona's section of historic Route 66, with its old-time gas stations and highway towns. Here the geology comes in shades of oranges and brown, and the sparse foliage of small shrubs and grasses is silver green. When we reach the badlands of Arizona, unusually beautiful colors abound. The layers of a flat-topped mesa can go from dark blue to bright red.

At the Petrified Forest National Park, Victor and I walk among the fallen, fossilized trees, pieces of which lie scattered on the red earth. The trees' rings gleam and twinkle like multicolored gem bracelets under the desert sun. Then we're back in the truck, and we drive west for another twenty-six miles. Nature continues to strut her stuff in this spectacle of colors called the Painted Desert, where hues of violet and lavender appear in the mesa's strata, along with vibrant red, orange, and pink layers. The colors create an earthen rainbow that is spectacular to look at.

At the moment, however, I myself am not so great looking. My concern is hair. Call me vain, but mine is thinning. These days, I wear a scarf tied tightly around my head and a man's Navy peacoat over a shirt and blue jeans. Mother Earth outdoes me in attractiveness. This makes my mood for romance almost nil.

That night, like most nights, we have a good sleep. The next morning, we ready ourselves for a tour of the great holes of the West. Victor drives us to the first one, Meteor Crater, which was created by a crashing meteor more than 50,000 years ago.

At the site is a sign that says the skin of the Apollo space capsule and its reentry shield are man's attempt to duplicate the material of meteorites. I wonder . . . could I be made of the same tough stuff? Perhaps my own internal resistance to the consuming fire of evil is just as durable. Familiar words echo in my head: *You're not going to get away with this. Murderer! You're not going to get away with this.* Along with the squares of white fire on black fire, these words sheltered my indomitable spirit with a protective grid and helped my soul withdraw from death.

As our crater hopping continues toward the Grand Canyon, I wonder about life itself. The canyon is more a gash in the earth than a hole, but the comparison will suffice. The

Grand Canyon is long and deep, formed by the rushing of the Colorado River five to six million years ago. When we arrive, we can only look over the area because, like Elvis' home, this place is closed to the public today. The park rangers order everyone to leave the park and forbid tourists to trek to the bottom of the canyon. Their concern is caused by an unusual, severe snow system entering the area.

Our route avoids the city of Las Vegas, and we head toward the next hole in the ground, which is Death Valley, California, the lowest point below sea level in North America. The land is flat and barren, some places so dry the ground is cracked and looks like cobblestones. Ironically, the name Death Valley becomes relevant when our truck overheats. As it starts to fume white smoke, Victor quickly drives off the road and onto the shoulder, where we come to a dead stop.

I look around us. There is not a car in sight. It seems we are stuck in the middle of nowhere. Grateful Victor is here, I try not to feel afraid.

Chapter 19

IT IS BROAD DAYLIGHT. All the windows of the truck are rolled down and the doors are wide open. Luckily, it is mid-December and not too hot. Concerned that this will turn into a full-blown, life-and-death drama, we sit inside our mini-pickup and say nothing. The road is still empty. I start to pray.

Luckily, we do not have to wait too long. A friendly truck driver slows down and pulls alongside us. The emphasis is on friendly. I guess he recognizes the situation.

"Bet you need help," he calls out.

"Yep. The truck overheated."

"I can drive you to get some water. Hop in."

Victor locks our truck and we get into the man's big truck. Our rescuer drives about fifteen minutes, then turns down a dirt road that leads to a modern wooden cabin. He gives us a gallon of water and drives us back to where we left our truck.

"Thank you so much," Victor and I both say.

"Good luck on the rest of your trip," he replies.

It seems fate is on our side. Luckily, there are good people everywhere.

One of those good people is Victor himself. With his help, I am fulfilling my first divine directive: move to the other side of the continent. What is luck, I wonder. Is it God responding to our needs or prayers? I am too much of a novice and have far too little knowledge about either meaningful coincidences or the metaphysics of God's grace to answer complicated, abstract questions. I need to learn more. Trusting my intuition is a good tool to develop.

We leave Death Valley without further incident and spend the night in a small motel. Early the next morning, we drive through a bit of Sequoia National Park and gaze at its huge, gorgeous, red trees. The air smells woodsy. Victor and I get out of the truck and hug a few of the redwoods. That feels comforting. Then we travel to Bakersfield and head toward the Sierra Madre Mountains.

We make the crest, north of Santa Maria. At the top of the range, the view from the highway opens up all the way to the Pacific. It is magnificent. This is first time I see the actual ocean, not just a picture in a book, and the panorama leaves me breathless. The Pacific doesn't look like the rough, gray Atlantic I'm accustomed to. The Pacific dazzles. On this sunny day, it shines a deep, turquoise blue.

We travel north on US Route 101, much of which runs parallel to the ocean. At Atascadero, we switch over to Highway 41, a narrow ribbon of an inland road. For twenty miles or so, the drive edges farmers' fields that go almost to the water. Next, we pick up the Pacific Coast Highway, a two-lane road and drive toward San Simeon, though we whiz past Hearst Castle, the architectural crown of William Randolph Hearst, king of newspapers and other media at the turn of the century. Located at the top of a grassy hill, the castle overlooks the ocean.

A few miles later, the road starts to rise as the highway hugs the foothills. Our side winds up and up, while the other lane is nearer to the edge of the hill above the ocean. The higher up, the longer the drop-off, and it goes straight down.

"Victor, when you take the curves, I get seasick. There are too many twists in this part of the highway."

"I'll slow down," he says. "I think it's worse for the passenger."

At Gorda, a cute hamlet nestled against the side of a mountain, we make a pit stop for gasoline. While Victor attends to the truck, I go into the general store in search of food and water. Besides the regular fare found at a corner convenience store, I also spot a tray full of hoagies sitting on the counter. Each one is wrapped in parchment paper. I point to the sandwiches and ask the clerk, "Are these fresh?"

"Yep. Made them today myself.

"What's in them?"

"Ham and cheese, with shredded iceberg lettuce, tomato slices, and mayo."

"They look good! I'll take two. And these." I place a large bag of potato chips, a jug of water, two apples, and a big chocolate bar with nuts and raisins on the counter and then pay for them.

Outside, Victor has finished pumping gas and is waiting for me. We travel a mile or so, then pull off the road at a spot where we have a splendid view of the ocean and have our picnic in the truck with both doors wide open. The sea air smells fresh and clean. From time to time, we can hear the roar of the waves as they crash against rocks at the shoreline far below us.

After lunch, we are back on the road. Then the drizzle starts. At first, it is only a light mist and easy to drive in. (So far on this trip, the weather has been excellent.) But about a half hour later, as darkness falls, so does the rain. Soon, it's coming down in sheets.

Because Victor has driven us from the Atlantic to the Pacific and done so well at it, I take his skills for granted and relax. But then I glance over at him. In the thick of this torrential downpour, he looks scared. His back is ramrod straight and he's staring at the roadway in full concentration. His face mirrors the white-knuckled grip he has on the steering wheel.

Now I'm frightened, but I sit still and keep quiet. Our little truck crawls forward, inch by inch along the highway as it winds around the face of the mountain. With the rain and the darkness, it's hard to see the edge of the road. Only the lines painted on the road guide us. Neither of us has ever driven in these conditions. Still we creep forward, not sure if the rain will lighten up or if our end is at hand.

"Myra, I can't drive much more."

"Okay."

"The wind is picking up too." His voice sounds tense. "We need to stop and spend the night."

"Okay."

The howling of the storm is all around us. The beam of the truck's headlights is weak, their light almost extinguished by the darkness and the blanket of rain.

"I need to stop at the first place we see."

"Okay."

Now the truck starts to sway from the force of the wind. Thank God, we checked the tarp after lunch. It is safe and secure. Perhaps we were concerned about the angle up the slope of the mountain, but neither of us had a clue that buckets of rain were in the immediate forecast.

Victor keeps driving. About ten minutes later, we spot a dim light ahead. It is stationary, so we know it's not an oncoming vehicle, and it's on the opposite side of the road, so maybe it's a boat moored offshore below us. We can't tell.

When we get closer, we see a small grove of redwoods, their huge trunks dark in the night. Our truck lights shine into the area and reveal a few cabins scattered among the trees. As we draw nearer, we spot a painted vacancy sign attached to a post by chains and shaking in the wind and the rainstorm. We've come to a motel!

On any other night, we would drive right past this old-fashioned motel and travel an hour to find a better place. Not tonight. Victor pulls off the highway and stops the truck near one of the cabins closest to the road. A soft light emanates from the window. We hope it's the office.

"Stay here, Myra. I'll go see if someone is around."

"Okay."

He pulls his coat from behind the seat and I help him get into it. Then he opens the driver's side door. The wind is so strong, it blows huge raindrops right at his face. He staggers out of the truck and heads for the office.

At the vacancy sign, he turns, and I lose sight of him.

It seems forever, but it's only a few minutes before Victor comes back and leads me to one of the cabins. A throwback to the fifties, it offers a wrought-iron bed with a filigreed headboard and a grandma-style, flowered bedspread. There's also a small bathroom with a tiny shower.

I grab one of the pillows and bury my wet face in it.

"Yes, Myra," Victor replies to my unspoken question, "the lady in the office said the towels and linens are clean."

We quickly strip off our clothes and get into bed, then lie curled up in each other's arms. While the storm howls outside, I feel safe lying next to Victor, and wonder about this journey we're taking.

When we started, my rule was for us not to smoke pot and for Victor not to drink beer. What if I had not laid down that law? The pot would have been okay, but not the beer. Could he have driven through this storm if he was drinking and maybe getting drunk along the way? Would he have been able to keep his focus and drive with a hangover and all worn out? He's not a heavy drinker, but perhaps not. Perhaps we would have gone over the edge of the road, crashed down the cliff, and died. I snuggle closer to him and feel grateful to be alive.

Chapter 20

OUR LAST STOP BEFORE VANCOUVER, Canada, is in a small town just outside Seattle. We arrive around midafternoon. Victor's family lives here in a modern house with teak furniture and Scandinavian décor. His father reminds everyone there how he and I first met in the tunnel on the university campus in London, Ontario, and he laughs when he comes to the part where all the coins fell out of my pocket.

Victor seems relaxed in his family's home. As for me, it's that old saying: the cat got my tongue. Though I'm generally shy and reserved when I first meet people, this is something altogether different. I turned into a mute. The members of Victor's family react differently to my silence.

His father seems disappointed. He expected me to have more oomph. Never mind that only two months ago, a stranger left me for dead on or near his Martha's Vineyard property. A couple of years later, when he will meet Marla, who is bubbly and vivacious, he will say, "That's more like it. What I expected of Myra that day." (But I am getting ahead of myself.)

Victor's stepmother greets me with a hug. She's both friendly and remote, which befits the stereotype of the introverted Norwegian. She doesn't say much and doesn't seem to mind if I don't say much either. Meanwhile, Victor's twin sister takes a decidedly different approach. A petite woman, she models for a fashion catalog and looks like Julia Roberts with the same, wide-open smile. When she corners me to have a chat, she talks for what seems like hours. I can't get a word in edgewise. My boyfriend's stepbrothers and his brother-in-law, on the other hand, don't pay any attention to me at all.

My time spent with Victor's family is now mostly a blur, except for the afternoon when all the guys and I take part in a sailboat race. The weather is rainy again, the ocean filled with huge waves. My role is to stay out of the way, which I do by sitting on a couch in the galley. I experience the whole excursion at a nausea-inducing tilt.

That night, besides still feeling queasy, I look a fright. Along with more thinning hair, there is still a red spot in one of my eyes, which is due to broken blood vessels. The doctors at Falmouth Hospital told me it could be an indicator of death by strangulation.

"Victor, come and check out my hair in the back."

"Sure." He pads over and takes a look. "Yaaah. A noticeable bald spot."

"What do you think it's from?" There is an anxious note in my voice.

Victor shrugs his shoulders. "Don't worry." He pats me on the back. "I'll talk to my dad. Maybe someone at the University of Washington School of Medicine can check you out."

I grab him around the waist, pull him close, and give him a kiss. "Thanks"

Victor unwinds himself, puts on his shoes, and leaves the bedroom. He's back in no time at all. Although it is the weekend, his father has already made arrangements for me to see his favorite intern.

That next afternoon, Victor drives me to the medical school building and waits in the truck while I go inside. The lobby is empty. A few minutes later, a man approaches. He appears to be in his mid-thirties and is casually dressed and looks athletic. After we exchange greetings, Favorite Intern leads me through the empty facility and into a large room. It contains a few desks, plus cabinets, gurneys, examination tables, and medical stuff under a bank of windows.

"Take a seat." He puts on a lab coat.

I hop up on one of the examination tables and sit with my back against a windowpane, my feet dangling over the edge of the table.

Standing close to probe my hairline, Favorite Intern asks, "What happened to your eye?"

"A perfect stranger strangled me and left me for dead."

The doctor lets out a chuckle and takes a step back.

His laughter hits me in the stomach like sledgehammer. "Are you laughing at me?"

"I am sorry. Guess I didn't expect that answer. What happened?"

"It was a nervous laugh, then, eh?"

He nods his head.

Leaving out the premonitions and transcendental aspects, I give him the police report version of when I met evil and died on Martha's Vineyard.

"I'm sorry that happened," he says when I finish. Then he gives me a brief examination. "Other than the eye and the hair, you seem okay."

Of course, Victor and his father ask me about Favorite Intern's prognosis. I do not mention his bedside manner. Instead, I say, "He's not sure why the bald spot showed up now, but the thinning is probably due to my having a traumatic experience and hopefully, over time, my hair will grow back and become thicker."

When the family visit is concluded without another incident, Victor and I drive to Vancouver, British Columbia, and arrive a couple of days later. Through the help of an artist friend, Cec, whom I knew from Windsor, we are able to rent the perfect place the same day. We unload and move our stuff into the new apartment on Haro Street. Then Victor parks the truck in the alley behind the building.

Cec and my other artist friend, Karen, a spirited blonde also from Windsor, came to Vancouver about a year ago. Cec, who looks like Liza Minnelli, prefers women and Karen, men. Other than that, they have the same vibrant personality.

About a week after our arrival, I hear a knock on the front door of our apartment. I've just stepped out of the shower. "I'll be there in one minute," I holler and then grab a fluffy, white housecoat to put on. With my hair still wet, I open the door to find an extremely handsome policeman.

"Hello, Myra Mossman?" He shows me his badge. "Is that your truck in the alley? I traced the license plate to this apartment."

I am surprised and suddenly nervous. "Yes. Sorry, officer." I start to talk fast. "It doesn't start. We came here from the East Coast. The truck died. We're not able fix it. We haven't the money. Is there a problem?"

The officer waves his hands. "No. No. I just want to ask, is it for sale? I want to buy it."

"Oh, great!" Relieved that he's not here about something more serious, I say, "But I'll need to talk to my boyfriend. He isn't home. You must have our number already, so give me a call later, and I'll let you know."

We sell him the vehicle that night, and a couple of days later, he arrives with a flatbed truck that has a hoist and a winch, and he takes our truck away. After that, Victor and I take buses, walk, or get rides to go anywhere in Vancouver.

We bought the Toyota mini-pickup secondhand from the Maintenance Department at the university in London just in time to leave the city and drive to Martha's Vineyard for a visit before my interview to become a hand bookbinder in Lawrence, Massachusetts. Like me, the truck died and was resurrected on the island. The mechanic got it running, and we were able to cross the United States and cross into Canada to my intended destination. The truck helped me fulfill the first of my five divine directives: move to the other edge of the continent.

❂

After he parked our secondhand truck in the alley behind the apartment building in Vancouver, Victor never drove again. Almost four decades later, in 2017, he will tell me that he had been petrified that night on the corniche of the Pacific Coast Highway near Big Sur in the horrific rainstorm. Once he safely got us to Vancouver, he vowed to never get behind the wheel again.

Chapter 21

CLEAN, QUAINT, AND SAFE, THE Vancouver area has a number of retired British expats and an array of international restaurants. Chinese, Greek, Italian, Indian, and Vietnamese cuisines can all be found within a fifteen-minute walk of our apartment. Best of all, Victor and I live just five blocks from the white, sandy beach on the Pacific Ocean.

Situated on the peninsula, called the thumb side of Vancouver (which looks like a hand on the map), our apartment building boasts an Art Deco style with lots of windows and wood floors. It is a half a block from the famous Stanley Park near the Lost Lagoon, a stroll around that takes me about fifteen minutes. (A quick walk around the perimeter of the park can take more than an hour.) Stanley Park's long walkway includes hilly terrain, and its midpoint comes at a natural cleft in the rock face. This is a favorite place for me. I like to stand inside this nook, encased on three sides with the sky above me and the ocean before me. I can be alone here, removed from the rest of the world. It clears and refreshes my spirit.

A couple of months after we've sold the truck, the telephone rings. "Hello, Miss Mossman," says a woman's voice. "I am the assistant district attorney for the Commonwealth of Massachusetts. We are handling the case against your attacker." Her voice has a calm, matter-of-fact tone. "You know we have Mr. Lasinski in custody."

"I recognize his name. Yes."

"He underwent a psychiatric evaluation at the Treatment Center for Sexually Dangerous Persons to see if he was fit to stand trial. He was held there at the center for about six months and then found fit. He faces three charges: attempted murder, attempted rape, and assault and battery. If he decides to go to trial, which is his right, would you be willing to come to Boston as a witness for the prosecution?"

I don't hesitate to reply. "Of course."

"Well, we are in plea negotiations right now. I will let you know if he decides to go to trial."

"I understand he was previously charged with an attempted rape while he was in the Army."

"Where did you hear that?" the assistant district attorney yells into the phone. "Who told you that?"

Her angry reaction takes me by surprise. "Well, it was the state trooper. When she visited me in the hospital. I can't remember her name now, but it was also mentioned in the *Vineyard Gazette* article. She told me about the attempted rape charge."

"That was an incorrect statement. Mr. Lasinski was never involved in a crime before this incident." Her tone is emphatic.

What can I say? "Okay. Okay."

A few weeks after her initial call, the district attorney's office phones me again. The Evil Man has pleaded guilty to the assault and battery charge, the lesser offense. There is no need for me to testify. His sentencing hearing will be later in the year. Before his release from jail, the state is requesting Lasinski undergo another psychiatric evaluation to see if he is sexually dangerous. I'm told this is not a usual sentencing condition.

As I hang up the phone, I ponder the Evil Man's fate and what justice will do to him. Before our encounter, I felt transparent. My high school English teacher once remarked, "Myra, you walk with your pores all open." Now I feel opaque. I have distinct boundaries.

It turns out my hair is getting thicker. The bald spot is gone. And OHIP will pay for most of the ambulance and hospital expenses incurred on Martha's Vineyard. Even so, my boyfriend and I still need to find work.

Victor finds a job as a line cook in downtown Vancouver, an easy bus ride from our apartment. Paul, the trendy restaurant's executive chef, and his girlfriend, Eileen, become our friends. She is an artistic weaver with her own studio. Originally from Nova Scotia, Paul stands five foot ten and wears a small mustache. Eileen is taller. At six feet, she is still down-to-earth. She almost became a fashion model but felt too gangly to be successful.

Karen, my friend from Windsor, helps me find employment by introducing me to two draft dodgers from the US. Fleeing conscription during the Vietnam War, they found employment as janitors and handymen in Vancouver, and now, in 1979, they own the publishing company where they first had such humble jobs.

One of the guys is a hippie who wears tie-dyed T-shirts and has long hair and a longer beard. The other is the "suit" of the company. The three of us reach an agreement. I will produce two hundred hardcover, handmade, and labeled books. The time frame for this special edition is three months.

When my contract job is done, Hippie Owner comes into my makeshift bindery and sits down on a folding chair. He is concerned about my wages.

"Myra," he says, "I'm convinced you figured it out."

I nod my head. "Yep. I undersold myself. But I like working here."

He looks me straight in the eye. "We don't want to take advantage of you and keep you working at your present contract price. However, the publishing company cannot pay any more per hardbound book. We are not putting out other special editions at the moment. But we like you and want you to stay on. The open position is running the paperback bookmaking machine. It's not a hand-binding job."

"That's fine."

"Instead of by the piece," he adds, "the pay is by the hour."

"That's fine too."

We agree on a wage, and for the first couple of days, I train on the paperback-making, perfect-binding machine. It is a large, rectangular device that applies hot glue to one edge of the bare body of a book. Next, the printed softcover stock gets pressed onto the spine, the cover is then folded to form the front and back, and then the book is trimmed. Although I am not certified to use it, the publishing company's head tradesman agrees to teach me. He is of Japanese descent and is a totally neat guy. Thin as a bone and immaculate in style, he belongs to an esoteric drumming group that plays both for sport and to make music.

Head Tradesman teaches me how to move around the paperback-making machine by listening to its sounds. Beeps and bops get coordinated into a rhythm and a dance, and the end result is a perfectly made softcover book. Moving with the machine invigorates me and relieves the boredom of the repetitive work.

After a few months in the shop, I notice a strange, unassuming man lurking around the place. He stays in the background and just watches us. I figure he must be a friend of the Hippie Owner and the Suit. The real word soon gets out: he is an efficiency expert.

One day the owners ask me into their office, which is a small, converted storage room. I take a seat on a folding chair.

Hippie Owner hands me a joint. "Here, have a toke."

The offer surprises me. I know that he and the Suit smoke marijuana alone in here on Fridays. "Thanks. But it's Tuesday. What's going on?"

The Suit, a blank expression on his face, says, "You're fired."

I nod my head. "The efficiency expert, eh?"

"Yep," Hippie Owner says. "His report concluded that you are an untrained tradesman and physically too small and, therefore, a hindrance to the company's profits because a man can lift heavier boxes than you can. And you should not have been using the two-handed guillotine or cutting machine. The report also said our tradesman needs more training."

I get up to leave. "Okay, then. While it lasted, thanks for the job."

The Suit waves at me to sit back down. "What are you going to do now?"

"My aspiration is to open a hand bookbinding business."

The Suit's jaw practically drops to the floor. "But how are you going to collect the money from your clients? You're too nice a person, Myra. What are you going to do when someone refuses to pay?"

"There are some solvency concerns in my plan," I agree. "But right now, my focus is on how to finish the small book press and the backing vice I've been making."

"What do you mean?" the Hippie asks, his face now aglow. "I used to be a candlemaker."

I smile at him. "You know our friend, Karen. Besides you guys, she introduced me to the head technician in the woodworking room at the University of British Columbia. For the past six months, I've been constructing a four-foot-high book press, a sewing frame, and a backing vice. I was given the hardware for the vice as a gift from my teacher, Vernon. The easiest thing to make was the sewing frame. I got the blueprints for the other two pieces of equipment," I add, "from Manly Banister's book on hand bookbinding."

The Suit's eyebrows go up. "Wow. That is enterprising."

"Thanks." I look modestly down at my hands. "After giving me a basic rundown on the electric saw and the electric drill, the head technician said I could sink or swim, it's up to me. He also set down two rules—don't expect any help from him and stay out of his way."

The Hippie Owner and the Suit both laugh at the guy's management style.

"I chose to swim," I tell them. "To get around needing his expertise and asking for help, I asked the clerks at the hardware store lots and lots of questions. Like, what does it mean to sink a bolt? How do you do it? What is a ready rod? Tell me about hardwoods and gluing them together."

Hearing how practical my plans are, Hippie Owner and the Suit offer to help me as best they can. They scrounge around for end-runs of book cloth and paper and provide me with letters of introduction to suppliers. They also wish me well and say they will send customers to me.

Not long after this, my friend Eileen introduces me to the property manager of her weaving studio, which is located in the oldest office building in Vancouver. Arrangements are made for me to rent space and set up my little handbook bindery there. I work in a long, bare room with only my three pieces of equipment.

Over time, I attract a few customers. One is a student who needs me to bind a copy of his doctoral dissertation before he graduates. Another client hires me to make a leather-bound book for a wedding gift.

Chapter 22

IT IS THE SUMMER OF 1979. I'm at the Vancouver Public Library learning more about one of my divine directives, meaningful coincidences. At first, my research focuses on precognition, then I move on to the works of Carl Jung, the Swiss psychoanalyst and founder of analytical psychology. He used the *I Ching,* or Chinese *Book of Changes,* in his studies, as did I before my death experience and still continue to use it.

Jung captivates me. He coined the term "synchronicity," which means "an acausal connection of two or more psychic and physical phenomena." Though noncausal occurrences might seem coincidental and have ambiguous significance, they have their own rationality. It can be highly significant when internal impressions meet outward phenomena and render the coincidence meaningful. I can see how synchronicity applies to the times I met Vernon and Victor's father. It can also apply to my precognitions on Martha's Vineyard, where I sensed the evil in the man we saw standing by the white van at Gay Head Cliffs.

One day when I'm at the library again to do more research on Jung and synchronicity, a man approaches my desk. He is tall, has long hair, and looks unconventional in his white, Nehru-collared tunic and pants. He squats down next to me and whispers, "I have noticed the forlorn look on your face. You're in need of a tarot reading."

His offer piques my interest because the tarot is also connected to Jung's work. And another of my divine directives is to learn a metaphysical or occult science. Like the tarot.

I see nothing sinister in the man's demeanor. "I've heard about it," I tell him, "but I've never had my cards read. Where should we go?"

"There is a teahouse around the corner. Buy me a cup in exchange for a reading."

I gather my materials and we walk to the café and take a seat at one of the empty booths. Tarot Reader takes a miniature deck out of his pocket. He asks me to choose a few cards, which he lays in a pattern on the table. I notice the medieval characters and symbols on them. They all look rather bland.

"This is the popular Rider-Waite deck," he says.

As he spouts his prophecy according to the cards, I become less impressed. There are no insights here. Nothing touches the depths of me.

Tarot Reader senses my indifference. "Why don't you accompany me back to my apartment? I have the most unusual tarot deck. It will surely capture your curiosity."

I could have taken his offer as a come-on, but I surprise myself and say, "Okay."

On the way, I contemplate my decision to go with this man. Less than nine months ago, a stranger left me for dead. Now I am walking with another stranger and we're on our way to his apartment! But I somehow trust him and myself. Even though I will never hitchhike again, the intuition honed during that time is still with me. After my encounter with death, I trust my intuition more strongly.

Tarot Reader seems sincere, even if he's not an inspiring reader. His apartment is close to the café, a tiny studio situated above a string of storefronts, his furniture is all crammed on top of one another. Yet everything is also neat and methodical.

"I want you to meet my boyfriend, Victor," I say. "He would find this interesting too."

"Okay. But first I want to show you these other cards. I use them just for my personal readings. First, I must put the Rider-Waite deck away. That way, it will not taint the other deck."

He puts the miniature deck in a drawer, then opens another drawer and withdraws a bundle wrapped in silk. He throws it on the bed, which also serves as his couch. I pick it up and unwrap the silk covering.

I find an oversized tarot deck. I'm suddenly excited. A tingling sensation flows through me as I look at the face of each of the tarot cards. They seem like jewels. Opulent, rich in visual imagery and colors. My heart sings with joy. I sense that a treasure trove of knowledge lies in my hands.

"This is the Aleister Crowley deck," Tarot Reader says. "Most people will not read from it."

"Why?" I shake my head in disbelief. "The cards are so vital. They captivate me."

"I have all of Crowley's books." He points to a collection on top of his bookshelf. "He had a reputation for sex, drugs, and magic, but he was really misunderstood. Most people consider him the vilest man on earth. So they'll read from the Rider-Waite deck instead of his."

"That deck seems a bore to me. I've never heard of Aleister Crowley." I take a minute or two to thumb through Crowley's books, but like the Rider-Waite deck, they have no draw for me. I am interested in his tarot cards, but not in Crowley, the man.

"Lady Frieda Harris was the real artistic inspiration behind Crowley," Tarot Reader says. "He thought it would only take a few months to create his deck. But thanks to Harris' psychic sensitivity and artistic talents, the project took over five years to complete."

In this moment, my love affair with the tarot cards begins. I intuitively know the cards mirror our differing states of mind. Tarot Reader is not my teacher, but the one thing he has taught me is to never be afraid of the cards. They have no power over me.

A few days later, I introduce Victor to Tarot Reader, and they get along really well. I also purchase my first tarot deck, the Crowley cards. This deck has positively affected me, though I realize it might not work for others. When I open the new package, I randomly pull out one card. It is the one card of seventy-eight to represent me. I draw the fifth Major Arcana card, the Hierophant. Also known as the Five of Trumps, this card can signify Divine Wisdom.

Chapter 23

AT ONE END OF HARO STREET is Stanley Park, at the other, Denman Street. Our apartment is halfway between the Lost Lagoon and an indoor mall with shops, a community center, and a diner that has big windows that look out onto both streets.

A few days after my meeting with Tarot Reader, I am at the diner eating a club sandwich and absorbed in a book. A burly, older man approaches my table. I can see he's looking at the book cover. "What are you reading?" he asks. He has a slight cockney accent.

"A book about meditation," I reply, but I do not say that one of my divine directives is to learn how to meditate.

"Well," he says, "knowledge of meditation comes from experience. Do you mind if I join you? My name is Stan."

"Sure. I'm Myra."

His eyes are intense, but I sense sincerity. Men who want to pick me up don't usually get into serious business that can lead to deep discussions. Besides, Stan has awakened my intuition. I pay attention as he squeezes into the booth and urges me to put the book away.

I am mesmerized as he begins to explain life by using forks, knives, spoons, and the salt and pepper shakers, which he sets here and there on the table to demonstrate the physics of existence and the function of consciousness. "Myra," he says, "humans are just energy that knows itself."

Next, he tells me about the spirit world and trance mediums who can see my aura and know who my spirit guides are. "I belong to this organization called the Great White Brotherhood," he informs me. "By 'white,' I mean goodness and nothing to do with racism."

"I'm glad you cleared that up! I lived in Windsor, Ontario, when the race riots happened in Detroit. It is not good when some people are treated less than others. Go on."

Stan nods. "I agree about racism. Anyway, the Great White Brotherhood is composed of all the avatars of peace and compassion. This includes all the prophets from the Bible, including Abraham, Moses, and Jesus, plus the Buddha, all the masters of the Near East and Far East and the Indian sages. All the great, good, and wise men who encompass all religions and beliefs in a benevolent universe."

"I believe this to be true," I say. "All types of gods can be revered as holy and divine. It does not matter if it is a different culture with an unfamiliar religion. I am Jewish, and in our religion, we have this notion of thirty-six righteous people. In Hebrew, they are the *Lamed Vav Tzadik*. They keep the balance of power for the good against evil. They're humble and pious, and not all of them are Jewish."

Engaged in our discussion as we are, time seems to fly. While Stan talks about his metaphysics, I look out the window and spot Victor. He is pacing back and forth and seems to be looking for me. I catch his attention and wave for him to come inside.

"Sit next to me," I tell him when he comes to our booth. "Victor, this is Stan."

The two men talk and seem to get along fine. I take a sip of the warm coffee and inhale the strong aroma. Luckily, it is not your typical, weak, American diner brew. Victor finally turns to me and tells me we have to go. Stan takes his leave too, and we walk out of the restaurant together. He follows us down Haro Street and into our building. It turns out that Stan's apartment is right across the hall from ours. A coincidence?

Later that night, Victor says he likes our new friend. This encourages me to join Stan the next evening and visit his spiritual medium. My belief system does not incorporate spirits and spirit guides, but curiosity compels me to go, though I remain objective.

Stan and I go to an average-style house, go up some stairs, and enter a room full of ordinary-looking people. From recent experience, I know the appearance of the ordinary can be quite deceptive. Stan is quite ordinary-looking, in his mid-forties and short and stocky. He grew up near the Liverpool docks in a rough neighborhood, where he trained in jujitsu, a Japanese system of martial arts and street fighting.

The lights in the large room are dim. Chairs are set in a semicircle around a large woman, the Medium. Dressed in casual clothes and looking unpretentious, she bestows spirit-guided wisdom upon everyone in her presence. Of course, I hope to gain some insight into the Evil Man, even though I haven't thought of him during these past few months. My focus more is on mastering the four remaining divine directives, since moving to Vancouver satisfied the first one. This involves learning more about meditation, martial arts, metaphysics, and meaningful coincidences.

In this room, I feel like an anthropologist. With three undergraduate years of anthropological training in university, I learned how to dispense with my own belief system to understand and hopefully gain practical knowledge from something totally unfamiliar. This moment makes me feel like I have come to a foreign culture. It excites me. I might learn something about myself, and meditation too.

At last, the Medium's gaze falls upon me. She draws in her breath and lets out a slow sigh. "I have never seen such a beautiful aura. It is this white light shining around you and then going into a radiant pink aura. And yet, young lady, there are these black splotches all over your aura. This is because your third eye is open, and you give hospitality to other people's negativity. You see the darkness of other peoples' fear states and let their fear inside you. You must learn to close off. I am going to give you a closing-off exercise."

"Thank you." I'm not sure if I understand, but I am eager to hear what she has to say.

The Medium shifts her weight and makes delicate gestures as she speaks. "Imagine yourself in a lovely flower. Imagine sitting inside the petals and being small. Now, I want you to see all the petals of this gorgeous flower closing up around you, giving you shelter from the outside world. Imagine this, and now place the flower at your third eye, all closed up and protecting you inside it. You will be protected from harm. You have an American Indian guide standing behind you. He is tall and also will protect you."

The Medium's words move me tremendously. Although I'm not convinced of the presence of my Indian spirit guide, I understand her impression of the spots on my aura. I used to relate to the darkness in others, which she said contributed to my insecurities. Surely following the path of the divine directives will move me forward, inch by inch, away from fear, doubt, and worry.

Back at our apartment building, Stan goes into his place. A few minutes later, there is a knock on my door. I open it, and he's standing there with some books in his arms. "Here. Read these. They will help to bring down the white light and shield you from negative energies."

After I've read the books, one mantra stands out in my mind. It is "I AM Light" by Ascended Master Kuthumi. I continue to use it, along with the Medium's flower petal meditation. Some mystics, no matter what their specific beliefs, can communicate with one another. I'm grateful for the conversations with Stan, but my search for a meditation teacher and my studies continue.

❁

It is late December 1979, the rainy season in Vancouver. When I'm outside, I always wear a big Stetson cowboy hat to keep dry. Some days, I feel great, but other days, my spirit is not so good. This place is far away from my family and is kind of lonely-making with days and days of gray skies and rain showers.

Jamie is doing great in his studies at the university, and Mom and Dad have split up. I hear that my mother is dating. Marla comes out for a vacation. It is wonderful to be with her. We visit Victor's family, and his father falls in love with my sister's vibrant personality.

Luckily, in addition to cooking, Paul and Eileen share my love of nature. When spring comes, Victor and I like to hike with them every other week or so. Sometimes we walk near or on Mount Seymour. Paul is an expert outdoorsman and has advised me on the proper hiking boots to buy. I feel safe with them and do not think about my experience in the woods on Martha's Vineyard. Being alone in nature is something else the Evil Man took away from me.

The four of us usually walk the trail in silence and in single file. Except for the birdcalls, the humming of the flying insects, and the wind whistling through the trees, it is silent. Someone might point to something interesting, like a rock formation, and we go "ooh" and "aah." Or we might ask Paul questions or converse while we eat our veggie sandwiches. But most of the time we are quiet.

Today, when Paul, Eileen, Victor, and I started out, it was a sunny morning. Now, a few hours later, we are walking in the darkness under the heavy canopy of Douglas firs, western hemlocks, cedars, and other kinds of vegetation that inhabit western

Canada. The air is thick with the fresh smells of the trees mixed with earthier aromas. I can see the clear blue sky up ahead.

Finally, the four of us stand on a rocky edge of the mountainside. What I thought was a meadow is now revealed in the bright light to be a grove of evergreens. Except the trees are all knocked down. Not like they were chopped down. There are no stumps to be seen, and the trees are sheared clear on one side. The branches and their pretty, fan-like needles otherwise remain intact.

"What do you think happened?" Victor asks. We all wonder about that.

I think the fallen forest resembles me. Metaphorically speaking, the Evil Man cut off one of my branches. The fearless hitchhiker is gone. My innocence is gone. Yet the tools honed by my wanderings and death are still with me.

"They look like western red cedars," Paul says. "This must be the result of a fast-moving avalanche. It must have occurred this past winter, only a couple of months ago." He points to the expanse ahead of us. "Unless we want to retrace our steps and walk for hours, we'll have to cross this."

The area is the size of a football field. I ask the obvious question. "How?"

"As usual," he says, "walk. Just follow me. Stay on the thick trunks, where your feet are secure, but move quickly. Whatever you do, look straight ahead. Don't look down." He starts forward.

Next, it's my turn. I step carefully onto a trunk, putting one foot in front of the other. I can't help but look down "Paul, I'm kind of scared."

Under my feet are trees upon trees. They are piled on one another like matchsticks, and the ones at the surface seem to have been most affected by the force of the avalanche. Their bare sides make an almost flat surface. I step back off the first tree trunk.

"Look straight ahead, Myra. Stay right behind me."

Eileen pipes up. "I'm scared too."

"Eileen," Victor says, "you go behind Paul. I'll walk behind Myra and make sure she is okay."

A bit of the tree trunk flakes off when my hiking boots hit the rough, reddish-brown bark. Yet it feels sturdy enough, and I start to walk faster.

We all make it safely to the other side of the fallen forest.

❀

As with hiking, I can also get absorbed and lose myself in my tarot studies. The Crowley deck comes in a cardboard box just like ordinary playing cards. Included is a small booklet. Most tarot decks have a guide to the general meanings of the cards; Crowley's booklet gives three different directories that provide meanings for each of the cards, a few essays, and a couple of diagrams. One shows a tarot spread used by the Golden Dawn, a Christian Cabalistic group, for their readings. The tarot spread, or layout, can stimulate the reader's intuition and perhaps inspire revelations. Where one places a chosen card is significant, as a position and its relationship to other cards evokes additional meanings.

Although the booklet helps guide my studies, over time I rely more on my own feelings and trust my hunches rather than a strict adherence to dogmatic interpretations of the cards. Reading the tarot involves developing logic and intuition. The logical, reasoning mind is necessary to familiarize oneself to the general symbolic meaning of a card or the significance of a position in a layout, but the images and symbols on the cards also stimulate the intuitive mind.

Another diagram in the Crowley booklet is of the Kabbalistic Tree of Life. Intended as a study aid, the tree shows the correlations between the Hebrew letters and the tarot cards. This fascinates me. Even though I attended Hebrew school, I know nothing about Kabbalah or the Tree of Life, especially from a Jewish perspective, and am totally unaware of the Tree of Life's relationship to the tarot. I want to learn more.

I pursue this research at the Vancouver Public Library and begin a reconnection to Judaism and my own spirituality. While I am still a student of Kabbalah and the tarot, I do not read for others. But I read for myself, which requires ruthless honesty.

To develop my intuition, my personal study ritual begins with shuffling the seventy-eight cards and roughly cutting the deck into four piles, which I place face down. Then I intuitively pick the pile that contains "my" card, the Hierophant. Of course, I always feel a slight trepidation. What if I choose the wrong pile? But I am developing even more trust in my intuition, that strong, small, inner voice that can guide me. Now I know. This is the inner voice we all have.

Chapter 24

AFTER STAN TELLS ME ABOUT his jujitsu training, I decide to tell him about my encounter with the Evil Man and what happened. Over coffee and a muffin at the corner diner, he listens to my story. When I'm finished, he says he wants to show me some self-defense moves. Later that day, he talks to Victor.

Now, in our living room, the three of us are barefooted and dressed in loose clothing. We push our makeshift dining room table back against the windows and place four huge pillows, which I sewed by hand, strategically along the wall as buffers.

"Myra and Victor," Stan begins, "if anything I do starts to hurt, just tap like this." He slaps his thigh. "If you're on the ground, do this." He falls down, lies on his back, and taps the floor a few times. "Or tap my thigh or arm. Okay?" He gets up and stands in front of Victor. "Ready?"

My boyfriend nods his head. Stan grabs his shoulders with both hands and gently pushes him to the floor and pins him down the same way the Evil Man pinned me down. Then they change places. On the bottom now, Stan twists his body and legs and throws Victor off.

Now it is my turn. Stan grabs me by the shoulders and pushes me down and then gets on top of me. He is built like a barrel-chested rugby player and is heavy. It is hard to get out from underneath him. Both of us break into a sweat, and the wetness is uncomfortable.

"Myra," he says, "try to rock from side to side. Good. Now try to lift your hips. Wrap your leg around mine and turn over."

I try to do this maneuver, but without effect. "I'm not strong enough, eh?"

"It will take practice." Stan puts his hands loosely around my neck. "Try to grab my pinky fingers. Gently. Just try to pry them off." He loosens his grip just a little for me to get some leverage and succeed.

I am five foot five, and Stan's martial arts style makes me feel even smaller. Once he is finished with his demonstration, he listens to my concerns and tells us about karate classes at the West End Community Centre. It is in the building with the diner, located at the top of Haro Street and just half a block from our apartment. Victor and I watch some classes over the next few nights. Then we sign up.

The club's head instructor is Yuwa, a fifth-degree black belt. A fantastic athlete, he is also finishing a master's degree at the university. His martial art is a mix of Okinawa styles that incorporate low stances and breathing techniques and favor multiple kicking combinations and punches.

Yuwa has a huge following. There are black belt assistants, all men, in all his classes. All these men are attractive and fit. Also, the senior-ranked students are mostly men. A sexual energy permeates the room, even though the sessions are conducted in a strict, regimented way. I wonder what lies under those white uniforms.

Commonly known as a gi, the martial arts uniform is usually white or black cotton pants and a white or black cotton jacket that is wrapped, tied on the inside, and then cinched in by a belt whose color displays the wearer's rank. To start, Victor and I wear T-shirts and shorts like a few other beginners. I am not here to be sporty. Remembering my vulnerability during the Evil Man's attack, I feel extremely shy, self-conscious, and intimidated by all the athletic types in the room. Before the class starts, I squeeze in behind the open door and the wall. This evasion strategy lasts until Yuwa peeks around the door one day.

"What are you doing, hiding in there?" He lets out a laugh. "Go and stretch."

A few classes later, I ask him what it takes to get a black belt.

Yuwa's answer surprises me. "Perseverance, Myra. Don't ever give up. Just remember that you cannot train only when you want to. You are shy. You must train even if you don't feel like it, even if you don't feel good. That indomitable spirit will make you a black belt."

The thought of a black belt seems far-off, but his words guide me. My first task is to not let the people and the energy of the classes overwhelm me. I always enjoyed watching games live or on TV. But watching is different from doing.

While I was in grade school, I participated in baseball, field hockey, basketball, and volleyball. In the eighth grade, I received a special reward. All the four sports teams I was on won their individual championships that year. This was probably due more to coincidence than my athletic abilities, but even so, the school presented me with a school letter at an annual awards assembly. The problem is that, decades later, Marla insists it was she who won the special recognition. But I know the honor is mine. And I could prove it with a phone call to the school registrar. But who cares? Let my twin sister think she was the one who won the letter.

Despite my early accomplishments, my involvement in athletic activities withered during my teen years. This was due more to vanity and self-consciousness over my naturally curly hair. When I took a post-game shower, the smallest amount of water that touched my hair gave it a life of its own. At the time, Cher's super-straight hair was in style, so, like many teenage girls, my sister and I wore wigs called "falls." Also like other girls, sometimes we even ironed our hair.

But now I have to forget about my hair. The imperative is to train in martial arts. I must fulfill this divine directive. I have no choice.

After two months at the karate club, Victor and I purchase the traditional uniforms. Yuwa sees our new gis and gives us the school's patch to sew on the back of the jacket. It is a circle of white cloth that shows a dragon outlined in red. The club holds classes Monday to Friday. Although Yuwa wants us there every day, I set myself a mandatory requirement to train at least twice a week. After about six months, this picks up to at least three times a week. Each class is an hour, with time added for individual stretching before and after the session.

One day, while I'm on the way to my handbook bindery, a homeless man sitting in a wheelchair asks me for some spare change. With a nudge of my shoulder, my bag swings in front me, and I reach inside to find my wallet.

The homeless man lets out a gasp. His hands fly out in astonishment. "You call that a purse? Jesus, it looks like a suitcase."

"Forget the snide comments," I tell him. "Just take the money."

What I didn't tell the man is that my bag holds all the stuff that usually goes into a lady's handbag, plus my martial arts uniform and a towel to dry off after showering. It helps to take these things everywhere I go, as I'm not sure if I'll catch a class that day. At least it eliminates having to go home and deal with the temptation to stay put. Along with hauling my gi and towel around, of course, there comes the endless chore of washing them and Victor's too. Without a washer and dryer in the apartment building, this means after every training session, they're washed in the bathtub and hung up to dry. It is not cool to show up in a stinky gi.

Another principle of martial arts is if you show up to train, you have to put out a 100 percent effort. Being small and lacking a killer instinct are just two of my disadvantages. Plenty of times, I don't want to go. Most days, all kinds of excuses arise. But my encounter with the Evil Man is the energy that propels me to show up. The divine directive—to learn a martial art and how to defend myself—must be accomplished. It overcomes any shyness or feeling tired or a hundred other excuses.

One weekday evening, it's a little early for class, so I stroll around the Lost Lagoon in Stanley Park and give myself my usual pep talk. I need it to get to tonight's karate class. As usual, the walk helps still whatever current excuse is rattling in my head and keeps me from going home and lying around. My headache is not at the level of a migraine, so there is no good reason to miss class.

My world is one of no excuses. Since starting martial arts, I have figured out something important. A part of my brain must be in my feet. My mind can be full of all kinds of reasons why I don't need to go or don't want to go or don't feel good, but I always end up walking through the doors of the West End Community Centre and getting changed into my gi. For me, discipline is developing in my feet. By the late summer of 1980, my feet help me mostly meet the mark on my weekly attendance at the club.

Then one day, I receive an unexpected letter in the mail. It changes everything.

Chapter 25

THE RETURN ADDRESS ON THE business size envelope is the Public Archives and National Library, located in Ottawa, Ontario. I draw out a single sheet of paper. It is an invitation to interview for the position of paper restorer. The letter says my hotel, food, and airfare expenses will be covered for this meeting with the chief of the Bookbinding and Paper Restoration department and his assistants.

So the archives has finally responded to my employment inquiry. I sent it at the same time as the one to the New England Documentation Center, which offered me an interview right away and, most probably, a job. After the attack on Martha's Vineyard, however, I ditched the meeting in Lawrence. My imperative was to fulfill the first divine directive and move to the other side of the continent.

A few weeks after receiving this letter, I attend the interview and am offered the position of paper restorer. I take the job at the Public Archives. The work entails the conservation and restoration of archival holdings, which include maps, manuscripts, and historical letters, and is considered "flatwork."

My tasks concern pieces that are done in either ink or pencil. The fine arts department handles paintings and other historical items colored with pigments.

One job requirement, of course, is to relocate to Ottawa. When I tell Victor about the job offer and my intentions to move to Ottawa, he goes quiet for a few minutes. The glow leaves his usually handsome face, and then he says, "Before we left Windsor, your father came to our room. I was alone. He sat on the bed and cried. He did not want us to get married or for me to take you to Vancouver."

I am slightly stunned. "He never said anything to me. And after all these years, you never told me?"

"Your dad said he liked me, but I am a lot like him. He thought it was a problem because we are too laid back. He thinks you're like your mother—too bright and with more energy than me. So I kind of suspected this breakup would eventually happen."

❈

Even though I left him behind and moved to Ottawa in November 1980, I was not too worried about Victor. Before we broke up, he was hanging out with this pretty girl who wore a big hat. I'm not sure if they slept together before I left Vancouver, but now he can, and I don't really care. I certainly had plenty of opportunities to cheat on him. But I never did.

❈

The problem is we are twins.

I finish the sentence and stop typing. My intuition tells me the time is right. I dial his phone number. The phone rings a few times. Then someone picks up.

I recognize the voice on the other end and say, "Hi. It's Myra. Victor, I've been trying to reach you for over a year."

"Oh, Myra. It must have been while I was on the East Coast. Ruth passed away She was in her mid-eighties."

"I'm sorry to hear about your stepmom. Well, the next time you talk to your dad, give him my love."

"I will. He's ninety-one years old now. Actually, I was thinking about you earlier today. About what if we had stayed together. But then you would not have accomplished all you have. I figure the problem is we're twins."

"Gosh, I can't believe you just said that! I'm taking this memoir-writing course, and I just typed those same words, 'The problem is we are twins.' And then I decided to call you."

Victor laughs. "Yep, that was our problem. We're both twins. We both have a kind of sensitivity that is not usual. It's a way of communicating deeply that I don't find in others. Anyway, I know it confused you. Sometimes, I was your lover and sometimes, I was your brother."

"I'll always love you, Victor."

After we hang up, I realize something. It is May 2016 and this talk with Victor is the one we should have had after the Evil Man killed me and I came back to life. But, again, I am getting ahead of myself.

❂

Back in Ottawa, I score a wonderful, one-bedroom apartment across the street from the Rideau Canal, the ribbon of water that connects the Ottawa River and Lake Ontario and cuts through the city. In the summer, boats and canoes stream up and down the waterway, while in the winter it is one of the largest ice-skating rinks in the world. A sidewalk above the water runs the length of the city section of the canal.

It feels special when I walk through the front doors of the Public Archives and National Library Building. The sound of my shoes echoes on the marble floor. Past the public access area and at the back of the football field–size lobby is a plain door for employees only. The hall beyond the door takes me into the bowels of the building. Down here is the fine art restoration shop, but I always head in the other direction toward the bookbinding and paper restoration department.

Situated on one side of the large room are the hand bookbinders and hand sewers, while the paper restorers are on the other side. Workbenches for both the binders and restorers and smaller desks for the sewers are set up in each area. On the back wall of the restoration side is a huge, multipanel, wooden board. It is the size of two public school chalkboards and is used to repair extra-large maps.

My job is to preserve historical information, which might involve the realignment of tears and repairs to small holes in the paper or the cautious removal of the backing on an old map or document and replacing it with something new. I always start the day with a clean workbench and end the day with a clean workbench. Materials might be left there to dry overnight or in some state of restoration, but I never leave my desktop in a mess.

One morning, I enter the restoration area to find a stack of thin boxes on the workbench behind mine. They look like small pizza boxes. When the assistant paper restorer walks toward me, I ask, "What's in those boxes? We make all kinds of boxes and portfolios for the archival holdings, but those are unique."

A tall, thin man from England who was trained at the British Museum, he lifts the top box. "These hold the British North America Act of 1867, the originating document that created the Dominion of Canada. Prime Minister Trudeau brought it back from England because he is bloody well bent on giving Canada a new constitution."

"I know what the act is about," I say. In my history classes at school, I learned that Britain still maintained control over Canada's constitution and could make changes to it, although the British parliament needed the consent of Canada's parliament. The new act would remove this British authority. "May I see it?"

"Sure." He opens the box and gingerly lifts out a single sheet of paper and hands it to me.

"Wow! Thank you. I appreciate your faith in me to handle this. Geez, I'm surprised at the lack of fancy filigree. And there's no silver or gold leaf."

"The chief decided to preserve the pages."

"How?" I ask.

"He ordered me to use Bostik."

My jaw drops. "You're kidding."

"Nope. I don't get it. Bostik! That stuff is not a natural material. As you know, the net-like adhesive feels like fabric, but when we heat it to adhere to the paper, it melts and fuses with the item we want to preserve. There is no reversing formula. There is no way to undo it if need be."

"And Japanese tissue, which is light and see-through, is probably too delicate if the prime minister intends to handle this a lot." I shrug my shoulders and shake my head at the use of Bostik, surely an unconventional preservation method for a most treasured national document.

The assistant and I reminisce about another questionable decision the chief of the department once made. This concerned the gift to Britain's Lady Diana and Prince Charles on the occasion of their marriage. The people of Canada presented them with a natural wood bedroom set. Not many people know that the head bookbinder was tasked with filling the bookcase with handbound books by Canadian authors. Unfortunately, the chief of Conservation and Restoration ordered him to tear off the covers of paperbacks and rebind them with hard covers.

This order was outrageous. In time, the inferior paper will turn yellow, become brittle, and break down at a faster rate than the fine quality paper found in first editions. A better process would have been to rebind those books.

One morning I come into the restoration room surprised to see Louis Riel's surrender note. Most Canadian schoolchildren are aware of this famous politician and founder of Manitoba from their grade school history classes. In 1885, he led the Métis nation, a people of mixed European and Indigenous Amerindian ancestry, in a failed revolt against the government. It resulted in his arrest, trial, and ultimate death for treason.

The small Riel document is in need of restoration. An experienced paper restorer has been assigned the job. Although its content is brief, the note sets forth lofty ideals. Written in pencil, it is on basically the same low-grade newsprint found in the books that Canada sent to Lady Di and Prince Charles.

Over time, the often-tedious work of restoration teaches me patience and develops my ability to concentrate. About two years into my position, I am called into an office on another floor of the archives. I'm somewhat nervous and do not know what to expect. Perhaps they found out that a supervisor and I snuck up to the top floor and smoked pot together. We did it a couple of times. It was a good distraction from the detailed restoration work that demanded our total concentration. I thought we'd found an isolated nook among the air conditioning units and large air ducts that would push the marijuana smoke outside.

An official welcomes me into the office and gestures for me to sit. He is a normal, buttoned-down, by-the-book, kind of fellow. "How are you?" he asks. "You look nervous."

I take in the small tape recorder on the desk, and then look back at him. "I'm okay. I'm just wondering why I'm here."

"Myra, to get to the point, we intend to assign you some classified materials to restore. You'll need to get the necessary security clearances."

Surprised and relieved that he's not going to arrest me, I feel flattered. At the same time, concern grips me. "What does getting the clearances entail?"

"Honest answers to a few questions. Most important, you must take an oath of allegiance to Her Majesty, Queen Elizabeth of the United Kingdom, Canada, Australia, and New Zealand and the head of the British Commonwealth." He nods at her photograph hanging on the wall above his desk. "Are you okay with that?"

"But, sir, I cannot take that oath. You see, I was born in Detroit, Michigan. My twin sister and I were about two months old when we entered Canada at Windsor, Ontario. At our first port of entry, we were declared Canadian citizens, but we were too young to take an oath. Now I cannot take the oath because I do not want to renounce my United States citizenship."

The official is silent, a pensive look fills his face. "Perhaps we can think of a workaround for you. Perhaps you can declare your assurances to keep these matters secret until the documents are declassified. Would you agree to do that?"

"Absolutely."

Some of the documents are later declassified. These are old placards from Paris during the Second World War, when the city was occupied and under German military control. On the placards are orders to male Parisians, young and old, to be at a certain place at a certain time. The men and boys who were rounded up were then executed in cruel retaliation for recent acts of sabotage conducted by the French Underground. The murder of innocent French citizens was carried out by firing squads. Sometimes they were marched to the outskirts of the city or lined up against the walls of the buildings where they lived and then were shot dead.

The placards affect me, even though I knew about the incidents. Surely no Jewish child is ignorant of the horrors of the Holocaust. I first heard about death at a young age. When other kids were reading *Green Eggs and Ham,* I was learning about gas chambers and piles of people's gold teeth and glasses. Almost from the crib, I knew about God. But I was not sure the Divine knew about me or about the six million

Jews who suffered and died from the atrocities of the Nazis. And so I became a mystic, a spiritual seeker.

There is nothing remarkable in a person who chooses to live life in a spiritual way. What can be remarkable is the mystic's ability to perceive a divine experience in the mundane world. It takes study, and practice, to develop this type of awareness. The divine directives are my process. The desire to master all of them is still in me.

Chapter 26

SO FAR, MY MARTIAL ARTS training is in Isshin-ryu karate, with an emphasis on multiple kicking techniques. Because Ottawa does not have a club in this Okinawan style, I check out a number of different schools and watch a few classes in each of them. Some of them seem more like a pool hall in a film noir. The atmosphere is low, the people look down and out, and the air is stale.

Then I hear about Taekwondo, a Korean martial art that emphasizes kicking techniques but has narrower stances than karate. The club is on the second floor above a downtown Italian restaurant. I walk up the stairs and enter a large room packed with people, a few of them seated in the spectators' section. An electric, almost sexual energy permeates the place. It comes from the intense physical engagement of the people. I can tell that Mr. Jung Park, the head instructor, and his black-belt assistants are top-notch athletes and strict on teaching Taekwondo techniques.

I sign up.

The martial arts classes offer me a particular dynamic balance to my quiet, focused paper restoration tasks at the Public

Archives of Canada. Training hard helps get my internal issues and concerns out of my system.

To fulfill my divine directive to learn to meditate, I am still seeking a competent teacher. The flower petal meditation the medium gave me in Vancouver is wonderful, but not sufficient by itself. For some reason, my first impulse is to thumb through Ottawa's yellow pages and search the category of parapsychologists instead of looking for a particular religious persuasion. The name Earl Curley seems to rise from the page. I've never heard of him before, but I decide to make the telephone call.

Earl and I talk on the phone for almost three hours. I tell him about my psychic premonitions and the strangulation incident. He tells me he is a famous Canadian psychic. In 1978, the year I was left for dead in the woods of Martha's Vineyard, Curley made a name for himself and received worldwide recognition for locating the wreckage of the Soviet *Cosmos 954* satellite that crashed in the Northwest Territories. He did this remotely, seeing from his office in Ottawa.

Impressed by our conversation, Earl invites me to his lecture free of charge. He turns out to be a short man, about five foot eight inches, with a head full of straight, black hair. Dark, penetrating eyes are his most outstanding features. There are also soft indentations on the sides of his mouth that offset his square jaw. Although on the smallish side, he is strong looking. After the lecture, he presents me with a cassette tape of his guided shamanic meditations.

Perhaps my American Indian spirit guide pulls me in this direction. I've done some research in the area and have come across the books on shamanism by Mircea Eliade, the famous professor at the University of Chicago Divinity School. Shamanism is one of the world's oldest spiritual pursuits, but unfortunately, people have pejoratively turned shamans into "witch doctors." Shamans can achieve altered states of consciousness using diverse techniques that allow them to connect with nonordinary transcendental forces, both good and bad entities. As a conduit to the transcendental world, the shaman aids in the physical, psychological, and spiritual health of his community.

On March 6, 1982, I experience my first guided shamanic meditation. Earl's tape first helps to quiet my mind. Then it directs me to visualize an underground tunnel to an imaginary place. Mine starts in that favorite nook in the rock formation along the pathway around Stanley Park in Vancouver. I imagine the tunnel going through the rock and down into a lovely cavern. I can invite nonordinary forces to enter. Although my ability to visualize the tunnel and the cave is excellent, the first time nothing happens. Hopefully, with practice, I will meet spirit forces and they will inform me about my specific concerns and issues.

That night, after my session with the tapes, I have a dream in which Earl Curley sits on a table with his feet dangling above the floor. With his arms open wide, he gestures for me to approach him. I see that he is blind. The dream ends.

A week later, I attend another of Curley's seminars and learn that he lives with a woman. When he pulls me aside and says he wants to begin a relationship with me, I tell him about my dream, which I see as a warning that he is blind to my needs and my integrity. He just shrugs his shoulders and looks downcast when I ask why he failed to disclose his involvement with someone else before he said he wanted to be involved with me. Then I leave. He is certainly not to be my meditation teacher. I do not trust Earl Curley and do not continue using his tape.

I am disappointed, but my resolve remains intact. I will learn to meditate. The next day, and for days after that, I ask everyone from the guys in my martial arts club to people at the Public Archives if they can suggest a meditation teacher. The name of Charles Laughlin, a professor of anthropology at Carleton University, comes up numerous times. I learn he is a published author and a Buddhist monk who is currently on sabbatical at a monastery in Nepal.

My intuition tells me to wait for his return to Canada. He is to be my meditation teacher.

About three months later, I hear that Charles is back in Ottawa and will hold meditation classes. Beginners are welcome. The sessions are twice a week and held off campus at someone's house. On the way to my first lesson, I'm excited but not sure what to expect. A noticeable odor of old socks greets me when I enter the home. The smell actually comes from the cleansing ritual in which sage is burned. Luckily, the sweet fragrance of incense also permeates the meditation room. I am surprised to find that Charles is a tall, Caucasian man who speaks with a slight Southern drawl and looks like the movie actor Gene Hackman. Except Charles wears wire-rim glasses.

About ten other men and women, most of whom seem to be about my age in their mid-to-late twenties or early thirties, are present at that meditation session. Charles is older, maybe in his late forties. Pillows are handed out, and then he instructs us in the proper Zen meditation posture, or zazen, where we sit on the floor with our legs in a pretzel-like arrangement. I cannot snake my legs together like that and resort to a simple cross-legged position.

Some of the attendees sit with perfectly straight backs. Clearly, they are not beginners, and many already know Charles and have meditated with him in the past. Next, we are instructed to close our eyes and place our hands lightly on top of each other in our laps. Now we begin to learn how to quiet our minds. Our attention is on the tips of our noses and we silently count our breaths. The idea is to later practice on our own.

The group meets twice a week. To start each session, we meditate for twenty minutes, then discuss our experiences. After a few more sessions, we are up to thirty minutes. We then move to more sophisticated forms of meditation called "insight work," in which the focus can be on an object, a mantra, or imagined colors. By six months, we are up to fifty minutes of meditation. In some of our sessions, the whole group holds hands. Over a few long weekends, some members of the group go on retreats that are held at a remote cottage in the woods. Sometimes seven or eight people will participate. We bring enough food for all of us and share in the chores.

Under Charles' instruction, the retreat consists of sitting quietly for fifty-minute sessions, three or four a day. Then there are the walking meditations. As we trek through a forest of maples and pines, he tells us to focus on just the light. Instead of seeing a rock, my attention is drawn to how the light plays on its surface or how it highlights an ivy-covered tree stump. Charles is a gifted Jungian. He later applies the noted psychologist's theories in the discussions about our meditation experiences. He tells us that "Focusing on the light can help us to own our 'shadow side,' and to learn from it and embrace the parts of ourselves that might bring shame or self-loathing."

Call it luck or call it fate. Charles' interests converge with mine when he invites our meditation group to begin to work with the tarot cards and the Kabbalistic Holy Tree of Life. Our purpose is not divination, but to use the cards as tools to facilitate the meditative mind as part of the epistemological realm, or how we gain knowledge.

For these sessions, Charles refuses to use the Crowley deck. "I don't want to meditate on a madman," he tells me. When I point out that his good friend and coauthor of some of his scholarly books uses this deck, Charles says, "And look how well he turned out. Probably the foremost authority on Carl Jung, and he's still a bartender. Huh!"

His sarcastic tone does not escape me. I do not see the Crowley cards the same way he does, and I am not interested in persuading Charles to use them. My belief is everyone must choose the cards that work best for them. It is imperative to have an intuitive connection with your deck, and if you are reading for yourself, you must be ruthlessly honest. Unfortunately, most people can't do that. I can.

Instead of the Crowley cards, Charles insists we each purchase the Builders of the Adytum, or BOTA, deck. These well-known cards are based on the metaphysical teachings of Paul Foster Case. His deck is a reinvention of the Rider-Waite cards. I purchased a used book on the BOTA tarot by Case when I lived in Vancouver and brought it with me to Ottawa. The unique aspect of his cards is they are printed in black and white. The user must hand color them, according to a formula laid out in the accompanying booklet. This process gets you intimately involved with the symbols and their basic meanings.

Members of Charles' meditation group must color their own decks. This is done in stages. When everyone has completed a set number of cards, we meditate on each one. It takes many sessions to color and meditate on all seventy-eight cards. Next, we help Charles draw a large Holy Tree of Life on a nine-by-six-foot sheet of butcher's paper. When it's finished, it is laid out on the floor and the group sits cross-legged around it as Charles instructs us on the meaning of the tree and its ten *sephirot*, or energy centers.

Simply speaking, the *sephirotic* system is somewhat similar to the better-known chakra system. There is a central channel that more or less echoes the rising line of chakras. However, the tree also has two other pillars that correspond to the right and left sides of our physical bodies.

The Holy Tree of Life and the ten *sephirot* are derived from the book of Genesis. In the first chapter of the Torah, or Bible, the words "God said" are expressly given nine times. However, the first declaration is internal, as God's inner voice conveying the desire or will to create. Kabbalists believe these ten energetic utterances generated the ten *sephirot*.

The Hebrew schoolteachers of my youth did not discuss these highly esoteric aspects of Judaism, but now my divine directive to learn a metaphysic calls me to learn more about the mystical Kabbalah and the tarot. My approach is a narrow and unique path: the study of the Torah, the Holy Tree of Life, and their correlations to the letters of the Hebrew alphabet and the tarot cards. Most orthodox Jews believe it is forbidden to practice divination. Not me.

In our meditation sessions, Charles places one of the Major Arcana cards on one of the twenty-two pathways that connect the ten *sephirot* on the tree. Only the Major Arcana cards can be placed on these paths. The group meditates on the total image. Charles then lays out more cards and we meditate on their arrangement. Not only do the sessions strengthen my understanding of Kabbalah, but they also help to create a Tree of Life spread that will enable me to do readings for others and myself. It will take time to perfect my knowledge, but I am a devoted student. Meanwhile, I use the Golden Dawn straight-line layout for my studies. It is also one of the diagrams in the Crowley deck booklet.

Besides the Major Arcana, there are four suits, called the Minor Arcana, in a tarot deck: pentacles or disks, cups, swords, and wands. The Minor Arcana cards are also associated with the four elements: earth, water, air, and fire, respectively. In turn, these correspond to the physical, emotional, intellectual, and spiritual worlds of the Kabbalah. Each suit has ten numbered cards and four court cards. All have specific placements on the Tree of Life, and for study and meditation purposes they are called "grammars." All the cards have symbolic meanings when drawn in a tarot reading.

Over time, I notice how the sheer size of the group's tree creates a reaction in me. This occurs while I am walking toward the glyph and just before we sit on the floor. The tree seems to evoke more meaning when I am standing than when I'm sitting.

My research on this point continues at the Ottawa Public Library. After hours of reading, I come to a conclusion. The diagrams in many books and articles show the *sephirot* transposed onto a human body that is erect and seen from the back, that is, the ten energy centers are seen from behind rather than in front of the body. This signifies our ability to directly connect with and embrace God. This Kabbalistic notion is unlike the images of the chakras and their associations to the human body in a sitting, cross-legged meditative posture.

When I stand before the Tree of Life, I try to sense the *sephirot* around and on my body. Just above my head is *Kether*, the Crown. Hovering near my right ear is *Hochmah*, or Wisdom, and near my left ear is *Binah*, or Understanding. These three energy centers are nonlocal, just as spirit and the mind are not located only in the body. Situated on my right shoulder is *Hesed*, or Kindness, and on my left shoulder is *Geverah* or Severity. Where my heart is, there is also *Tiphareth*, or Beauty. On my right hip is *Netzach*, or Eternity, and on my left hip is *Hod*, or Splendor. At my genital area is *Yesod*, or Foundation. My feet stand on *Malchuth*, or the Kingdom. There is also a quasi-*sephirah* called *Daat*, or Knowledge, that is located at the back of my neck. In *Daat*, we can hear the whispering of divine guidance.

Everyone can practice the exercise to locate the *sephirot* on his or her own body and then stand before God. Kabbalists talk of God's desire for "face to gaze upon face."

From my own studies, I came to realize the Holy Tree of Life glyph Charles drew for our meditation sessions is from a Christian Cabalistic perspective. This is like the Golden Dawn glyph, which is also found in the Crowley deck booklet. My research reveals a somewhat differently shaped tree associated with the rabbinic or Jewish form of Kabbalah. It also has different alignments for the Hebrew letters, but little is written about their relationship to the tarot. I study both schools. There are three accepted spellings for the term: "Kabbalistic" is traditional Jewish, "Cabalistic" is the Renaissance (mostly Christian) spelling, and "Qabalistic" is the spelling used in modern ceremonial magic (which is mostly Christian).

One day, Charles does a tarot reading for me using the Celtic Cross layout. Before we begin, he says, "For the reading, give me five dollars. It is an exchange of energy."

I thus learn from a Buddhist monk that an honest and professional tarot reader charges money. As he tells me, if it costs something, people will take their reading more seriously. The fee is not to make a lot of money, nor is it to connive a client out of their money. It's an exchange of energy.

Chapter 27

THE BITTER, TWENTY-DEGREES-BELOW-ZERO Ottawa winter means wearing two coats, a sweater and a hoodie, two pairs of pants, heavy socks, and sturdy boots when I walk to the club, where I then have to change into my martial arts uniform and take classes in bare feet. After about a year and half of training with Yuwa Wong in Vancouver, and more than a year of training at Jung Park's club, things are physically starting to click for me. As they say, I now own my kicks and punches.

At the club, I am good friends with Ron, a Japanese Canadian, and Lucas or Luu, a recent refugee from Vietnam. We often watch martial arts VHS movies all night at Ron's place. He knows stuff and tells me about General Choi, a South Korean and the founder of our style of Taekwondo. The next highest ranked is the general's first lieutenant, our head instructor in Ottawa.

I am a brown belt, which is two levels lower than a black belt. I wear my hair with a nod to dreadlocks. A bit just behind my right ear is braided and dyed soft pink and worn long. You can see it better when my hair is tied up, like when

I'm training in martial arts. Perhaps as a counterbalance to Ottawa's diplomatic dullness, my amorous attention is soon drawn to a handsome Rastafarian and reggae musician. The Rasta Man is a percussionist in a local band.

After a night out with him and the group's singer, I receive a telephone call from my mother.

"Your father died last night. I tried calling you."

The news hits me like a punch in my stomach. A punch I cannot block. "Sorry, Mom. I was out with friends and didn't get home until after midnight." Between sniffles, I add, "When we talked earlier this week, you said Dad was coming home from the hospital. The heart attack was minor, and he was fine. That's why I didn't go to Windsor. He was going to pull through."

"It was his second attack in twelve years," she says. "This time his heart just stopped."

"I'll catch a train to Toronto and come home with Marla."

"Your brother is coming to Windsor for a week for the funeral and to sit *shiva*. Then he has exams and will have to go back to Harvard."

It is 1982, and Jamie is studying for an MBA. It will be good to see my brother and good for my mother to have us all home. "I love you," I tell her. "See you soon, Mommilla." I made up this Yiddish-sounding name and use it to show her my affection.

Although the winter weather does not affect my journey home, I feel empty on the train to Toronto and on the bus to my sister's apartment. I'm feeling emotionally numb and my movements are mechanical. My sister shares an apartment with Chris, my former high school boyfriend, and another guy. She and Chris are like brother and sister. He kindly offers to drive Marla and me from Toronto to Windsor. Even though it's snowing so hard we're in a blizzard, and on Highway 401 there's a whiteout, Chris gets us safely home.

It is still extremely cold on the day my father is buried.

Even though snow is piled up everywhere and the city is closed down, his funeral goes forward. Everyone my father and our family know, and more, has come to his memorial service. On the way to the cemetery, our car gets cut off from the long line of other vehicles. Just then, I notice a single, red rose lying in the middle of the road, its scarlet hue bright against the dusting of white snow that covers the street. For just a moment, it blocks our way forward. My mother loves Joy perfume, which is made from rose petals. I think of my father. Perhaps he is saying goodbye to her with this rose. I watch the flower as the car drives past it.

For seven days, we sit *shiva* and hold a Jewish *minyan*, or prayer service, in the morning and at night. The required ten men plus more friends show up (with food) at my mother's apartment. These gatherings help us get through the mourning period. Because my parents had been separated, Marla and I stay a week longer to assist Mother with cleaning out Dad's apartment. It all feels odd.

Back in Ottawa, I continue to mourn my father's death in silence. With his passing, my romance with the reggae artist slowly fizzles. He stole $250 worth of my stuff and that is just the last sputter.

A year later, when I'm living in Toronto, I'm leaning against the wall of a low-lit, trendy bar when the Rasta Man walks by. He doesn't see me, but he sure feels my presence when my hand juts out, grabs him by the throat, and gently guides him over to the wall. The speed of my action surprises him. While he is not in any pain, he is pinned in place. I tell him he owes me $250, then loosen my grip on his neck so he can speak. But I keep my knee shoved between his legs and hold his back against the wall. He informs me he doesn't have the money. My intention is not to hurt him, but to let him know I can.

But I am getting ahead of my story.

Back in Ottawa, through the Rasta Man's connections (and before our relationship completely ends), I create and participate in a performance art piece held at a local art gallery. My coworkers at the Public Archives help me to artistically reinterpret the Martha's Vineyard strangulation incident. Even Earl Curley agrees to let me tape him saying a few lines. During the performance, his rich, hypnotic voice will sound through the loudspeakers. "You're here for a reason. You are here to learn something. You are here for a reason. You are here to learn something..."

One night, John, a gifted bookbinder and paper restorer, helps me take pictures of the bright beam of the spotlights around the archives building. With the cutout stencils we made, I manipulate the light, and he takes the shots. Later, he helps me to turn them into photographic slides. These are intended to mimic the white fire on black fire squares. During the performance, John operates the slide projector and the fade-out machine, which casts images of the squares moving in geometric regression onto a blank wall next to the stage. He also helped me to draw, paint, and then hang a large, seven-by-seven-foot canvas of the tarot card, the Hierophant. This is the backdrop for the performance. Michael, the assistant head paper restorer, acts as my attacker. But he doesn't succeed in killing me. Instead, I kick and punch him out.

The preparation for the show takes months. While he is working on the performance piece, John falls in love with Karen, who lives across the street from his apartment. He told me he watches her longingly through his front window. Then one day they meet. It turns out she is also a member of Charles' meditation group. A pretty, perky girl, she wears retro clothes and her blonde hair in a bob with bangs that conceal an extremely bright mind. She bakes first-rate pastries too. We become best friends, and she and John become a couple.

After the performance, I sense that something is missing in my life. Vernon, my bookbinder teacher and a great friend, warned me about this the last time we talked on the telephone. An actor and director himself, he said, "My dear, when your art piece is over, it might feel anticlimactic."

It does.

Soon my life picks up again. Karen is special, because she is deep and can grasp nonordinary things and experiences. Also, she and John are highly artistic, and he likes to cook too. Together, they hold tea-and-dessert parties and embark on an afterwork project to design a line of unique, asymmetrical, women's clothing. A dress shop in downtown Ottawa hosts their first fashion show. It's a big event, and I am one of the models.

A few months later, Karen tells me Charles wants to invite me to go camping with him and some friends.

"Oh," I reply, "I don't have a tent. I'll have to rent one."

"Myra," she says, "he wants to share his tent with you."

Although he still practices the faith, Charles has ceased to be a Buddhist monk, and so I ask, "You mean like we're boyfriend and girlfriend?"

She looks at me like I'm an idiot. "Duh! He's falling in love with you. He said I should talk to you and test the waters for him."

I shake my head. "No. He's too old for me. Anyway, we are just good friends, and he is my mentor. A romantic relationship could ruin everything."

Over the next few days, my method is to say nothing about this conversation to Charles. Perhaps he told Karen about falling in love with me, or maybe she surmised it. Nothing is said about my declining his camping invitation, and Charles and I continue to carry on as the good friends we've become.

All this creativity on top of my work at the archives, my meditation practice, my personal tarot and Kabbalah studies, and my martial arts training keeps me active. As far as pursuing the path of the divine directives, I am doing great. Yet, despite the incredible progress I'm making to learn more about meaningful coincidences and Jung's notion of synchronicity, I find myself feeling depressed. It is like I feel short in my own skin. Perhaps, a caterpillar feels the same way while it's in the cocoon. Metaphorically speaking, I don't know if I'll ever become a butterfly.

Change does come in the summertime of 1982. I plan to notify the Public Archives of my intention to leave at the beginning of November. I could have had a lifetime job as a paper restorer, but instead, I choose to go back to school at Carleton University and study full-time with my mentor and friend, Professor Charles Laughlin. I'll still attend his meditation sessions twice a week. At school, I hope to learn more about meaningful coincidences and transpersonal states of consciousness from him and the other teachers.

In 1983, I am admitted to Carleton University. My goal is to complete the courses by the spring of next year and obtain an honors bachelor of arts degree in anthropology.

Chapter 28

A SMALL, MURMURING CROWD FORMS and pushes me forward. We are all wondering why a limousine flying flags and emblazoned with the insignia of the People's Republic of China is driving into the Greyhound bus terminal in downtown Montreal. When it stops, a young man steps out of the vehicle. He is Chinese but dressed in casual Western attire. Then a man and women, both wrinkled with age, exit from either side of the limo. They are dressed in traditional Maoist clothing with the long, high-collared tunic and pants.

The old man, who gazes out over the crowd as he walks, stops in front of me. He winks and gives me two thumbs up, then a big smile spreads across his face. My first reaction is to feel flattered. Then the realization comes. He is acknowledging the image on my powder-blue sweatshirt: the name Taekwondo and the drawing of a martial artist doing a high kick. Even though the style is Korean, this old Chinese man singled me out from the crowd.

"Who is he?" I ask the young woman standing next me when I hear her speaking English, instead of French, to her friend.

She shrugs her shoulders. "Someone from the embassy. I don't know."

The murmur from the crowd gets louder as we are exchanging speculations about these people.

I soon board my bus to Ottawa and take a seat close to the front by the window. The younger Chinese man from the limousine sits down in the empty seat next to mine and after getting settled in introduces himself. "I am the deputy cultural attaché of the People's Republic of China."

My eyes go wide. Then I introduce myself. His friendliness encourages me to say, "Mr. Deputy, if I may inquire, why are you taking a bus from Montreal to the capital of Canada? Your arrival in the limo at the bus station surprised everyone."

"To be honest," he replies, "it is no secret. Our plane was delayed, and I must get back to the embassy in Ottawa tonight."

"If I may, one more question?"

He smiles. "Please, go on."

"The older gentleman who was with you. He stopped to give me two thumbs up. It is my sweatshirt. This is the club where I train." I point to the image.

The young man laughs. "We are in Montreal for a film festival. The man and the women are legendary actors in martial art films. Although they are quite old now, they are much revered."

"One of my favorite things to do with my friends is watch martial arts films!"

He nods his head, and then we both are silent. Lost in my own thoughts, I do not mention to the deputy why I am in Montreal and on my way to Ottawa.

I am now a red belt, which is one level below first-degree black belt. My training schedule for the past year has been at least four times a week in special classes with the members of our club who are on Canada's Taekwondo national team. By the time I finish these three-hour sessions, my hair, and my gi are both soaking wet. All the guys in my classes are black belts and some have two and three degrees. I do demonstrations and competitions with them too.

Two days ago, we did not do so well at the international board-breaking tournament held in Quebec City. At that event, the guys went first, and I waited for my turn in a room off stage. They returned with disgust and dejection written all over their faces.

Mr. Park's first assistant, a talented Vietnamese named Phap, said to me, "Those boards were sabotaged. Someone must have soaked them in water last night." His statement is strange. He won the entire event last year.

My part in the demonstration was to come next, so concern was evident in my voice as I asked, "Why? What happened? Tell me." My task is to break boards with the knife edges of my hands.

"Myra, I cannot let you go out there," he says. "You'll shatter your hand. None of us could break even one board, no matter if we used our hands or our feet. Not one of us! I can usually break two or three easily. Take off your uniform, Myra. You are done, here."

A couple of hours after my conversation with Phap, we head out of Quebec City. The atmosphere in the car is gloomy. Used to being a winning team, the guys are quiet and depressed. Their mood propels me to make an alternate plan. Just outside Montreal, I ask the guys to drop me off.

At the nearest phone booth, I make a surprise call to my friend. A brilliant professor of mathematics, he teaches at both McGill University and Carleton University, where I first met him in a coffee shop in downtown Ottawa. After he commented on a book I was reading, we got into a deep discussion about Edmund Husserl's notion of phenomenology. At the time, my future friend was doing creative mathematical research. He said his solutions to math problems came to him in his dreams. He also agreed to my request to interview him for my honors thesis, "Discovery within the Scientific Enterprise."

Now when he answers his telephone, I say, "Hello, Professor. It's Myra. I was just in Quebec City for a martial arts tournament. The guys dropped me off in Montreal. I have a favor to ask."

"Ask."

"May I sleep on your couch for one night?"

"Of course. No problem. I'll be home. My only plans for this evening are to drop some acid and play the piano. You can join me on the trip. I have enough for two."

"Thanks for letting me stay overnight, but I'll skip the acid. Pot's my thing. But you go ahead."

He gives me directions to his place via the bus and the metro system. By dusk, the math professor has dropped the acid and is sitting at his piano. Surprisingly, he plays smooth jazz, though later on, he switches to more soulful tunes. I am stretched out on his big couch in the next room, and the music lulls me to sleep.

About two or three o'clock in the morning, I wake up and find the professor, coat in hand, ready to go out for a walk. "Hi, Myra. Do you want to come along?"

"Sure."

"Okay. I'll wait."

I rummage in my suitcase for a sweater and grab my purse. "One of my favorite things to do is to wander around cites," I tell him, "like an anthropologist. To view our current urban culture."

We head out and hit the quiet streets of Montreal, our arms intertwined. In low voices, the professor teaches me a wonderful folksong, "Sometimes I feel like a motherless child." We sing it in a delicate harmony.

Back at his house, I take a long nap on the couch. After I wake up again, I wash my face, change my clothes, and say a quick goodbye. Then I head to the nearest Greyhound bus terminal and purchase a ticket for the trip back to Ottawa. Outside the station, I watch as a limousine from the People's Republic of China enters the terminal.

As my daydreams and memories end, I break out of my reverie to glance over at the deputy cultural attaché sitting next to me. On the chubby side and with a smooth face and hands, he is more an intellectual than a physical specimen. He smiles, and we start to talk. He tells me his country has undergone a time of renewal and moved away from Chairman Mao's policies. In 1981, China's Central Committee adopted the Resolution on Certain Questions in the History of Our Party Since the Founding of the People's Republic of China. It was, he says, a way to reconcile the failed Cultural Revolution.

We continue our discussion until the bus reaches Ottawa. Before departing, the deputy says, "With your anthropology background, Myra, you made for an enjoyable companion on this unexpected bus trip. Please, may I have your address? I wish to invite you to an embassy event."

"Of course. I am honored. Thank you. That would be wonderful."

Chapter 29

A FEW MONTHS AFTER MY Father's death, my mother and I went to Puerto Vallarta for a two-week vacation. Even though they had been living separately, his passing was hard on her. And me too. The trip helped her to unwind.

Or so I thought.

When she came to visit me in Ottawa a couple of months later, we got into an argument about what movie to watch on TV in her hotel room. Somehow this minor problem escalated. For no apparent reason, she screamed at me, "Your father hated you. He hated you. He hated you."

I did not believe her. But her words cut me to the core.

Even though she later apologized, an inner discomfort still clings to my soul and arouses my insecurities and abandonment issues.

Perhaps this is why I keep making the wrong choices in men. After my split with the Rasta Man and brushing aside the possibility for true romance with Charles, along comes a real firecracker of a guy.

One day, while I'm warming up before a Taekwondo class, a handsome guy tells me he is a policeman. "You better watch out for that fellow you were with yesterday," he adds.

"Who?"

"The James Dean–looking one. He's an ex-con and is highly manipulative."

He's just described the Firecracker.

I try to sound tough and say, "Well, I know he did time in jail. It's written all over his character. Since I've known him, he's bartered a lot of his stuff away. That is what inmates do. Thanks for the concern. But I'm okay. We are just friends." The last part is true.

After my time in Quebec City and the detour to Montreal, I have not seen the Firecracker for several days. When we talked on the phone, he sounded pissed off. Instead of going on a date with him, I stayed that extra day in Montreal at the professor's place. While I was gone, and no doubt to let off some steam, he bartered away his bedroom set.

Now I see a pathetic mattress lying on the floor of his apartment. The Firecracker is cute and usually has a lot of energy, but sexually speaking, we've only kissed. I walk out of his apartment and think, *the Firecracker is really the wrong kind of guy for me.*

I don't hear from the deputy cultural attaché until a few weeks later when a beautiful invitation arrives in the mail. The event is to be held at the embassy of the People's Republic of China. It is for a guest and me. I am excited to go and ask my good friend, Professor Charles Laughlin, to escort me.

The embassy is housed in a three-story building that looks like a schoolboys' academy surrounded by huge stonewalls. The décor of the main entrance and waiting area is in the elegant Ming style. I am wearing a black dress and heels. We walk past dark furniture, long silk scrolls, and paintings that cover the walls of the lobby. In another room, glass showcases display antiquities and ancient objects of art. In a larger room, wine is being served and waiters are passing hors d'oeuvres similar to dim sum.

There is a buzz in the air. As soon as we enter, some Chinese women surround Charles. Their multicolored frocks flutter as the ladies chirp, "Ooh, you so tall," and, "Ooh, you so big."

As a big grin spreads across Charles's face, I leave him and his group of admirers and walk into the room with the display cases. Intent on greeting the deputy cultural attaché, I see him across the room standing with a few people. When the group starts to break up, I approach and lightly touch his shoulder. It is a friendly gesture, my usual manner. Yet he shrugs me off and moves away. Out of habit, I touch his arm again. He shrugs it off and walks away.

I do not need a third try. Rejection fills me. It is time to go find Charles.

A few minutes later, the deputy enters the room where we're standing. He sees me, walks over, and whispers in my ear, "Not here. Don't touch. It's not proper." The Chinese have strict rules against public displays of affection: no holding hands and definitely no kissing. Even a simple gesture of friendship is taboo while the deputy is involved his diplomatic duties.

Charles and I attend more events at the embassy of the People's Republic of China. I have learned my lesson about touching. Although my light taps on the deputy cultural attaché's arm were casual and friendly, I have no romantic interest in the man.

❖

Under Professor Charles Laughlin's tutelage, I am able to pursue the divine directive to learn more about meaningful coincidence. In my university studies of Jung and phenomenological and transpersonal anthropology, I discover more about shamanic and other cultural experiences with the Divine. This helps me to understand nonordinary occurrences and where "the self does not stop at the skin."

During the school year, I present a paper at the Canadian Ethnographic Society annual conference. My topic is "flow," or the experience of the mind-body connection while performing martial arts katas, which are patterns or forms of imaginary fights against multiple attackers. For my talk, I wear a designer outfit. Dark gray, and made of heavy cotton, it mimics an ancient Japanese warrior's uniform. Later that night, Charles says, "Your presentation was well received. I could tell from the audience's spontaneous applause."

For my honors thesis, I submit an essay titled "Discovery within the Scientific Enterprise," which addresses the intersection of intentionality and nonlogical factors in creative scientific research. For my fieldwork, I interviewed an anthropologist, a physicist, an architect, and my friend, the professor of mathematics. Two of my interviewees found inspiration in their dreams, one through meditation, and the fourth through sculpture.

Finally, I complete the necessary coursework for my degree with excellent grades and make the Dean's List. In the spring of 1984, I graduate with an honors bachelor of arts degree from Carleton University.

In the process, after I gain some academic prominence, a competitive fight breaks out between my current school and the New School for Social Research in New York City, both of them vying for my attendance in their master's degree programs. The New School's Anthropology Department boasts a leading authority on the shamanic and transpersonal experience, Professor Michael Harner. A fierce contest next begins as each graduate school offers me more scholarship money to attend its institution. The New School's offer includes automatic admission into its doctoral program after I complete the master's degree. Carleton does not offer a doctoral degree in anthropology.

Meanwhile, at the martial arts club, I am gearing up for my black-belt test. The head instructor, Mr. Jung Park, is on a world tour with General Choi. They are testing third-and fourth-ranked black belts and creating an encyclopedia of Taekwondo. We expect him to return to his Ottawa club in a few months to oversee our test.

But then I hear Mr. Park will be back next week. Black-belt testing will be held in two weeks. It is August 1984. He is at least two months ahead of schedule.

I train hard for the upcoming test but break my routine when the deputy cultural attaché telephones and invites me to come to see him at the embassy. During our last discussion, he informed me that China's highest-ranking Kung Fu martial artist would be coming to Ottawa. Of course, the deputy intends to invite me to that event. Now, he says he wants to give something to me. Uncharacteristically, he tells me to wear a shirt and a button-down sweater and to sit in the first chair in the long hallway.

The next day, I pass through the embassy's security and take the appropriate seat. The lobby is empty. A few minutes later, the deputy walks over to me. Expecting him to shake my hand, I remain seated, but instead, he bends down and kisses me on the mouth. His soft tongue finds mine. I am shocked! This is a total lack of decorum. Then he slips a large VHS cassette inside my sweater, after which he bows and walks away. Feeling numb, I rise and leave the embassy grounds with the VHS cassette undetected by the guards.

That night, I watch the video at Ron's place. Luu is here too. We see an unbelievable display of martial art skills. It is nothing like the hundreds of other martial art videos we've watched during the past few years. My two friends have access to all kinds of underground movies, but this is a secret documentary of Shaolin monks training in an esoteric Kung Fu style and displaying weapons inside an ancient monastery.

When the video ends, Ron makes our usual movie-night dinner of curried fish over steamed rice. For the past year, my diet has changed to mostly stir-fried, lean proteins and a lot of vegetables. Ron's recipe is simple. Cook the rice. In another pot, heat a can of cream of mushroom soup and douse it with curry. Then cut up a bunch of green onions and green peppers and throw them into the pot. Let that simmer and at theend, mix in a can of tuna. The result is a flavorful meal that is also gentle on the stomach. The apartment gets infused with the aromatic spices. We eat Ron's dish and discuss the video we just saw.

"Those katas were powerful and done in perfect unison," I say. "And, Ron, this curry is delicious." A minute later, I add, "Hey, did you guys notice the stone floor of the monastery? Some areas were so worn down. Probably from centuries of use."

"Yeah," Ron responds. "And the Shaolin monks performed more complex techniques with a long whip. They snapped it around their bodies and did flips and headstands. And when they lay flat on the ground and bopped up, an inch from the floor and still stretched out, while the whip whirled around them, it was amazing."

"Whip made of metal. I see in my country." Luu looks at both of us and continues in his broken English. "Not easy learn."

I laugh. "It puts New York break dancers to shame, eh?"

"Yes." Luu nods his head. "Metal whip break bones. Or kill."

After watching the Shaolin monks on the secret video, I'm totally focused on my upcoming black-belt test. Surprised by the sudden switch of the test date, I prepare by training six hours a day. "Nervous" does not describe how I feel; fear, doubt, and worry are present in full force. I need all my mental faculties to hold these emotions at bay. I also protect myself by spending the first part of the day of the test in meditation.

The memory of my death at the hands of the Evil Man has been my companion all week. Tonight I will reclaim my power and overcome any lingering identification as his victim.

One cannot win against all attackers, but at least now I have an idea about what to do if someone attempts to assault me again. And yet, I still have my concerns.

Tonight all the techniques I learned in the Taekwondo repertoire will be tested. The examiner is one of the highest-ranked martial artists on the planet. Like me, three other senior belts are going for their first-degree black belt, and seven, first-degree black belts are going for their second degrees. One of them is Jung Park's wife, and some are on Canada's national team, as are the two black belts going for their third degree. Phap, the acting head of the club while Mr. Jung Park was away, is going for his fourth-degree black belt.

Ron, Luu, and the rest of the club, plus many visitors, are here to watch the black belt tests. Their whispers fill the room with a soft hum. My special guests include Marla, who took a train from Toronto to be here; my friend, Professor Charles Laughlin; and another good friend Jim, who recently received his black belt from the Therien Jiu Jitsu & Kickboxing club, where the number one ranked kickboxer in the world trains. I've studied privately with Jim and his gifted nephews to develop my weapons skills.

I met Jim by accident. It happened just off the walkway along the Rideau Canal, where I was going through some martial arts routines in a secluded spot hidden on three sides by tall bushes. Suddenly I heard a voice, "What style is that?" It was Jim, dressed in full biking gear and standing beside his three-speed bike. He stepped forward and explained that he'd been training for many years in jujitsu. We became good friends.

Now it is my turn to be examined. During the test, I feel strong and prepared. This gives me confidence as I perform the required techniques.

When all the Taekwondo black belt tests are completed, instead of going to the dinner ceremony where the results will be announced, I head home. Early the next morning, I say goodbye to my sister.

A few days later, Mr. Jung Park awards me with a black belt and my first-degree certificate. As for the results of the martial arts test, I ranked third overall. Phap came in first, and one of the guys going for his third degree came in second. Unlike me, the late bloomer, both of them have trained most of their lives in the martial arts. I am extremely proud of myself.

Chapter 30

THE BAD BIT BEGINS IN my apartment. My old feelings of abandonment are in full rage. "Don't go!" I shout as I look into his face.

The Firecracker reaches for the door and pulls it open.

Just a few weeks ago, I vowed not to see him again. Now I follow him into the hallway, down the back stairs, and out the door. It is dark outside; the street is empty. Walking a few paces ahead of me, the Firecracker does not look back. In no time, I catch up and grab his shoulder.

Now he turns to look me. His eyes are dark. His face is mean. "Let go."

But I'm caught up in my insecurities, and my voice is meek. "Why can't you stay? We can talk. You like to talk."

"Let go."

My stubbornness surfaces. I tighten my grip. "No."

"Let go." His voice is stern.

"No."

We stand a few inches apart. The heat of his breath is hitting my face. Then he shoves me back against the brick wall of a building and something connects. All I can see are stars. And not the kind that are shining brightly in the night sky.

I don't know how long the stars last.

Then there is a nudge on my arm. I open my eyes. Two unfamiliar people, a girl and a guy, are standing over me. I'm still curled up on the ground. I manage to sit up and lean back against the brick wall.

The girl stoops down. "Are you okay?"

"What happened?" I look around. Nothing seems familiar. "Where am I?" My head is throbbing. I can taste blood in my mouth.

"On Elgin Street, near Argyle Avenue," the girl says. "We were back there, down the street." She points behind us.

I recognize the street names. I'm only a block from the side entrance to my building.

"We saw the man hit you," says the guy. "You went down. But not before you kicked him. He limped away." He points in the opposite direction.

Somehow, I find my way to my apartment and telephone the Firecracker.

"What happened? I don't remember."

"We got into a fight."

"Geez. Someone saw you throw a punch and crawl away. What happened?"

"You kicked me in the groin. Man, it still hurts."

"It hurts? So what?" I taste the blood in my mouth again and discover a chipped tooth. "You sucker punched me."

I didn't see the punch coming, which has me concerned. But my kick came out automatically, which is good. There was no time to think. It seems my front snap kick made contact with the Firecracker's pelvic area. He is only moaning, which means he got lucky. Out of some compassion, I just gave him a tap. He should be grateful I didn't kick harder and break a bone.

The Firecracker lets out another groan.

"You'll be fine." My headache is on its way to a full-blown migraine. "Got to go."

Of course, he is the wrong kind of guy for me. He is the opposite of marriage material. Charles is probably a better choice. But marriage is no longer a defining principle of myself. Instead, I must learn and master the remaining divine directives.

A few days after the black belt test, the Taekwondo club is scheduled to do a demonstration at an open-air event in Ottawa. After getting sucker punched by the Firecracker, I don't want to take part, so I invite Mr. Park to come to my apartment to talk and to see the documentary of the Shaolin monks doing Kung Fu. Not having a Beta V8 video machine or a TV, I rent them before his visit.

Mr. Park arrives on time. He loves to walk and wears a dark suit in the hot weather. After we watch the martial art video, I tell him about my recent fight. "I didn't even see the punch coming," I conclude, "and I got knocked out."

Mr. Park replies in his broken English, "Myra, you too hard on yourself. Difficult to think someone who is friend will punch you. Even if you argue, you still think friends. Your guard was down."

I nod my head in agreement. "When guys hear I take martial arts, they get testy and want to take me on and fight. This guy was edgy, and I got stubborn. But you're right. I didn't expect him to throw a sucker punch. Although I was able to kick him, what concerns me, and why I want to talk with you, is because my martial arts stopped working when I fell. With the Shaolin monks' Kung Fu, they can fight on the ground. The monks learn how to fall. Taekwondo doesn't teach this. I cannot do the demonstration with the club."

"Interesting," he says. "You see the faults and I come with offer. I want you to move to Winnipeg. Help my wife and me open a Taekwondo school there. You will join Canada's national team. I personally will instruct you. Our International Taekwondo Federation demonstration team will compete against the World Taekwondo Federation. The International Olympic Committee must decide to admit the sport and which style."

I'm astonished. "Wow! I am honored. Thank you so much for your consideration. But I will need to take some time to think this through."

Something else makes sense. A couple of months before I left the Public Archives, it sent a few people to Canada's Olympic center for testing. I was one of them. We didn't know why we were being tested. The nurse who took my blood pressure said, "You're as fit as an Olympic athlete."

Now I wonder if that was just random testing of me, on behalf of the Taekwondo Federation. During that same period, I trained with members of Canada's Taekwondo national team, at least four times a week for three-hour sessions.

The Firecracker's sucker punch taught me a lesson. If I am to fulfill the divine directive about training in a martial art, I still have a lot more to learn. Mr. Park's offer would require three to four years devoted to doing katas, sport fighting, and tournaments. My clandestine weapons training in jujitsu with Jim is a lethal art. My focus is working out with nunchucks, a short staff, and a small blade.

With lots of practice, each of these traditional weapons can translate to modern-day items. No nunchucks? Use your necklace, a belt, or a TV cord. No short staff? Use curtain rods or a broom stick handle. No knife? Then use a pen, a screwdriver, or scissors. Not all sticks and not all stones can break your bones. Practice. Practice. Practice. Because any weapon can be taken away and used against you.

I turn down Mr. Park's offer.

A few weeks later, all the members of the Taekwondo club are invited to attend a day-long skills retreat held at a camp in the woods near a shallow lake so we can take a swim after the training sessions. Following the group warm-ups, all the black belts are led to a barnlike structure. An old man dressed in a well-worn gi greets us. His belt indicates a high rank, which is also indicated by the frayed cotton and dullness of its black color.

We are told the old master is here to teach us killing techniques. His area of expertise is deathblows to the torso and head. The black belts gather around him as he begins to demonstrate the lethal hits on a mannequin. A translator tells us what he is saying. "A short jab to the chest. Do not punch through the bones of the rib cage. They react like windowpanes and will shatter like glass. You might be able to punch in, but when you pull out, the broken bone chips will tear up your hand."

We are instructed where on the body to strike and where to deliver a one-, two-, or three-month punch. When done correctly, these hits will set up vibrations in the internal organs and cause death in one to three months.

These hits are done at close range. It's inside fighting. Different strikes have their individual sounds, a light tap at the ribs or a smack near the kidneys. With my training, I know I own the jab and the blows to the torso. The old man's strategy could work for me, though the Hollywood-looking punch to the head is not likely in the range of my capability. My only chance would be a perfect quick strike to the temple. Anything else would crush my fist. I bet only 15 percent of the men on this planet actually have that punch.

Back home, I ponder these new martial arts techniques. Still, it is not enough for me to continue in Taekwondo. I need to change my style. This might be one reason I feel short in my skin. I need to get to Harlem in New York City and train with people who know how to survive on the street.

And this is one reason why I accept the offer from the New School for Social Research.

Chapter 31

MY PLAN IS TO USE the inheritance I've received from my father to help with the expenses involved with my relocation to New York. Before the big move, I also use some of the money to visit Marla, who lives in London, England, with her art director boyfriend. They have a home in the swank Chelsea district, and my sister takes art history classes at the famed Sotheby's Auction House. In our long-distance telephone conversations, she tells me about the fun trips she takes with two of her classmates. They've gone to Bath and Windsor. I'm looking forward to seeing her and meeting them.

London is a city made for walking, which is one of my favorite things to do. Marla and I stroll the perimeter of Buckingham Palace. Walking along the Royal Mews, we get close enough to smell the stables and see elaborate, golden, horse-drawn carriages. We also saunter past the classic Greek columns and into the Tate Gallery. Known for its collection of J. M. W. Turner paintings, the Tate is one of my sister's favorite art museums.

One morning, Marla persuades a security guard to let us into the Royal Horticultural Society's famous Chelsea Flower

Show. At first, he objects. "It is before Queen Elizabeth and her regal entourage have seen the show. You can't come in. It's unheard of."

Marla launches into news press speak and uses enough jargon to convince the guy she is a photojournalist at a famous paper. She points to the expensive collection of cameras hanging on straps around her neck.

The guard is convinced. He gives us a wink, nods his head, and says, "Never mind, go on."

Now we're in the showroom tent, an overwhelming perfumery of scents, musk, and wet soil accompanying us as we roam the aisles. Row after row are displays of beautiful flowers and different kinds of English gardens.

One night, we head to a trendy Soho restaurant, where a low murmur of chatter fills the room. The crowd is cool but well mannered. Marla's two girlfriends from Sotheby's are already there and seated at a table. Both are pretty, one is a blonde, the other has raven-black hair. Their accents are not quite British.

After an hour or so of listening to Ms. Dark-Haired Beauty talking, I'm becoming agitated. She's monopolized the conversation and has not made one remark about my sister. Not one comment about Marla's highly evolved esthetic eye.

I reach my boiling point and stand, push my chair back, and snarl, "Enough of this conversation. Let's go, Marla. Let's leave. Now."

Ms. Dark-Haired Beauty shuts up. The other girl looks astonished.

My sister glares at me, like I am a madwoman. Then she calmly stands. "Sorry," she says, "but Myra is probably just tired." She wisely puts enough money down on the table to cover our bill. "Myra still has some jet lag and doesn't really feel well."

Then we hustle outside, where Marla gives me an earful. All the way home, I reflect on the outrageousness of my outburst. I should have restrained myself.

A few days after my public disaster at the restaurant, I take a train to Heathrow Airport. My intention is to meet Mr. Rhee Ki Ha, the head of the British and European International Taekwondo Federation. Prior to my trip to London, Mr. Park made arrangements for us to meet.

The baggage area is full of people, but I notice Rhee right away. He is a handsome Korean man, known as the Golden Boy because of his dark hair, sparkly eyes, high cheekbones, and thick lips, not to mention his strong body and smooth skin that glows from his being so fit. His first assistant is also present. He tells me he serves as a bodyguard to Saudi Arabia's royal family when they visit London.

I laugh when Rhee bounces a small handball over to me. The three of us play ball and giggle like little kids for about half an hour while we're waiting for the men's luggage to arrive. After we have dinner together, Rhee drives me back to my sister's place in his gold-plated Jaguar. Marla greets us at the door, and I introduce them. As we follow her into her living room, she asks him, "Can I get you something to drink?"

"Yes," Rhee says. "A glass of milk, please."

On her way out of the room, my sister rolls her eyes at me, and a minute later we watch as Rhee drains the large glass of milk in one gulp. He puts the empty glass on a side table, smacks his lips, and says, "Feel my fists. Go ahead. You first."

He turns to me and holds one hand in front of me, all balled up. I squeeze what feels like a rock. His straight punch could definitely crack a skull, Hollywood-style.

My sister squeezes his fist too. "Oh, you're so strong!"

"Compared to my friend, Muhammad Ali, mine is much stronger." A huge grin spreads across his face.

Of course, I develop a huge crush on Rhee. But nothing happens.

❁

Now, back in Ottawa, it is the night before I move to New York City. I can hardly sleep. My stomach aches. I am not sure it's the right decision, because it involves leaving my dear friends Karen, John, Ron, Luu, and Jim, and my friend and mentor, Charles. Despite the scholarships from the New School of Social Research, I feel unsure about my future.

Once I reach New York, loneliness settles in and stays with me for several days, even though I'm bunking at my brother's place. I've always admired Jamie, and since my father's death I feel a need to be closer to him. He has graduated from Harvard with an MBA and is currently employed in the financial industry. He spends long hours at his job. Meanwhile, my days are spent hunting for a room to rent. And roommates I can get along with.

Today, it is sunny and cool and the air smells fresh. That will change. The spicy aroma from the shawarma seller's stand mixes with the doughy fragrance of the fresh-baked pretzel cart and the beefy musk from the hot dog vendor. Even some sidewalks in New York emit odors. Thanks to decades of decayed dog poop and throw-up, the stink seems to be embedded in the concrete. It is late November 1984. I hear the trash and filth were a lot worse a few years ago.

Walking around Manhattan is a workout in itself. I weave along on sidewalks full of people. We race down stairs and run to the subway cars. We climb the stairs at breakneck speed. Walk. Bob and weave. Wait to catch the bus. Sit. Walk. Climb. Race. Repeat. Repeat.

The energy builds inside me. Not able to train in martial arts for the past few weeks, I now feel the need to do some moves. An ideal place is a semienclosed outdoor area. While roaming the streets and avenues, I come across the long, narrow entranceway of a building on a deserted side street. It has walls on three of the sides, which are about forty feet in length. Compared to the hustle and bustle on 5th Avenue and 14th Street, it's empty. No one has walked out or gone in for the last fifteen minutes.

I decide this is the perfect place to do a mini, martial-art workout. After a quick warm up facing one of the brick walls, I begin to do a black belt, up-body kata. I do it again and again and again. I get lost in my routine.

Suddenly a man's voice interrupts my concentration. "Where do you train?"

I turn around to find a handsome, casually dressed African American man. One of his arms is in a sling. Right away, I like his smile and his spirit.

"Nowhere," I reply. "I don't belong to a club. I just moved to New York."

"Well, I train in jujitsu, at Little John Davis' club."

"Oh, I've heard of him. He's a ranked martial artist." The happenstance of our meeting is similar to how I met my friend Jim in Ottawa. "Your teacher's teacher was Moses Powell, eh?"

"That's right. And you're Canadian, eh?"

"Yep. You can tell from the ehs, eh?"

The man laughs and extends his free arm to shake my hand. "My name is Cleveland."

"I'm Myra. Hey, where am I? I mean, what is this building used for?"

"You're on the campus of New York University," he says. "This place is one of the student residences. Up the street is Washington Square Park. Hey, if you're up for it, why don't you come to Sensei Little John's club with me? I'm not training these days 'cause of this." He raises the arm in the sling slightly and winces, but then the grin returns to his face. "The club is in Harlem, near Morningside. I'm driving up there tonight. You can get a lift with me."

In this moment, my mind flashes back to my hitchhiking days. Never did I expect to experience these feelings again. Yet here I am, contemplating whether or not to take a ride with a stranger.

"Yes. Sure."

We decide the best place to meet up is on the corner nearest to my brother's apartment.

"Okay," Cleveland says. "I have a red BMW. I'll pick you up on the way to Harlem."

"Sounds great! Thank you."

That evening, I leave Jamie a note before heading out the door. "I am going to Harlem to do some martial arts. I'll be at Little John Davis' jujitsu club. If you do not hear from me, check the hospitals in the vicinity."

While I'm waiting at the corner for Cleveland, I think back to the sucker punch, and about Mr. Park's offer to be on Canada's national Taekwondo team and the Olympic demonstration team. It still feels right to have turned him down. Just then, the red BMW pulls up to the curb.

The club is nondescript. The students show great respect for Sensei Little John Davis, who is short, broad, and looks strong. Like Cleveland, he is African American and likable. Sensei welcomes me into his club, even though my black belt was not awarded by him.

There are about thirty people in the class. Some of the men are tall, some have long dreadlocks. The women are tall, short, wide, thin, and in-between. Some wear the headscarves of the Black Muslim faith. Everyone is some shade of African American, and all are dressed in different styles of black and white and mixed-color gis, unlike the Moses Powell group, who all wear light blue uniforms. I'm wearing a clean, white top with no insignia, my black belt, and plain black pants. My friend Jim gave me the top when I gained my first-degree black belt. The owner of Therien Jiu Jitsu & Kickboxing club had awarded it to him after his black belt test. I am honored to wear it. Mr. Jung Park gave me the black belt when I passed my test.

After class, Sensei Little John Davis unexpectedly orders the wildest-looking guy there to spar with me. Before our fight starts, we circle each other in the middle of the room. My opponent is a black belt with no front teeth. Even though we wear mouth guards, his lack of teeth signals me he won't be shy to come in close. I go back to my corner, where Cleveland is sitting on a bench, a big smile on his face.

"Why were you laughing at me before?" I ask him.

"I thought you were going to blow up when the class did the hundred sit-ups. Your face was so red."

"Yeah . . . well, I got through the sit-ups." I haven't trained for a few weeks and my conditioning has suffered.

"I don't know why sensei picked that guy to fight you."

His comment about my opponent makes me nervous. "What do you mean by 'that guy'?"

A serious look crosses Cleveland's face. "He's a nasty fighter, Myra. Do you know how to defend against a leg sweep?"

"Nope."

"That's his specialty. When you start to execute a kick, he'll knock out the leg you're standing on."

"Then I'll use my high-turning kick. Go for a light tap to the cheekbone. It's fast. I'll try not to telegraph it."

Cleveland nods his head, but he does not look convinced.

Lucky for me, sensei calls off the fight a minute later. Sure, I was scared. But I want to learn how to avoid a sweep, how to properly fall down, and how to fight on the ground.

Chapter 32

I ARRIVE EARLY FOR MY scheduled meeting at the New School for Social Research with Michael Harner. He is the famous anthropologist and author of the renowned book, *The Way of the Shaman*, which made the shamanic experiences and methods accessible to the masses.

In pursuit of my divine directive to learn metaphysics, I have so far focused on the Kabbalah and its connection to the Torah and the tarot. I've also come to understand Judaism has its roots in shamanism. This explains the occurrences of animal sacrifice. (Abraham, a shaman, almost performed a sacrificial ritual on his son, Isaac.) There are also shamanic echoes in today's evangelicals, who will explain natural occurrences like hurricanes and floods as due to human's moral decline.

Professor Harner walks into the room and takes a seat across from me. "It is obvious you are a psychic," he says after introducing himself. He smiles and then frowns. "But I am concerned about when you work with shamans. Metaphorically speaking, they can consume a weak person. We'll see how well you do just by thriving in New York City. That's your first test."

Our conversation goes on, and afterwards, I leave the room deep in thought. Harner's perception of me was insightful and yet contained a caution. Perhaps he sensed the inner battle of my own insecurities. If one's self-confidence is built on shifting sands, and the person is not solid in his or her self, a shaman has the advantage.

Harner's assertion that my surviving the trials of New York City might be important, but my first order of business is still to find a place to live. I totally appreciate my brother's kindness, but it is not good to hang out at his place and sleep on his couch for too long. I don't want to overstay my welcome, so I study the New School's bulletin board and look for rooms to rent, thinking that real weirdos would not post in such a public place. Well, it turns out some semi-weirdoes do post notices here. At one apartment, the renter tells me he is on the night shift and intends to share the same bed and room, but at different times. Really? Not with me.

Finally, a pretty woman named Jackie escorts me around her apartment. She offers to rent me a tiny bedroom and share the bathroom, kitchen, and living room with her and another girl. I agree to take it. Located between 2nd and 3rd Avenues on 21st Street, it is only a few blocks from the New School, which is on 5th Avenue and 14th Street.

My next task is to find a part-time job. The New School's curriculum is geared toward people who work during the day, so classes are held in the evenings. Miraculously, employment comes to me in a book publishing company. Perfectly situated at the corner of 5th Avenue and 20th Street, it is only a couple of blocks from my apartment and a few blocks from the school.

Michael Roger Press makes blank books and the ledgers used by the New York Police Department. The owner is a man in his early forties who has spotted a trend. He hires me to create a line of blank books for use as personal journals. He also trusts me with the keys to his office, and over time, he agrees to pay to ship the bookbinding equipment I made while

I lived in Vancouver to his Manhattan office. This includes the backing vice, the sewing frame, and the standing press, plus the gifts of movable type and the type holder from Vernon. These are currently stored at my aunt's place in Huntington Woods, just outside Detroit.

New York's skyscrapers, all the concrete and glass, make me feel sealed in and choked off. Central Park is a blessing, a green bath in the middle of a cement world. A walk along the East River Promenade provides some good moments with its proximity to water, but some of my schoolfriends say, "I don't want to walk through the A, B, C Streets to get there." It's 1984, and the city has lots of bad places with bad reputations.

One afternoon, Cleveland and I decide to take a stroll around Washington Square Park. Today, it is packed with people, dogs on leashes, and vendors with their pushcarts. I have a class in an hour at the New School, which is just down the street. Cleveland lives in one of the NYU student residences that are close by. A few years back, he completed a degree in film at the school and still occupies a room on campus. After graduating, he became a crime photographer for the New York Police Department and held that job for many years. Now, thanks to his extensive training in jujitsu, he works as a corrections officer on Rikers Island. He tells me he has to watch the worst of the worst, men who get into trouble while doing their time in New York's infamous jail complex.

During our walk around the park, Cleveland points out things only his detective-like sensibilities notice. "Myra," he says, "did you catch the police handcuffs tied to the side of that lady's belt." I did not. We turn around to scurry past the woman, then turn around again and walk past her so I can get a look at the cuffs, mostly hidden by her open cardigan sweater.

"Myra, did you see that naked guy?" I did not. Again we retrace our steps, and he points out the naked man lying stretched out on the ground, under a patch of thick shrubs that hide him and make him almost invisible. Only Cleveland's keen eyes could spot him. We run over to 5th Avenue and tell a cop about the naked fellow.

It's fun taking walks with Cleveland.

Vernon calls me. Charles visits me in New York. It is good to see and talk deeply with my friend. When he is gone, however, I realize that something is amiss. Except when I'm in my anthropology classes at the New School, my interests are generally too esoteric to talk about with most people. Except while at Michael Roger Press, I am left out of many conversations about the day-to-day working world and how to make money. The city is filled with commerce. Although my brother is at home in New York's district of high finance, I do not discuss financial matters with him, and he does not talk about the Kabbalah or the tarot with me. This is the pattern with most people I meet. No one is particularly interested in mysticism, metaphysics, or shamanism. Everyone wants to talk about making money and profit margins. The power of wealth is obvious in the Big Apple.

When I was a student at the University of Western Ontario, I found it mentally stimulating to discuss theoretical aspects of capitalism with Marxist anthropologist Professor Silverman and my fellow classmates, Kathy and Paul, who are smart and cool people. But the actual functions involved with free enterprise seem foreign to me. Other than the sad experience of my father's bankruptcy, I have little understanding of mortgages, credit ratings, debt, stocks and bonds, and how the financial markets work. The other day, when I was speaking to a young man who told me he was in the securities business, I took it to mean he sold high-end house alarms and fancy doorbells.

Jamie took an opposite route from mine in life, and while I admire his expertise in mathematics and finance, the ways of money remain mysterious to me. What most people see as ordinary about commerce seems alien and somewhat dangerous to me. These negative feelings are probably due to the trauma my father's bankruptcy inflicted on his health and our family's circumstances. At a young age, I bought into the spiritual belief that money is the "root of all evil."

My conviction that money is aligned with malevolence has clouded my understanding of commerce. But having to survive in New York makes me realize my need to learn, explore, and somehow participate in the financial aspects of my life. My curiosity soon takes priority over my shamanic studies with Professor Michael Harner.

Sometime in 1985, I decide not to finish the courses at the New School. I move to Windsor, Ontario. It is sad, of course, to say goodbye to my friend Cleveland. We've trained together all these months and become really good buddies. I pack the bookbinding equipment and the gifts Vernon gave me into a large box. Before I turn the office keys over to the owner of Michael Roger Press, he agrees to ship the box back to my aunt in Michigan.

Except I never see my bookbinding equipment, the hand tools, or the moveable type ever again. I've called the owner of the press many times about it. I even went to see him. I checked out his story and came up empty. It feels like I've lost my children.

My plan now is to teach the martial arts-style fitness classes I've designed and to live with my mother at her apartment and sleep in the den until I get a place of my own. But ambition calls, and I take my self-defense workout program and move to Toronto, where I find a bed-sitting room to rent on the second floor of a converted mansion. Located in a neighborhood of tree-lined streets and big houses with landscaped lawns, my place is a short walk to one of Toronto's main intersections, Bloor and Yonge Streets. The outstanding feature of my room is an outdoor deck. The owner's family lives on the floor below me. The renters' communal kitchen is one floor above me. Two other rooms are rented out on that floor, and there is a third in the attic.

I contact a number of health clubs to demonstrate my martial arts fitness program and hopefully get on their schedule of classes for their members. The Women's Club offers me a small contract and I acquire a few private clients, two of whom are actors who are currently in hit shows on Canadian television. One is the police drama series *Night Heat,* and the other is *Seeing Things,* about a journalist who solves crimes with the use of ESP in the form of psychic visions.

I do not have many friends in Toronto, and I'm lonely, so my Saturdays and Sundays are spent in the movie theaters. After watching a one o'clock matinee, I might see two more movies that same day. Between movies, I grab lunch and supper, maybe Chicken McNuggets or a Whopper with fries and a Coke. I feel lost and my good eating habits suffer. There is little magic for me in this city. Nothing connects for me. Overcoming death, accomplishing my divine directives, having a university degree, and being a hand bookbinding and paper restorer all mean nothing now. I feel like Ms. Nobody.

To maintain my kicking and punching skills, I train at the headquarters of Canada's World Taekwondo Federation, located at the corner of Bloor and Yonge. This is the style in competition with my former Ottawa club, which will be designated an official Olympic sport by the 1988 Olympic committee. Sparring with the head of Canada's World Taekwondo Federation tests my black-belt qualifications and allows me to teach classes too.

But I still feel like Ms. Nobody.

One night I have a dream. It takes place in a garden surrounded by oak trees. The land is neatly hoed with clean but empty rows of well-turned soil. The sun is shining, and it's a beautiful, late spring day. All of a sudden, my dream-self is in another part of the garden, where it is dark, and the plants are in various states of decay. Everything is damp and smells of mold. I feel tiny and afraid.

Then the word FALLOW appears before my dream-mind's eye.

When the word disappears, the dream continues, and my dream-self walks out of the dark side and into the sunlit side of the garden. Here, my hair is blonde, and I am naked, lithe, and beautiful. On this sunny side of the garden, pieces of burlap cover each of the garden rows, now planted. I trust that the seedlings and baby shoots are growing under their protective cloths.

Then, all at once, the garden comes alive with full-grown, magnificently colored flowers. An old woman wearing a long, black dress and a black babushka wrapped around her head pulls a garment rack behind her. It is the type one sees in the fashion district of New York City. On the rack hang many small, transparent bags neatly clipped onto hangers. Each bag holds a new white brassiere and panties. The dream ends here.

I awake feeling refreshed and feminine. (I don't wear frilly underwear, anyway.) The dream seems to speak about my depression. Decay and decomposition are not bad, they are necessary. Every seven years, or so, a traditional farmer will let his garden patch go to rot and decline. This fallowness enables the soil to replenish its minerals, and the land becomes fertile again. This practice helps to ensure a good harvest. The dream has shown me that when nothing seems to be happening, it is really my soul lying fallow and rejuvenating itself. The underwear seems to represent a personal harvest yet to come.

My depression lifts.

Chapter 33

LUCKY FOR ME, MY LONELINESS in Toronto starts to subside when I reconnect with Ron, an artist and photographer and old friend of Marla's. We first met when my sister lived in the city and we'd visit him together. On one occasion, the conversation somehow turned to porn movies, which I had never seen.

"What?" Ron said in disbelief. He walked into the TV area, where he pulled a video from a stack. "Come and sit over here, Myra. I am going to put this on. You watch some porn. Marla and I are going to talk photography at the kitchen table."

"Okay."

Now, Ron's funky loft-studio on Davies, which I often visit, becomes a haven of creativity and comfort to me. He is a wordsmith, bright, nonjudgmental, and "laugh until your cheeks hurt" funny. We have great discussions on all kinds of topics. I really like his perky girlfriend, MK, and Barney, her extremely smart dog. We frequently take walks together and cruise the shops and stores. After our walks, Ron usually makes a huge salad with exotic leafy greens, such as dandelion, romaine, and watercress, and dresses it with the best olive oil and red wine vinegar. We scoop it up with hunks of warm, artisan bread. A yeasty fragrance fills the room.

He believes forks and knives will wilt the greens and change the nutrition in them, so we are forbidden to use utensils when we eat. His salads always taste delicious. I think Ron might have a point. Speaking of food, when I talk to my twin sister on the telephone (she still lives in London, England) and we mention what we had to eat that day, Marla and I either ate the same thing or had a craving for it.

After my portentous dream about the fallow garden, I continue to have vivid dreams and write them down on a yellow legal pad I keep near my bed. There could be two or even three dreams a night. To work with these dreams even more and gain personal insights into their meaning, I seek out the help of a Jungian analyst.

Our sessions are always the same. After making Xerox copies of my notes on the past week's dreams, I head over to the office of my therapist and give him a set. We sit across from each other in high-backed chairs, a few paces apart, in a small room with many windows.

I read the first dream out loud. My dream-self is at the national Gatineau Park, in Quebec, near Ottawa. It is nighttime with a full moon and millions of stars. The first thaw from the winter season has started. Thick ice is on the lake, but it is not completely frozen over in a few areas. A tree is by the shoreline. My dream-self sits on a log underneath the tree and watches people pull a wood-framed house out of the water. Everyone is bundled up in winter coats, hats, and scarves to ward off the cold air. The people had submerged the house before the ice came. Now that the thaw has arrived, it is time to retrieve it. I marvel at a man who dives into the freezing cold water to pull ropes under and around the house, which then enable the people to raise and drag the building ashore.

When I finish reading the dream, there is the briefest silence in the room, while the therapist gathers his thoughts. Then he asks, "From a Jungian perspective, if all the things and people in the dream are symbolic of you, what does the house mean?"

"I don't know," I admit. "Maybe frozen assets, frozen self. Time to bring what is submerged and hidden in me up into the light? I don't even know if people ever did this to their homes."

The therapist nods his head. "Frozen assets. I like that. What assets do you hide, Myra?"

"My intuition and my psychic self. I think a lot of people do too."

The therapist nods again. "Interestingly, the dream occurs in darkness with a bit of light cast from the bright moon. Do you think this also has to do with hiding yourself?"

"Yes. Actually, I experienced nighttime in Gatineau Park the weekend I was tested for my black belt in Taekwondo. But that was in August, not in the early spring. You see, I did not go to the banquet following the exam but stayed home to prepare for a camping and canoeing expedition the next morning. I was going to the park with my buddy Jim, who came to my black belt test, and his sister and her four kids. Plus, a friend of Jim's sister who brought along a large, personal telescope and a tripod to view the Milky Way and the rings of Saturn."

And on and on we talk about the personal meanings and symbols in this dream and the others. When the hour is over, I feel deeply listened to, more insightful, and eager for next week's session.

Another happenstance contributes to lifting my sadness. While walking around downtown Toronto, I can't seem to shake thoughts of Vernon from my mind. Suddenly I spot my bookbinding instructor with his wife and son. (I first met the boy when he was only eight years old.) Like Father Nolan, but minus the priestly vestments, Vernon is a tall, proud man who walks with the confidence of someone who feels comfortable in his skin. He now tells me his family is in town for medical help with allergies and proper diet, and they are booked up with appointments. They still live in London, Ontario, which is about a two-hour train ride away. I give them all a big hug and bask in their warmth and love.

I soon make friends with the woman who rents the converted attic in the mansion where I live. Late one night, I give her door a light tap and say in a soft voice, "Knock, knock."

Attic Girl greets me wearing a colorful, Chinese, silk kimono, red sweatpants, and a matching red feather boa around her neck. "Come on in," she says. "I just have to finish some chores." Her room is small and decorated in a girly-girly style. There are lace curtains, more colored feathered boas are hanging from the corner of a mirror, and a multicolored, fringed shawl is draped over the shade of a standing floor lamp. A burgundy velvet love seat with a matching chair completes the front area. A dresser and bed are tucked into the corner at the other end of the room.

Her décor is the opposite of what I expected when we first met in the communal kitchen. I was at the stove cooking my dinner when Attic Girl barged into the room. At almost six feet tall and close to 220 pounds, she occupied a lot of space in that tiny area. We introduced ourselves and made small talk about my meal, curried tuna over rice. With her hands on both hips, she looked straight at me and said, "I'm a dyke, you know."

Her statement seemed rhetorical, but coupled with her posture, I took it as a challenge that needed defusing. "Okay," I said. "Well, that's cool. I'm looking for a husband. It started when I was a baby in the crib."

She laughed. "Give it up. Men are no good."

I could not help myself. "Why do you say, 'I'm a dyke'? Why not say, 'I'm gay,' or 'I'm a lesbian' or 'I'm into women'?" My curiosity was not about labels, but to hear how she defined herself.

She shrugged her shoulders. "I found out I'm a dyke last spring. You see, one day I was dressed kind of loud, as usual. I needed to buy a double-headed dildo." She noticed me squirming and raised one eyebrow. "You with me?"

"Oh, I'm a bit of a prude and not into sex toys. But go on with your story."

Attic Girl rolled her eyes. "It's not porn, honey. Don't worry. Anyway, so I ride my bike over to the sex shop. It's the one off Queen Street. They have a huge dildo with a white side and a chocolate-colored other side. I point to it and the guy behind the counter takes it out of the display case and hands it to me. I ask him to put it in a bag. He tells me they don't have one large enough. Now I have to ride up Yonge Street with one hand on the handlebars to steer and holding this giant, double-headed dildo in the other."

There was a dramatic pause, then she continued. "All of a sudden, it starts to rain. At first, it's a light drizzle. I can handle that. But then it turns into a steady downpour. The sex toy gets slippery. It falls out of my hand and starts to roll down the street. I have to turn around to get it. So now I'm a mess, holding this large dildo and maneuvering the bike on the wet roads. Everyone's staring at me. They're all gawking at me like the circus just came to town. That's when I knew it. I'm a dyke. Only a dyke can do that, Myra. Only a dyke could pull that off. Most girls would have let the dildo go."

I couldn't help but giggle. "Your story is fantastic."

Because of Attic Girl's colorful dress, straightforward manner, and fearless attitude, we develop a friendship. When she is short of money, I put $20 to $50 in an envelope, slip it under her door, and know it will be paid back when she gets some cash. Whenever my pot or hash stash runs out, she gives me a small numblette or we'll smoke some together.

Now it is around midnight. Sitting in Attic Girl's chair and reminiscing with her about how we met and her stories, I wait until her tasks are done and she is ready to smoke.

"What are you up to these days?" she asks as she rummages

around in a dresser drawer.

"In the morning, I have a one-day Kelly Girl assignment," I reply. "It's for a criminal attorney. His usual receptionist is sick, and he will be in court all day." My martial arts fitness program is not enough to financially sustain me in Toronto, and I need to supplement my income. Because the city has few opportunities for hand bookbinders or paper restorers, I have signed up for part-time work with a temporary agency and become a Kelly Girl.

"No martial arts clients?"

"No. My private fitness business slows down in the summer, so I take temporary jobs. You know . . . do clerical work or answer phones in professional offices for a day or two."

While waiting for Attic Girl to find whatever she's looking for, I pick a book up off the floor. Its title suggests it's a collection of love affirmations. With my eyes closed, I fan through it and let my fingers settle on a page and find an affirmation to contemplate for the day ahead.

"Today, you will make a decision. It is no ordinary decision. It is the kind of decision that leads men into battle and nations are created."

Wow. This is not the kind of "love saying" I expected. My intuition tells me to stay alert. Something's up.

The next morning, I arrive at the Kelly Girl assignment to find the law firm's door open. A long, narrow hallway leads to the receptionist's desk, where I start to settle in. A thin, young man wearing a narrow tie and no jacket saunters over to me. "Hi," he says, "I'm the articling student."

"Hi, I'm Myra Mossman, the temporary receptionist for the day. What do you mean, 'articling student'?"

He cocks his head to one side as he talks. "Well, the year before the bar exam, you have to work, or article, for a lawyer. They make a report about it to the Law Society of Upper Canada. After that, you become a lawyer. And you know what?"

"No. What?"

"I really want to be a musician. My parents want me to be a lawyer. But I don't want to be a lawyer." A look of anguish spreads across his face. "So my advice to anyone who wants to be a lawyer is don't. Don't do it unless you really, really want to."

Just then, the phone rings and the articling student walks away to go and brood elsewhere. The criminal attorney is on the other end of the line.

"Something strange has happened," he says. "Court is cancelled all day. I am coming back to the office."

"I look forward to meeting you," I reply. I did not expect to encounter him at all today.

He arrives about twenty minutes later. As he walks down the long hallway, I get a few seconds to size him up. He is handsome, maybe a bit taller than me, and a few years older. The only apparent downside is his coffee-colored suit, which blends in with the wainscot paneling that runs throughout the law firm's offices.

He introduces himself, and we talk at the receptionist's desk for about a half hour. Then he calls me into his private office, which is large and has built-in shelves filled with law books. A delicate aroma of furniture polish is apparent. I take a seat in front of his desk as he sits in the brown leather chair behind it.

"Myra," he begins, "you are bright. Have you ever thought of becoming a lawyer?"

"Nope. Never."

"Well, I sit on the board of admissions at the University of Toronto Faculty of Law school. I could get you in. What do you think?"

Both his compliment and his offer surprise me. He just made an offer to get me into the most prestigious law school in Canada. Compared to my brother, the genius and golden child, I have never considered myself bright. "Geez," I say. "Thank you. But I don't feel prepared for law school. For the past eight years, I've focused on making books by hand and restoring paper and on metaphysics and martial arts. I'm currently working in the everyday world as an office temp."

"That's fine."

"And my BA is in anthropology. I studied the notions of the self and the divine cross-culturally."

"No problem," he says with a smile.

And just then, a quickening happens in my body. It feels like a charge of energy is running through me. It awakens my intuition. The "love affirmation" I read in Attic Girl's room flashes into my mind. I know my destiny is being revealed in this moment. Going to law school and becoming a lawyer is the important decision I must make.

Criminal Attorney continues to talk about his school and tells me anecdotes from his practice. Then he says, "You know, I also train in martial arts."

I am surprised again. "What is your style?"

"I do a bit of this and a bit of that. I take private lessons."

When he tells me the name of his instructor, I recognize the name of a man who has a reputation for teaching unconventional stuff. This puzzles me. Why would a lawyer study with that kind of person? I know the Criminal Attorney is well respected. There's a clue on the firm's stationary. Following his name are the letters QC, which stand for Queen's Counsel. Queen's Counsel is a meritorious title given to lawyers and barristers throughout the British Commonwealth. In the past, this title enabled distinguished attorneys to handle matters on behalf of the Crown.

"How about you?" he asks me. "Where do you train, Myra?"

"I've trained in a few different styles during the past eight years. Now it's Kuk Sul Won at the club on Bloor Street."

"I've never heard of it"

"It's rather esoteric."

"What does that mean?"

"Come to the club and watch us."

"Well, give me an idea. Punching and kicking?"

"Yes, but stealthy. Lethal. Imperial guard skills with high kicks, multiple hand techniques, grappling, joint locks, takedowns, throws, rollouts, walking on walls, and using the long sword when you reach the black-belt stage. All good stuff for self-defense."

The lawyer is staring at me. He leans back in his chair and remains quiet. My words seem to have disarmed him. Perhaps our common interest in martial arts can cement his commitment to help me. I do want to be a lawyer now, and I might need him to get into law school. The year is 1987. He tells me there are not many women lawyers these days.

"Instead of talking," I say, "why don't you come down to the Kuk Sul Won club with me? You know, it's easy to spin a story about my skills, but you can't lie about them. Either you have it, or you don't. So come watch us."

He lets out a laugh. "I know what you mean. Maybe I will."

It feels comfortable to sit in Criminal Attorney's private office, relaxed and open, surrounded by books. We talk some more about law and martial arts, and then he stands up. "Because court is out all day, I'm taking off early. You don't have to stay. Can I drive you somewhere?"

"Actually, I could use a lift to the martial arts club."

I fetch my purse, while he goes to talk to the articling student. A few minutes later, the lawyer guides me outside to his Jaguar parked behind the building. In the car, he turns on the radio and finds a classical music station. "Do you like this kind of music?" he asks.

"Not really. I was born in Detroit and grew up in that area. I like music with some soul. Or rhythm and blues. Something deep. These days I'm into reggae."

"What's that?" He looks at me for a second, then back at the road.

"It's Jamaican, with a strong offbeat. It can be spiritual. Oh, never mind."

He is happy to change the subject. "You'll have to take the LSAT, you know."

"What's that?" I ask.

"The Law School Admission Test. And then you'll need to apply to my law school."

"Geez. That's a lot to do."

By now, we've arrived in front of the club, and he pulls the car up to the curb but leaves the engine on. "I can't come in today," he says. "Maybe next week."

Next week comes, and I catch sight of Criminal Attorney in the public gallery at the front of the club. He's dressed in his business suit and leaves before the class ends. I enjoy it when people watch us train. Spectators boost my energy and give me an edge that transforms the training session into a performance that can help develop confidence. I feel like a star. Even when I'm learning something new, I understand how to be teachable and to not act out.

A few days later, Criminal Attorney is back in the public gallery. After class, I find him pacing outside the club.

"Do you have time for a coffee?" he asks.

"Sure. Let's go across the street to the donut shop."

I order a coffee and a carrot muffin. He gets something too. We take seats near the window.

"Wow, Myra. You're into some intense stuff. Finish-them-off techniques, eh?"

"Yeah. I was training in Taekwondo at the club on Bloor and Yonge when I went to a demonstration by this Kuk Sul Won club. Their skills intimidated me. It took me almost a year to get enough courage to start training with them. It is powerful yet artful. In Kuk Sul Won, you have to show you've killed your opponent. Finish him off, but with elegance."

The lawyer has a serious look on his face. "Why are you into this kind of deadly style?"

"Well, to make a long story short, when I was on Martha's Vineyard a few years ago, I saw the back of this man, a perfect stranger, and sensed he was evil. The next day, he dragged me into the woods and started to strangle me. He never said a word, he just wanted to kill me." I take a sip of coffee, check out the lawyer's body language, and evaluate his level of interest. He seems attentive, so I continue. "I let go into death. I didn't know how to defend myself then, and I was too exhausted from the struggle. I let go into death but came back into life. Among other things, I had to learn martial arts after that." I have decided to not talk about the other divine directives. Maybe at another time.

"I'm sorry to hear what happened to you," he says. "It is good you're training. As a criminal attorney, I know people do bad things for all kinds of reasons. Was he ever caught?"

"Yes, he was. Anyway, that's enough about me. How did you get into martial arts?"

"Well, because of the hard-core criminals I deal with, I never know when someone might lose it or take out a contract on me. How they'll seek revenge if they don't get the results they anticipated. I imagine I'll have to fight my way out of a dark place." A few seconds pass. Then, "Why don't you come to one of my private lessons? You'll find it interesting." Criminal Attorney looks more closely at me. "The club is in downtown Toronto." He tells me the address, and we talk about the LSAT exam and law school applications.

Over the next few days, I find myself eager to train with this lawyer and meet his infamous teacher. When the day finally arrives, my feet seem to fly up the stairs to his club. Once I'm there, however, my initial reaction is disappointment. I am used to modest training places, but this place is dingy and filled with the pungent smell of mildew. His instructor is a wiry, blond-haired guy about six feet tall. He looks like the actor Richard Widmark when he played the neurotic gangster Tommy Udo in the movie *Kiss of Death*.

At least his club has two changing rooms, which is a step up from mine. Not many females train in Kuk Sul Won, so we girls have to kick the master out of his office and change in there.

Now, changed into my always-clean uniform, I join Criminal Attorney in the workout area. We do a few stretches and warm-ups, then Wiry Instructor begins teaching us some rather inelegant street moves to gouge out eyes and ram fingers up nostrils.

Chapter 34

IT IS A BEAUTIFUL, SUMMER afternoon in Toronto. As I walk home from a Kabbalah study session with a friend, I think about buying a Bible. I need it to further my divine directives to learn about the metaphysics and the mystical aspects of the Torah, the tarot, and the Tree of Life. All of a sudden, a loud clattering sound interrupts my contemplations. Not exactly sure where the noise is coming from, I stop and spin around and look in all directions. Usually the streets around here are fairly busy, but now there is neither a car nor another person in sight.

At the corner of the intersection a few yards away, I notice dozens of Canadian quarters scattered on the pavement. Are these coins responsible for the clatter and jingling I just heard? I didn't see anyone throwing the money down. I pick up $5.25 in quarters. They seem like a gift from God. Tomorrow, I'll use these coins to purchase the Jerusalem Bible. I like this translation because of its depth, footnotes, and commentary. Hopefully, one of the used bookstores on Yonge Street will have a copy.

When I head out of my apartment bright and early the next morning, the stores are not open yet. To pass the time, I wander back up the street and get a coffee and hot apple pie at the McDonald's. My plan is to window-shop along the street and move toward the bookstores. Hopefully, one will be open soon.

While I'm looking in the window of a dress shop, a tall and attractive man comes up behind me with a key in his hand. He opens the shop and says, "Good morning. Beautiful day. May I help you?"

"I am just looking at the dresses." I turn to face him. "From your accent . . . are you by chance from Israel?"

"Why, yes. My name is Mir." He sticks out his hand.

A wide smile crosses my face and I shake his hand. "Oh my goodness. My Hebrew name is Mirca."

The man laughs at the coincidence. "Yours is the feminine version of my name. As a verb, it means 'to give light.' It is like turning on a flashlight in a dark room."

"I didn't know that," I say. "I'm on my way to buy a Bible at one of the used bookstores down the street. It's for my Torah studies. If I come back, will you write my Hebrew name in it?"

"Of course."

I leave and head over to the see if the booksellers are open. One is, and on the back wall of the shop, I find a paperback copy of the Jerusalem Bible in good condition. The price marked on the first page comes to the amount I found on the street yesterday, plus twenty-five cents.

Afterwards, I walk back to the dress shop with my Bible in my hand. My new friend from Israel writes my Hebrew name, Mirca, at the top of the last page. He writes it in script style. Under my name, he writes in English, V. To give light.

❀

A few days after the workout with Wiry Instructor, I receive a phone call from Criminal Attorney.

"Myra, I need to talk to you. In person." His voice sounds anxious. It's unusual for him to call me at night. Which leaves me to wonder . . . what's up.

"Can't it wait?" I ask.

"No. Come over to my place. It's important. I'll send a taxi to pick you up." Criminal Attorney hangs up the telephone.

I'm not sure what the urgency is, but I am eager to talk to him. Tonight might be an opportunity to learn more about the criminal mind. I want to ask him why a perfect stranger would kill me. But as I change into a long, flowing, summer dress, a subtle sense of unease comes over me. It was apparent the first day I met this attorney, but I dismissed it then, figuring it was aroused by the color of his suit. To me, a brown suit signifies ambulance chaser, whereas a dark blue suit seems more elegant.

My ambivalence about tonight's meeting also stems from our martial arts session the other day. It was raw, and the lawyer's judgment to train with Wiry Instructor continues to make me suspicious. In any sport or profession, you want to learn from the best. Criminal Attorney's teacher, however, is a nasty street fighter cloaked as a martial artist. My guess is that he was involved in a crime and the lessons might be in exchange for legal representation. But these thoughts get pushed aside by the sound of the taxi horn.

Criminal Attorney greets me at his door and proceeds to give me a tour of his home. "This condo," he says, "is what's left after two divorces. Otherwise, I would be a multimillionaire by now."

To avoid a conversation about his lost money and failed marriages, I comment on the modern décor and the muted colors set against the dark wood, which I like. Noticeably absent are the brown hues. When we reach the master bedroom, Criminal Attorney takes my hand and guides me inside.

The air is motionless and thick with intensity. I have a strong urge to open a window, but this is not my bedroom.

"I want to tell you something," he murmurs.

As I sit on the king-size bed, a lump forms in my throat. Is he going to withdraw his offer to help me get into law school?

Criminal Attorney starts to pace around the room. "I'm falling in love with you, Myra. I'm sure you've guessed it."

"No. Not really." I sense something unspoken. "What's wrong?"

"There's someone else. She's been out of town for three months. I need to tell her in person, my, uh, girlfriend, or, well, my former girlfriend."

He continues to walk around the room and talk. However, once he uttered the word "girlfriend," I shut him out. I am not interested in his drama. Finally, his soliloquy seems to end, and he plops down on the other side of the giant bed, lies back, and stares at the ceiling. I lie on my back and look up too. The moment feels more therapeutic than romantic. Criminal Attorney takes hold of my hand.

After a few minutes of silence, he squeezes it a little harder and says, "It's not going to work out, eh?"

"No. It is not."

We get off the bed and head downstairs, where he calls a taxi for me. I never did have that talk with him about the Evil Man.

And after that night, I do not hear from Criminal Attorney again. It does not matter. Preparations for the LSAT consume me. After the test, there are applications to fill out and send to law schools. I learn that the University of Windsor offers a joint program with the University of Detroit Mercy. You can earn law degrees from both Canada and the United States. A high grade point average is required every year, and before each semester, an academic panel must preapprove your course selections. Extra classes are mandatory during two summers.

Still, it is the only curriculum in North America that grants law degrees from both nations. I think it's well worth the extra effort because of my dual citizenship. Windsor becomes my first choice on my applications. The University of Toronto, where the Criminal Attorney sits on the board of admissions, becomes my hedge and second choice.

Once the LSAT is over and before the application deadline to the law schools has passed, I decide to go see Criminal Attorney again. It is a few months after our disenchanted evening. Despite what happened that night, my intention is to hold him to his offer to help me get into the University of Toronto Faculty of Law school. One afternoon, I have an intuition that tells me to go to his condo, not to his law firm. I put on black jeans, a white T-shirt, and my favorite black walking boots and grab my purse and a sweater on the way out the door.

I notice a bistro at Criminal Attorney's building. Its wall of windows faces the condo entrance, about fifteen yards away. Inside the eatery, the smell of fresh baked goods hits me. I order a coffee and a carrot muffin and then sit at a table next to the windows. It has the best view of anyone entering or leaving the condos. My plan is to stand when the lawyer passes, catch his eye, and then go speak to him.

As soon as I sit, a man in a wheelchair draws up to the table next to mine and sets his drink on it. "Do you mind watching this while I go to the men's room?" he asks me.

With one eye on the windows, I take a quick glance at him. "No problem."

He rolls away. A minute or so after he is a gone, Criminal Attorney exits his building. Another man and a woman walk out with him. The good news is he is walking on the side facing me. Their animated gestures show me the trio is deep in conversation. Before they pass, I stand and wave my arms, hoping to catch the lawyer's attention. (Splayed across the glass, I probably look like a Gumby character.) Unfortunately, the lawyer does not see me.

My body goes limp, and I slump back down into the chair. I take a bite of my muffin and think about running after him. That is probably not wise. I would look even more foolish.

Anyway, the fact that he did not see me is a sign.

My misery is interrupted by a voice. "Thanks for looking out for my drink." It is the guy in the wheelchair. "Excuse me," he adds, "but you look kind of sad. When I left, you seemed happy."

"Yeah, well . . . When you left, my plan to get into law school was easy. But I just found out I'll have to get in on my own merits and without anybody's help. Thanks for asking."

The man has a pleasant, round face and longish, dark hair. He appears to be in his thirties. "Well, you know," he says, "interestingly enough, I'm kind of in the same boat."

"What do you mean, same boat?"

"Do you mind if I move over and talk with you?"

"Please, do." I clear a space for him.

He rolls over and sets his drink down on my table. "If I went to the mineral baths at least once a week, I wouldn't be confined to this." He slaps the sides of the wheelchair.

"Are you serious? What's stopping you?"

"It is hard for me to do it alone. Getting in and out of the wheelchair and then into the mineral bath hurts. So I wait for my sister to come and help. I always feel some pain anyway. But honestly," he pauses, "I'm just lazy. That puts me in the same boat as you. My life has to change. I need to do it on my own merits, just like you said."

"I get it. But wait a minute—I'm not lazy. I never even thought about becoming a lawyer before this attorney recently said he could get me into a good law school. It was his idea."

Round Face nods. "I didn't mean to imply you're lazy. It's me who's lazy." He tells me about the car that smashed into him when he was walking home from high school and the subsequent nerve disorder to his spine and loss of feeling in his legs. He tells me why he's in the wheelchair and about his doctors and his desire to change. He answers my questions in a straightforward and sincere manner. When he talks about all the physical suffering and surgeries he had to endure, it causes tears to well in my eyes. I cannot believe he is too lazy to help himself relieve the pain.

Our meeting is no accident. It is a sign that I must rely on my own merit to get into law school. I must never be lazy. I must approach law school with the discipline of a martial artist. I take a sip of coffee and sit with my thoughts for a moment as my fingers tap out the beat to the reggae tune coming from the boom box behind the bistro's counter.

"I like reggae," Round Face says.

"Me too." My face lights up, and I let out a laugh. "Liking reggae can be taken for code, you know."

"What do you mean?"

"It can mean you like to smoke weed."

Now his face lights up. "I do."

"What a minute." I rummage through my purse for a special little sack. "Found it. I have a chunk of hash and a pipe," I whisper. "Do you want to celebrate that from now on we're going to change our lives?"

"That sounds great."

We gather up our stuff. On our way out, I grab a book of matches from the dish on the counter. Outside, the spring air feels crisp. I take hold of the back of Round Face's wheelchair and push him along as we wander down the street, on the lookout for a secluded spot. Soon we come across a clean-enough alley situated between two closed establishments. After Round Face wheels into the narrow area, I follow and stuff a bit of hash into the bowl of the pipe. I hand it to Round Face for the first hit. We each take a few puffs. The small space quickly takes on the telltale sweet smell. Once the stuff in the bowl is finished, we continue to roam the streets, seeking out more good spots to take more good puffs.

Along the way, we tell each other wonderful stories about how our lives will change and what lies ahead in our futures. Happy, strong, and certain of my destiny, I am now intent on getting into law school. Becoming a lawyer is now my sixth divine directive.

Round Face has his own ideas. "I am going to take long

walks in the forest and on the beaches."

"In law school, I'm going to learn about finance and the corporate and business world. I know nothing about these things."

"Gosh, if someone heard our quixotic conversation, they'd think we're nuts," he says.

"Wow," I say. "That's such a big word."

"What? Quixotic? From *Don Quixote*."

"Never read it. I am a tarot card reader. In the deck I use, we epitomize card seven of the Major Arcana, the Chariot. Whatever the Charioteer imagines, he can manifest. And do you know what?"

"No. What?"

"The Charioteer holds the wheel of fortune in his hands. The wheel could also be symbolic of your wheelchair."

Round Face is silent for a moment. Then he says, "Yes. I love that image." After another minute of silence, he adds, "Do me a favor?"

"What?"

"When you go to law school, don't talk about tarot. Don't even mention that you read the cards. I know a bit about the legal and business worlds because of my injury and my experience in courtrooms. The guy whose car hit me didn't believe the nerve damage was caused by the accident and so we went to trial. I won and was awarded lots of money. Promise me you won't say anything to anybody about being a tarot reader. Never. Not a word. Most people will probably think you are flaky, which is not an appropriate reputation to have as a lawyer."

"Okay, I promise. But only while I am in law school. After I pass the bar exam, I want to practice law and be a professional tarot reader too."

Chapter 35

BY NOW, I HAVE MOVED back to Windsor and once again live with my mother in her apartment. Like the last time, I sleep in the den. Actually, we share the room during the day and in the evenings to watch TV together.

A few months after that fateful meeting at the bistro, a formal invitation arrives from the University of Toronto's law school. As part of the evaluation for admissions, a meeting with me is requested. This face-to-face conversation will help narrow the list of prospective students. Although the legal profession seems exotic, I am ready to learn and am armed for the meeting with the martial arts principles of perception, an indomitable spirit, and a strong sense of discipline.

There is no indication that Criminal Attorney is involved in the law school's selection process. I will never see or hear from him again. The same is true for Round Face.

It is a beautiful summer day on the University of Toronto campus. I feel confident when two girls greet me at the steps of the law library. They represent the selection team and will conduct the interview. I am a bit surprised. I am in my early thirties. The two girls appear to be ten years younger.

One of them motions to me to follow, and they lead me inside the library and down the stairs into the bowels of the building. We move in single file and in silence between the shelves of books in the stacks. On the way, I detect a faint, moldy smell. It gets more pronounced as we pass a caged area against a wall. Inside it are shelves full of old, leather-bound books. I can see the wear and tear on their raised spines. This must be the law school's rare book collection.

A few feet more, and we come to three folding chairs. We each take a seat. Surrounded by shelves of law books, it is close quarters and dimly lit. The girls take turns asking questions. Why do I want to be a lawyer? Why their law school? Why did I become a bookbinder?

Why? What? Who? On and on it goes.

The problem is, I am distracted. My mental martial art skills slip away as the odor of leather bindings wafts over to me, and the neat rows of books almost compel me out of my chair. I'm feeling a strong desire to hold them, to read their titles. This is why my answers are halfhearted. Although I respect their earnestness, the girls' questions sound like chatter.

Interview ended, I leave the library feeling dejected. On the train ride home, I reflect on my poor performance. It was inexcusable. Was it self-sabotage? Or was my intuition at work? Did the school interviewers purposefully pick that location as a test? Perhaps they did not want their current students to see me and bias their admission decision with unwanted telephone calls to support or not support a candidate.

Back in Windsor, I must now wait to hear the results from the various law schools' admissions departments.

❈

It is close to midnight when my mother and I sit across from each other on the pink, floral loveseats in her living room. The atmosphere is easy. My mother and I are chatting about all kinds of things.

Then, out of nowhere, she says, "Myra, remember that time you were strangled? Marla and I went to Cape Cod. We were there by your bedside."

"Of course I remember. I appreciated you being there." Despite my dropping out of the New School, I am eager to hear a good word about my recovery. In anticipation of some motherly stroking, I lean forward.

"Yes," she says, "we got a flight out the next morning to see you. But no one was there for me." Her voice is soft and full of self-pity.

I feel a rage roaring inside me. Tears begin to flow down my face. Before she can say anything else, I run out of the apartment and take the elevator down to the ground floor.

The night air feels warm. I take off my sweater. My mother's place is air-conditioned, but I don't need the sweater out here. It is way past midnight now, and the street is almost deserted. The hotel across the road beckons but I forgot to grab my purse. With no money, I have nowhere to go. Going back inside is not an option, and it's too late to call my friends.

An idea pops in my head. Some might call it foolish. Others might be scared. I walk five blocks toward the familiar iron gates of the Windsor Grove Cemetery. They are closed. Never mind. I hop up and climb over the stone wall where it is the lowest.

After my experience with death, I have no fear of ghouls or goblins. It's live people who can shake me up.

Luckily, there is a bright moon. My plan is to find a grave that's hidden from view. Something seems to guide me, and in no time, I find the perfect spot. On three sides of the plot are tall shrubs. It is too dark to read the headstone, but I can feel and "read" the carved letters. I think it says James Caldwell. To pay homage to whomever, I say a brief prayer, then put my sweater back on and lie down on the warm ground of the grave. Surrounded by the scent of fresh grass, I feel snug and safe and instantly fall fast asleep.

Early next morning, a light rain awakens me. No one is around, so I push myself up off the ground and walk back to the gate, then hop over the fence. I head to a friend's place and find him walking his dog. A gentle fellow and a pastry chef by trade, he lets me sleep on his couch that night. The next morning, I walk over to my girlfriend Tara's place. She's way cool, and her open-mindedness knows enough not to ask any questions. She tells me my mother called. She is looking for me.

"She said you have a job interview at the London Chop House for the hostess position. Geez, you could make a lot of money."

"I know. When I was a kid, my mother told me about that restaurant and nightclub. All the rich and famous go there." About a week ago, Tara had told me about the full-time position and I had applied. The restaurant was looking for someone with a natural elegance, and she thought of me. I felt flattered.

"But I have nothing to wear," is all I can say.

"Your mother says she's sorry. Whatever. You don't have to tell me what it's about. Anyway, she wants you to come home. She will lend you something to wear."

"Okay. Good."

"Hey, you can stay with me 'til you find a place of your own, but don't come back unless you get the job at the Chop House." Tara laughs and gives me a big hug.

❋

Lanie Pincus, the owner of the famous restaurant and nightclub, is a thin, elegant woman who swears by her potato diet. She hires me on the spot. Part of the job is to look gorgeous, which means I'll need more clothes. My mother is thrilled to help me pull together a wardrobe for my work. I've regained my own fashion sense during my travels, but I still defer to my mother's and my sister's tastes in clothes, along with my Aunt Gladys and cousin Bonnie, with whom I started shopping or got trendy hand-me-downs from when I was a toddler and into my teens.

The seating arrangements at the restaurant demonstrate the diner's status. Reservations for dinner are made weeks in advance, and matchbooks printed with the guests' names are set at all seats. The hostesses do this printing on a small letterpress in the office. A hostess might also be called on to wrap up fancy cigars and exotic and expensive perfumes for the guests. The air is permeated with the floral fragrances as the patrons spritz on samples and makes their choice. The wine cellar is world class, and the restaurant brags about having a sommelier who is the first woman to achieve the honor.

Although most of Detroit's hoi polloi cannot afford to eat at the London Chop House, people come in from the business, political, sports, and music industries. When the musical duo Hall and Oates come in without ties, I loan them rather loud ones from the house stock. Bob Seger cries on my shoulder one evening. Blair Underwood, an actor in the TV series *L.A. Law*, is extremely charming, and with Lawrence Taylor, a linebacker for the New York Giants, I just get tongue-tied.

Because my hours can go past midnight, eventually I get my own apartment. It is a one bedroom, across the street and down one from my mother's place.

A couple of months into my working at the Chop House, a letter arrives. This one is from the law school at the University of Windsor. After my sad presentation at the interview at the University of Toronto, a slight case of anxiety has been consuming me. Instead of reading the letter right away, I need to pace around my apartment for a while. Once I'm calm, I tear the envelope open.

I am accepted.

Wow. This school was my first choice. It is a great honor. I immediately pray to God. It seems appropriate. My prayer begs the Divine to work beside me on this legal journey.

Certainly, law school is an opportunity. Like an anthropologist who comes to understand the aspects of a culture, I can gain knowledge of the seemingly esoteric world of contracts and money, corporations and business law, real property law, torts or civil wrongs, and, of course, criminal law. There are required courses in constitutional law and civil and criminal procedures.

To keep mentally focused and physically fit while I'm in law school, I cook lean proteins and vegetable stir-fries in a wok. It is a quick and healthy way to eat. I like to use fermented black beans and garlic, which taste pungent, woody, and salty. Some dishes are made with the sweet, fishy flavor of oyster sauce. I eliminate fast foods from my diet, because I find them heavy and they make me sleepy in class.

I try out something new and take classes in aikido and jump rope in my ground-floor apartment. One day I hear that the 1988 International Olympic Committee has admitted Taekwondo as an official sport for the 2000 Sydney games, but they chose the style from the Toronto club, and not the one from Ottawa.

These days, I am either working, working out, going to law school classes, or doing homework. I still have my Kabbalah and tarot studies too.

Because of the Socratic method used for teaching case law and legal concepts, I must express myself in front of my fellow students. There is no place for shyness in law school. The instructors and professors do not tolerate timidity. In the moot court classes, specific requirements are to be assertive and persuasive in your presentations. Over time, these skills give me a wholesome sense of self-confidence.

The fact patterns, or the facts that form the basis of a legal cause of action and the issues that arise, in the contract law cases visually come alive for me. Often having to do with real estate agents or a broker's shenanigans, they are relatively easy for me to picture and then understand. Over time, I come to rely not only on my logical, rational mind, but also on my intuition to learn more about economics and the law.

By my second year, my grade point average is good enough for me to be accepted into the joint law degree program. My brother makes a generous contribution to support my studies, my sister buys me a car, and my mother chips in too. I am grateful to all of them. During my first year, I took the bus to the University of Windsor. Now the car is useful because some of my courses are still there, while others are across the border at the University of Detroit Mercy, where the law school is located downtown on East Jefferson Avenue. Sometimes I have to speed through customs to make it to a class on time. Luckily, the toll guards and the customs officers come to recognize me.

Again, I fill my studies with the subjects I know the least about—income tax law, international business transactions, jurisprudence, and the conflict of laws. I soon form a study group with a classmate named Jim and a few other students. This is helpful, but I find the legal courses are mostly self-taught, even though you attend lectures by legal experts. I also pray a lot to God for guidance.

Although the legal principles are similar, tackling law schools in two different countries can be extremely demanding. It might seem counterintuitive that neither country recognizes the other's law as authoritative. Canadian citations can be made to English statutes and common law or to other countries within the British Commonwealth, such as Australia and Fiji, but generally not to American legal precedents. There is one area of Canadian jurisprudence that recognizes the United States' legal authority, however. This has to do with property law and not categorizing one's wife as chattel, or the husband's personal possession. In the United States, only a few legal references can be made to the English law, such as the statute of frauds that governs which contracts have to be in writing. Some oral agreements are not enforceable.

While I'm in school in two countries, I quit the Chop House and begin a part-time research position with Professor Howard Abrams, who is currently writing about American copyright law. My focus is on the "work for hire" rules, as distinguished from the US tax code. Next, to do honorable legal work based on years of reading about the Nazis, I take a clerkship with an important law firm in Detroit known for its civil rights and police misconduct cases. All the attorneys and staff in that firm are people of color. I am the token white person, and for some of the paralegals and secretaries, their first contact with a white person.

In my third and final year, I clerk at the Goodman, Eden, Millender & Bedrosian law firm for Bill Goodman, one of the founders of the National Lawyers Guild, a leading, national, civil rights organization. My work for him centers on his police misconduct litigations. He likes the way I reduce the content of voluminous transcripts to bite-size, handwritten documents on yellow legal pads. They help him get ready for trial.

Chapter 36

A HIGHLY, RESPECTED INVESTMENT BANKER, Jamie is married to a Grace Kelly look-alike who is both beautiful and sensible. They now have a gorgeously handsome baby boy. My young nephew is bright and alert, just like his parents. Do I sound biased? Who cares. I still live in Windsor, and so does my mother. Marla resides in Santa Barbara, California, and is pursuing a certificate from the Brooks Institute, a world-renowned photography school. While I'm visiting her during my law school breaks, I become enchanted with the city.

It is now late spring of 1992. I've recently earned two law degrees but did not attend the convocation ceremony at either the University of Windsor or the University of Detroit Mercy. Like the uncomfortable feeling I get when people compliment me, formalities that even slightly focus on me have the same effect and cause me to want to leave. Maybe it has something to do with being the second-born twin who wants to hide behind her sister. Anyway, I deem these types of events unnecessary and just don't attend them.

When a letter arrives from the State Bar of Michigan, I feel some trepidation. I open the envelope and find a letter congratulating me for having passed the most recent bar exam. I'm so excited, I want to call the Criminal Attorney, and share this moment with him. Why I think he would care, I don't know. I have not seen or talked to him since that fateful evening almost four years ago at the bistro in Toronto. Never mind. I call operator assistance and ask for the telephone number of his law firm. Then I place the call. A receptionist answers and refers to him as the judge. When I ask about that, she tells me he was appointed to the criminal bench a few years ago and is currently out of the office. I don't leave a message.

It's time to move on.

On the basis of having passed the Michigan bar exam, I line up job interviews with leading civil rights firms in the Detroit area. Goodman, Eden is not hiring any associates at the moment, but it gives me an excellent letter of reference. A few law firms call me back for second and third interviews. A prominent firm even offers me a job. But now my mind is made up. I do not respond. My plan is to visit Marla in Santa Barbara.

This beautiful city, which is nestled between the Santa Ynez Mountains and the Pacific Ocean, is an ancient sacred site of the Chumash, an indigenous people. They believe the Great Spirit guided them to Santa Barbara more than five thousand years ago. I feel pulled to Santa Barbara too. My sense is that Santa Barbara is a suitable city for me to be both an attorney and a professional tarot reader.

A mystic entered law school and emerged as a lawyer. With two law degrees from two countries with differing legal systems, my concern is whether or not the legal profession will forever silence my questing soul. Now, my soul beseeches me to not keep the mystical parts of myself hidden any longer. Round Face warned me about the consequences of talking about the tarot in law school, and I kept my promise to keep quiet. The legal community in Michigan is not even remotely interested in understanding the metaphysics of the tarot or its relationship to the mystical Kabbalah.

Plans for my upcoming trip to Los Angeles and Santa Barbara include some solid job interviews with a few firms that handle federal law matters. Okay, I still need to get sworn in to the Michigan bar, but that is just a ceremony conducted by a judge, plus some more paperwork to file. As with my two graduation ceremonies, I choose not to participate in the big swearing-in ceremony for the Michigan bar. Instead, I visit Marla.

I've always dreamed about living in California, where I can look out my windows and see palm trees. A Los Angeles law firm that specializes in immigration cases hires me part-time to assist in its appellate cases for the Court of Appeals for the Ninth Circuit. Once I am sworn in, in Michigan, one of the lawyers agrees to sponsor me for admission to the Ninth Circuit Court. My ambition is to get onto the Ninth Circuit's court-appointed criminal appellate panel, which handles appeals for defendants who meet a standard of indigence. I have no idea how to go about this. Nor does anyone else I contact, not even the clerks at the Ninth Circuit. But even though they have no idea what I am talking about, I must heed this legal calling.

My job for the immigration attorneys involves researching federal law and drafting appeal documents relevant to denials of applications for political asylum. This concerns internationally recognized human rights. My task is to write a persuasive argument showing the immigration judge was wrong, and the applicants do have a well-founded fear of persecution or death if the United States denies them entry and sends them back to their countries of origin. Although I will live in Santa Barbara, the plan is for me to commute to Los Angeles when necessary. As an independent contractor, I can do most of the work on my own.

After a month-long visit and getting my job details squared away, my sister and I fly back to Windsor to pack or sell my stuff. We intend to drive my car back to Santa Barbara. While in the Detroit area, I arrange to get admitted to the Michigan bar, even though I missed the big swearing-in ceremony a couple of months ago. This admission includes the state courts and the federal Court of Appeals for the Sixth Circuit. It also makes me eligible for admission to all the other federal appellate courts, such as the Ninth Circuit.

When I telephone Mike, an attorney at Goodman, Eden, he agrees to be my Michigan sponsor. He is a great lawyer—fun, bright, and hip. Jamie cannot make the trip to Detroit, but he sends me a gift. It's a gorgeous, black leather, Mark Cross briefcase. My swearing-in ceremony is held at the famous Wayne County Courthouse in downtown Detroit. Wearing a stunning, shocking, pink business suit with a floral, short-sleeve top, I feel and look great. Marla is in her original Jean-Paul Gaultier outfit. Mike looks debonair in a dark blue suit. Mom looks beautiful too, but she's somewhat depressed because she knows I am leaving town for good. I will miss her too.

The judge is an attractive, young woman. She addresses Mike, who stands and says, "I am Myra's sponsor. After working with her, I have found she has the qualities that make for an extraordinary lawyer."

A couple of days later, Marla suggests I put a classified ad in the *Windsor Star*. "Have a yard sale," she tells me. "Sell everything, and let's get the hell out of here. Fast." Sifting out what I'll really need from my saleable belongings becomes a matter of size rather than importance. Everything going with me has to fit into my car. I have no money to ship goods and no room for storage, as I plan to live with my sister.

Sale day is a beautiful, sunny day. A law school friend from Senegal stops by for a look-see. "Myra," he tells me, "you ask too much money for your goods. These things should be way less expensive."

Nevertheless, he buys me out of pots and pans. Others come and shop too. With some regrets, every single piece of my furniture, my pictures, clothes, shoes, and books are sold. I even sublet the remainder of my apartment rental agreement.

After the sale, Marla, my friend from Senegal, and I attend a political rally in Detroit together. The gathering is for Bill Clinton's vice-presidential candidate, Al Gore. We drive across the border and park downtown. When we walk to the rally, our trio happens to bump into Bill Goodman, the famous civil rights lawyer I clerked for. He is on his way home from a day at the law office.

A few days later, my car packed and our goodbyes said to our mother, my twin and I take off for our road trip to Santa Barbara, California. Because of the Al Gore rally, we have decided to make a detour and visit Arkansas, where Bill Clinton is completing his last term as governor. He hopes to become the forty-second president of the United States. But many of the folks we meet in Arkansas are upset with him. They say he made them a promise and broke it when he ran for higher office.

Chapter 37

ALMOST SIX MONTHS AFTER MOVING to Santa Barbara, I receive a phone call. It is my friend Mike from the Goodman, Eden law firm. We chat a bit, and then he tells me that Bill Goodman wants me to move back to Detroit to handle an international case for the law firm. It originated across the border at a strip club in Windsor. I can't help but laugh. My hometown is the capital of Canada's strip clubs and fur coat stores. Then I get more serious and want to know more about the case.

Mike fills me in.

When he is finished, I feel honored that Mr. Goodman would ask to work with me, but don't want to move back east. Mike is disappointed to hear I won't take the job offer. Instead, I provide him with names of people to question about the incident. They might help establish some of the facts of the case. One person is a girl called Betty the Boop. She is the driver of the strip club bus that tos and fros the guys from Detroit to the Windsor clubs. Then there's my friend, whom he has met. She is the former stripper who now owns a shoe store. She'll know all the gossip. Also, I know a criminal attorney in Windsor. He handles a lot of cases for strippers. Finally, there's my third cousin on my father's side who owns the big strip club on Riverside Drive.

Mike thanks me, and I invite him to visit me in Santa Barbara.

A few months later, he does come for a visit. He tells me Bill Goodman almost fell out of his chair laughing when he gave him the names of my colorful contacts. But they turned out to be fruitful.

The truth is, I want to live in Santa Barbara. It is a walking city. The stunning Spanish architecture of some of the buildings are theaters for my eyes. Strict ordinances prohibit any structure from being more than two or three stories high, which gives almost everyone a view of either the mountains or the Pacific Ocean or both. The weather is mostly great. Well, sometimes it's too hot, but California is in a drought right now. I am told there has not been a cloud in the sky for years.

❧

By 1995, my association with the immigration law firm has ended, and for the past four years, I have been assisting various attorneys in Santa Barbara and Los Angeles. Because I am not admitted to the California bar, my work is limited to doing legal research and drafting documents. It hasn't always been easy. My brother and sister have aided me financially and emotionally, and my mother is always available to talk on the telephone. But I do not want to burden my family and friends, so I have sought the help of Jungian therapists in interpreting my dreams. I also take Kabbalah workshops with a number of rabbis.

While I'm doing legal research, my professional tarot reading business, called Insight Tarot, starts to blossom. It might be due to my working deeply on myself during this "black and blue" period.

I even gain an event-booking manager. He found me through my tarot reading ad in the classified section of the *Santa Barbara Independent*. We've never met. He arranges everything by phone and leaves my check under his front door mat. My only requirement for doing tarot readings is to get paid beforehand.

Thanks to the event manager, I do a number of tarot reading events, such as a private wedding held at the Cold Spring Tavern, which features the country-blues-rock-jazz music group, the Marshall Tucker Band. The Tavern is a California landmark. Once a rest stop for stagecoach travelers and their horses to relax and eat on the journey through the San Marcos Pass, it now features great bar food and local bands.

The late afternoon air is still warm, which is good. The event hostess sets up my tarot table outside the old saloon. Around me, performers dressed in rodeo and cowgirl outfits and jugglers from the Old South mingle with the guests of the soon-to-be bride and groom. Excitement is also in the air. This is a precursor party. Their wedding is in two days.

Because of the number of people waiting for readings, the readings are limited to ten minutes per person. One person I read for is a woman who was once the personal secretary to an important person in the White House. Her husband is into kinky sex and sneaking around. A divorce is imminent. Later that evening, I read for a man who is into extremely, unconventional sex. I put two and two together. He's the woman's husband.

Even though she lives in Washington, DC, the woman becomes a regular client of mine. After she's done some of her tarot homework, she schedules additional sessions to be conducted over the telephone.

At the two-day Renaissance Faire near Ojai, my booth is adorned with large landscape photographs taken by my sister, gorgeous images in contrast to the day's rain and the mucky grounds. Despite the drab sky, I notice this attractive man who seems to glow. Next to him is a blonde woman pushing a baby stroller through the mud. A few minutes later, she and the baby and the stroller are in my booth. Turns out, the man is a former, third-string quarterback on an NFL team. The cards reveal a love-at-first-sight romance, a wedding with another man canceled at the eleventh hour, new beginnings with the quarterback, and a lot more.

At Santa Barbara's Summer Solstice Celebration, I do readings for a dollar a minute. Because of the long lines, I read for four hours straight. The same timeframe applies at a Big Dog corporate event and at the California Association of Flower Growers and Shippers annual convention. In a few years, my event manager arranges for me to be the guest tarot reader at the famed San Ysidro Ranch for its New Year's Eve, New Millennium Party. (But I am getting ahead of myself.)

Thanks to these events and my advertisements, I acquire a few private clients. Two are professors from Stanford University who encouraged me to write an article on the World Court for inclusion in the publication, *Human Rights Encyclopedia* (Sharpe Reference), with a foreword written by Aung San Suu Kyi. Another man owns a Las Vegas casino and talks like the gangster, I am still sure he is. I also intuit that a woman I read for is currently under the US Federal Witness Protection Program and is using an assumed name and identity.

For the tarot readings, I now use the Tree of Life layout and have dropped the need to test my intuition by first picking the pile that holds the Hierophant card. Instead, I open a private reading session, or begin an event, with one of the oldest Kabbalistic prayers, the *Ana Be'Koach*, which is related to the Tree of Life and is built on the forty-two-letter Hebrew name of God. I also say this prayer as a meditative chant each morning.

After doing hundreds and hundreds of tarot readings, I've yet to meet a dull person. Everyone has extraordinary qualities, but many people are blocked or conflicted. The tarot allows people to perceive inclinations that are below the level of everyday consciousness and gain insights into their circumstances. Working with the Tree of Life reading can bring individuals back to a state of balance and unblock their energetic flow. The intuitive understandings help to see a way forward when before they cannot see the way.

※

On the personal side, while I do not belong to a martial arts club, I now train in my own routines and workouts. Besides that, I jog along the oceanfront walkway or up the foothill behind Marla's condo, and she and I go hiking in the mountains around Santa Barbara twice a week.

My friend Trevor Goss, the famed artist, introduces me to Chris, a sea captain who looks like the actor Robert Mitchum. Within three seconds of meeting him, I know we will date for a long time and be friends forever. Chris has bright blue eyes that show the depth of his character. Although he looks rugged, our talk soon takes on a spiritual tone. His mystical knowledge and innate leadership skills inspire me. I like his sense of style and immediately fall in love with him.

※

It has been almost two decades since my encounter with death on Martha's Vineyard. Most of the time, I have been focused on mastering the five divine directives given to me after the incident and, given ten years later, the sixth directive to become a lawyer. This pursuit has led me to move to the other edge of the continent and to learn meditation as a way to connect to my inner voice and with the Divine. I was also motivated to train in martial arts and to come in touch with the knowledge within my body. Stirred to learn about meaningful coincidences, I wrote my honors thesis on the topic of creative discovery in the scientific enterprise. My death experience inspired me to learn about metaphysics, the tarot, and its association to the vast mysticism of the Kabbalah. The sixth directive was met when I earned my two law degrees and became a Michigan lawyer and was then admitted to the Court of Appeals for the Ninth Circuit.

Some aspect of my death experience is always playing out in my mind. It is the metaphorical crystal that I keep in my back pocket and take out to view the world. In all this time, I have blotted out from my memory the Evil Man's actual name. I don't even know what happened to him. The fact that my memory has failed me here is ironic, because in law school a student must have a good memory. I relied on mine to pass all those exams and during my clerkships. As a lawyer, I still rely on my memory.

But now, everything seems to remind me of the Evil Man and when he strangled me. I'm watching TV, and I click through the channels and come upon a Canadian drama series named *Two*. I have never seen this show before. It involves a professor framed for murder. He discovers he has a twin, who is the probable person who committed the crime. This week's episode has the FBI's profile team assembled to address the topic of serial killers. The real-life team is famous for its unique type of investigating. They pull together facts from evidence the detectives have gathered and create a personality prototype of the likely suspect.

In tonight's show, one of the FBI profilers says, "If a serial killer is married, then most often he kills when he is on a leave of absence from his family. For example, while on business trips or during visits alone to take care of personal family business and when the spouses are on separate vacations."

This remark intrigues me, well, the fictional twin angle not so much, but I remember something the Massachusetts state police officer told me in my hospital room. She said the Evil Man was married. His wife had red hair, whereas mine is dark brown. They have a child. He and his family lived together in Syracuse, New York. The officer said he went to Martha's Vineyard with only his brother in tow. He was away from his wife and child. Considering, the police office said, that he had a prior claim of attempted rape while he was in the military, the Evil Man fits the FBI profilers' description of a serial criminal.

Okay. Okay. I know. It's a television show. Nevertheless, I think it's time to get this investigation of my murder going again. I need to learn things about the Evil Man. But all I can remember is the name of the facility where he was held while the experts were determining if he was fit to stand trial. The Sexually Dangerous Institute might be a mnemonic I made up, but now I have to find out about this place and what happened to the man who left me for dead.

Chapter 38

EVERY COUPLE OF MONTHS, MY dear friend Gail throws a Sunday afternoon salon at her home, which features a large, wraparound, outdoor deck and a world-class view of Santa Barbara, the mountains, and the ocean. For a $15 donation, attendees are serenaded by the smooth sounds of Woody on the piano and Hank on the bass, and their world-class jazz group. A cold and hot buffet from the Fresco Café includes the best-ever eggplant parmesan that's loaded with thick slices of aubergine. All the proceeds received from the huge crowds who attend the famous salons go to charities.

Gail is a "babe." We met about four years ago when I was looking for independent contract work assisting attorneys in Santa Barbara with legal research and drafting documents. At the time, almost everyone I met referred me to her. It could have been the function of the crowd I hung out with, for they all remarked on how highly ethical and fair she is.

An imposing person, both in the physical sense and in her personality, Gail is also a glower. Her smile and spiritual warmth emanate from her being. Big boned by nature, she has an even bigger heart, though she can also be as tough as a tank. She is about thirteen years older than me, but I often think she is my age. Gail is the recipient of multiple awards, such as the Santa Barbara Foundation Woman of the Year and other state and local commendations.

From her, I learn more about the soul engaged in good citizenship and best business practices. Initially a student volunteer for the Legal Aid Foundation of Santa Barbara, she eventually rose to become its director. She is also a pioneer advocate for alternative dispute resolutions and has been a mediator for more than eighteen years. She was one of the first in the nation.

It is now the spring of 1996. At Gail's monthly salon, I chance to overhear a distinguished and uniquely colorful gentleman, who is wearing a bright beanie and a vest, say he is a forensic psychiatrist and has just been to a play about Carl Jung. His name is Ron, and he is also a lawyer.

I introduce myself and ask, "Ron, have you heard of the Sexually Dangerous Institute?"

He responds with a long-winded story that does not quite answer my question, then finally confesses, "I've never heard of the place. Why do you ask?"

But I have another question for him. "How long does it usually take to determine if a person, a defendant, is fit to stand trial?"

"Honestly, within five minutes of talking to someone, you know if they are rational or delusional. However, a fitness determination could take as long as two to three weeks."

Our talk now turns to another subject, and when I say something about spirituality, he looks straight at me and asks, "How do you define spirituality?"

"I am beyond the dictionary stage in my understanding."

"Myra, have you ever had a spiritual experience?"

"Yes. Plenty. I refer to them as transcendental or mystical experiences."

"Tell me about one of them."

And so, for the next few minutes, Ron listens to the story about the Evil Man. Because I know he's interested in Carl Jung, my telling stresses the transcendental aspects of the experience, something I kept from the Massachusetts State Troopers and the Martha's Vineyard and Boston police.

"I am an internet fanatic," he says when I finish the story. "And I'm the head of a chat group. I promise to send an email to my forensic psychiatrist cyberspace group and ask them about this Sexually Dangerous Institute you mentioned. Someone is bound to have heard of the place."

"The institute existed in 1978," I tell him, "but I'm not sure if it's in Massachusetts or somewhere else."

"If it's there, we will find it," he assures me. "Give me your email address, and I'll let you know."

The week after I meet Ron, replies to his inquiry start arriving in my email inbox. The first one says, "We've hit pay dirt with Bridgewater." Most responses point to a place in Massachusetts called Bridgewater State Hospital and the Treatment Center for Sexually Dangerous Persons.

Pieces of the puzzle are starting to fall into place. I wonder about the Evil Man's behavior and demeanor. It must have been disturbing enough to compel the judge to order a determination of his fitness to stand trial. Simply speaking, "Competency to stand trial" is a not a decision about criminal responsibility or a finding at trial that someone is insane or is not guilty by reason of insanity. A concern about someone's fitness to stand trial arises in the initial phase of the court proceedings. A determination must be made that the defendant understands the charges against him (or her) and the legal consequences and that they can aid in their own defense. If found "not fit," a defendant can be confined to an institution for care.

More memories of the Evil Man begin to surface. I remember the newspaper article that Victor brought to my hospital bedside. It stated my name and also named the man being held in police custody. The first time I read the piece, it made me furious. The *Vineyard Gazette* reporter probably obtained his information from reading the police reports or talking to the officers. I felt the newspaper had invaded my privacy and maybe jeopardized my well-being, and my twin sister's too, by reporting my name. Now I am hopeful that the newspaper's librarian can give me the Evil Man's name. I search the *Vineyard Gazette*'s website to get its telephone number. Because there is a three-hour difference between the West Coast and the East Coast, the newspaper would be closed now. I will call them tomorrow morning.

Dawn finds me in a bit of a daze and slightly nervous. I need to figure out what to say. "Hello, I'm the girl you wrote about over nineteen years ago who was strangled on your island" seems too brash.

Instead, I make the call and ask the receptionist if she can transfer me to the librarian, to whom I say, "Please, can you help me locate a newspaper article that was published around the fall of 1978? It would have been late September. It was in regard to an attempted murder of Myra Mossman."

"Yes, I can help you with that. One moment while I take a look." A few minutes later, the librarian is back on the phone. "There was no article accessible under the name Myra Mossman. I've been on staff since 1980, and maybe the prior librarian had indexed it differently. Can you reveal a little more of your story to me?"

I give her a brief description of the events.

"I have an idea," she says. "Perhaps it is in our rape file. Hold the line."

"Yes, go ahead," I say, "but I wasn't a rape victim." It's interesting how everyone seems to view this crime as a sexual one rather than a murder. The Evil Man was charged with an attempted murder.

The librarian is back on the line and somewhat out of breath. "I found it."

"Wow. Thank you. Please, can you tell me the name of the man held in custody?"

"The article is dated September 26, 1978. It is about a Canadian girl named Myra Mossman being the victim of an attempted murder and attempted rape. The article goes on to say the suspect in custody is John S. Lasinski—"

"Can you repeat the name?"

"John S. Lasinski." She spells it out for me.

Now I have it! I had totally buried the man's name, hidden John S. Lasinski from my consciousness. After all these years, now a door begins to open. I try to keep my voice calm. "Are there any follow-up articles?"

To my surprise, she says yes. There are two other articles. "One moment," she says, "while I look over the next article." Again, I hold for a minute or two. "Okay," she says. "It concerns the psychiatric finding that Lasinski was not sexually dangerous and the plea of guilty to assault and battery. The next follow-up was due to some local interest in the case. It was the first time someone on Martha's Vineyard had been confined for so long in the county jail. Two and a half years." She offers to mail me copies of the three articles. I give her my address and express my appreciation for her help.

My stomach starts to hurt.

Chapter 39

I ONLY HAVE TO WAIT a few days for the copies to arrive. The envelope is a standard business size with the newspaper's logo as the return address. It is hand-addressed to me. How quaint. I rip it open and a single sheet of paper flutters to the floor. I see photocopies of the three articles, reduced in size and arranged to fit on one page.

The first report I saw when Victor brought the newspaper to me in my hospital room. The second is new to me.

Gay Head Attack
Victim Recovers

A 23-year-old Ontario woman has recovered from the serious injuries she sustained when she was dragged from a Gay Head road and nearly strangled to death Sept. 23.

The man charged with attempted murder, attempted rape and assault and battery in the matter pleaded innocent to all charges in his hearing before the Dukes

County District Court. Judge Herbert C. Tucker ordered John S. Lasinski of Syracuse, NY to Bridgewater State Hospital for a 20-day observation period.

The 30-year old defendant was arrested within six hours of the incident, his vehicle recognized by police from the victim's description.

Myra Mossman says she was returning to a friend's Lobsterville home from a beach walk when Mr. Lasinski's truck parked ahead of her. About three quarters of a mile from her destination, she says, Mr. Lasinski grabbed her from behind and dragged her into the bushes.

The victim says she remembers fighting violently with her assailant until she lost consciousness. Miss Mossman says she next recalls recovering to discover the man gone. Her blouse was torn from her body in the struggle.

Victor Frankel, 27, the victim's friend, heard her screaming. From his father's house, he says, he spotted Miss Mossman running up the driveway.

The Communication Center was immediately alerted and Mr. Frankel and Miss Mossman say Kenneth Belain, the Gay Head police chief, and Officer Michael Marshall were soon at the house.

The police got a description of the man and the truck he was driving from Miss Mossman before transporting her to the Martha's Vineyard Hospital in the Tri-Town ambulance.

Miss Mossman was transferred that evening to Falmouth Hospital. She remained in intensive care three days. The hyoid bone in her neck was broken but her stay was lengthened because doctors were troubled by possible damage to her windpipe and resulting respiratory complications. Fortunately she says, no serious problems were found.

W. James O'Neill Jr., the first assistant district attorney in Philip Rollins' office, says he expects Mr.

Lasinski's 20-day observation period to be automatically extended upon request by hospital officials.

If the defendant is found to be incompetent, Mr. O'Neill says he could be committed by the court to the state mental hospital. If there is some uncertainty, he said, a probable cause hearing on Mr. Lasinski's charges and the matter of criminal responsibility is likely.

(Date Stamped October 13, 1978.)
(Used by permission of the *Vineyard Gazette*)

The third article is also new to me

Convicted Attacker Will Serve
Term in Dukes County Jail

Thirty-year-old John S. Lasinski is the first long term resident anyone can recall in the recent history of the century old Dukes County Jail. Wednesday, it was determined that Mr. Lasinski is not a sexually dangerous man.

Mr. Lasinski's two-and-a-half year sentence was made directly from the bench of the Dukes County Superior Court. Choosing to waive his right to a jury trial, Mr. Lasinski pleaded guilty to a single charge of assault and battery before Judge Joseph S. Mitchell Jr. The more serious complaints – assault and battery with attempt to rape and assault and battery with attempt to murder – were not pressed by the Commonwealth.

The Syracuse man appeared before the county's highest court after an incident last September. He attacked a Canadian woman, a visitor to the Vineyard, as she walked down Lobsterville Road in Gay Head.

This week in the third and final week of criminal and civil business, Dr. Charles Saltzman, a private psychiatrist and a consultant to Bridgewater State

Hospital, told the court that Mr. Lasinski is not sexually dangerous.

Dr. Saltzman said the defendant does not need further evaluation at the state hospital nor did he need to be enrolled in the facility's sexually dangerous treatment program. Dr. Saltzman examined Mr. Lasinski at the Dukes county jail. Judge Mitchell returned Mr. Lasinski to the Dukes County jail. He has been there since early winter, painting, building and sprucing up the old jailhouse where cell doors are still locked and unlocked with a single, large church key.

The bricks, all exposed and all chipped, were scrapped and scrubbed by Mr. Lasinski and painted. The colors may not be bright – the floors are gray, the walls and ceiling white – but it's clean and infinitely more livable, Christopher S. Look Jr., the county sheriff, said.

Sheriff Look figures Mr. Lasinski's labor – supervised by the jailer on duty – have saved the county almost $5,000 in labor costs. The work done to date was required by the state correctional department demanding certain minimum conditions in all jails.

For Mr. Lasinski, the work has kept him busy and closer to his family. A wife and young son can more easily visit him on the Vineyard, he said, where there are relatives with whom they may spend weekends and overnights.

Mr. Look said the county is also saving the costs of incarceration in Barnstable. "It would cost us $22 a day for someone staying there and we get nothing out of it. This way, it costs us only $8.00, all the jailers have to be there anyway, and we've gotten a hell of a lot of work done."

When a Gazette reporter visited the county jail, Mr. Lasinski was painting the bars a predictable gray. On the second floor, a separate sitting room has been made by fencing off access (or escape). There, Mr. Lasinski and the jailers have made a bookshelf for a reasonable, if small, collection of books and magazines. A portable television gives a constant if blurry picture.

"I'm grateful to be able to stay here, and I don't mind the work," Mr. Lasinski said.

(Date Stamped Friday, June 1, 1979.)

(Used by permission of the *Vineyard Gazette*)

I was never interviewed for those newspaper reports. They are not factually accurate. Police Chief Belain was not present at Victor's house that day. Maybe he was outside having a cigarette, but I never saw him in the living room or when the ambulance took me away. The October 13 article mentions that I experienced a loss of consciousness. What I actually told the police officer was I let go into death. The "loss of consciousness" is not factually true. And I was dragged through the woods, not just bushes. The June 1 article failed to mention that before Lasinski is released from jail, he will have to undergo a psychiatric evaluation. The court wants a doctor's finding that Lasinski is still not sexually dangerous and should not be confined for a longer duration.

Also, the reports of Lasinski as the first-ever Martha's Vineyard resident to be convicted of a violent crime plays on my mind and leaves me feeling unsettled. "First ever" sounds like "making history" to me, the history of a quaint, upper-crust, New England enclave. But those on the island don't know the half of it. They might have a sense of a historical first, but they don't have the whole picture. Neither do Lasinski, the state troopers, the Coast Guard, the doctors, the nurses, or anyone from the district attorney's office. Believing these people would not understand, I never told any of them about my intuitions or the transcendental and psychic nature of my experiences before, during, and after the attack that left me for dead. I never mentioned or alluded to the five divine directives. And now, ironically, the sixth directive to become a lawyer gives my story more credibility.

My phone conversation with the librarian left me feeling sad. Now, after reading the articles, I am depressed. Lasinski didn't get a prison sentence. He was awarded a paid vacation on Martha's Vineyard. Surely, his wife also had a treat when she visited him.

Maybe a walk to the Old Mission Santa Barbara will do me good. Maybe it will calm my sense of injustice. Still an active church and a retreat center, the Santa Barbara Mission, built by the Franciscan monks in 1786, is the tenth in a string of twenty-one missions strung along the coast of California. The building is about a half-hour trek from my apartment. A few years back, I did some hand bookbinding with an old monk who ran the mission's bindery. Now as I walk, I think about the articles I've just read and the newly found facts concerning the Evil Man's arrest, conviction, and incarceration. But as I come closer to the mission, my internal dialogue changes. *You're here for a reason. You're here to learn something.* These are the same potent words that filled my thoughts right before Lasinski attacked me and left me for dead.

The middle of the day is the hottest part. By the time I reach the mission, the sun is blasting down on Santa Barbara. This old church is capable of transporting me out of time and cleansing me of my negative moods. I bathe in its cool shade, then head for the rose garden across the road. Even though it is too early in the day for most of the roses to release their scents, I stick my nose inside a few of the blooms and inhale their velvety fragrance. Because of the heat, I am somewhat reluctant to walk any farther, but at the same time I am pulled toward a small, woodsy area to the left of the flowerbeds, a series of dirt paths running through trees and a grassy meadow.

The trails beckon. Minutes later, they coax me to go farther. I find myself in an unfamiliar area. Just ahead, hidden by trees, stands what looks like a heap of large stones. Once I get closer, I see the rocks are not a heap, but an old ruin. Then I see the wooden sign in front of the stone structure: Jail House. Only one room remains. I walk inside and reach out to touch the cool, bare walls. It is a small space. Even though the roof is long gone and there is no door to shut, I suddenly feel like an inmate confined in this ruin of a jail cell. Standing here brings alive in me a sense of the Evil Man's punishment. I rush outside and sit on the nearest large rock.

I'm suddenly convinced there is meaning to this coincidence. I've found a jail. It feels like a personal, private, anthropological discovery. I know of other ruins in the area: old tannery vats and a stone reservoir constructed about the same time as the mission, but the old jail is new to me. My walk to the mission was meant to help me process Lasinski's sentence, which the newspaper described more as a retreat on an island resort instead of time served for a violent crime.

As I sit beside the old jail house, the mission bells ring out, connecting me to a sense of community. The music guides me to contemplate a society's duty not only to justice but also to mercy. My compassion deepens. I feel a new empathy for all who are held captive.

Now the ringing stops. Soon the surrounding area—and my mind—become quiet again. I begin to meditate, breathing deeply and calming my thoughts. Suddenly I can see Lasinski. I imagine him after he attacked me. Sitting in a bar, having a beer with the bartender. A black and white police car is parked out front. I'm outside the bar and can see the car's flashing lights under the dark night sky. The doors of the bar open, and Lasinski is brought out in handcuffs. They have Mirandized him and warned him of his legal rights. Lasinski is put in the back of the police car, and it takes off.

I imagine I am in the car too. Within minutes, Lasinski slumps down in the seat, sniffling and wailing. He seems to be out of control and is muttering something about "killing her, killing her." When the police book him, he appears to be a broken wretch standing behind the bars of his cell. I feel his fear, his hopelessness, his despair. I feel his exhaustion. The officers need corroborating evidence to match Lasinski's story that he killed someone. They arrange a photo array to be prepared for me. At his arraignment, the judge wonders if this guy is even fit to stand trial.

This is my imagination at work. I'm guessing about Lasinski's behavior. It is behavior that would cause the police, the district attorney, and a judge to wonder about the suspect's capacity to stand trial.

I sit in contemplation on the large rock near the old jail a little longer, then go home.

A while later, I do an internet search, this time for John S. Lasinski from Syracuse, New York. Another result shows his name on a church organization committee sponsors' dinner. Well, well, well. Lasinski might be a white, married, God-fearing Christian, family man. In many American communities, he would be considered the "perfect neighbor." He would be someone no one would suspect of committing murder.

Perhaps I could notify the pastor and ask him to arrange a meeting with Lasinski and me. But what would I say to the pastor? Hello, I am the girl who was strangled and left for dead by one of your parishioners. Or at least I think it was him. Could you arrange a meeting, so I can ask if he was the one who killed me?

But just the thought of meeting the Evil Man again dredges up old fears. I drop the idea.

Chapter 40

SPIRITUALLY SPEAKING, KNOWING GAIL IS saving my life in Santa Barbara. Since we became friends, I feel rooted here. She gives me a sense of family. We celebrate the Jewish High Holidays together. Our connectedness has become more acute because I'm so far away from my family. Marla has moved to Venice Beach, near Los Angeles, to pursue her art. She currently has a fantastic show, Persona Portraits. It's a series of self-portrait photographs that are hand-colored over and around her face to express totally different characters. Jamie and his wife live in Connecticut and now have a second child. My handsome nephew is alert like his older brother and cuddly, but also good at playing possum. My mother lives in Windsor for part of the year, and in the winter migrates to North Miami Beach, where she stays in my brother's condo until May.

At one of her monthly salons, Gail pulls me aside and says, "I want you to meet this intelligent woman. Brightest person I know. You two will get along fabulously."

"Okay," I reply. Over the years, Gail has introduced me to many wonderful people, and so I follow her toward a thin, mannish-looking woman with short hair and neatly dressed in pants and a jacket.

"Myra, this is Victoria. She was a child prodigy. Her poetry and artwork were published in *Seventeen* magazine. Now she's an accomplished playwright and director, and I've produced a few of her plays in Santa Barbara. Victoria, Myra reads the tarot."

"Oh, you do! How interesting. What deck do you use?"

"Crowley's."

Victoria tells me she designed her own deck, and we immediately get into a deep discussion about the cards. I also learn she is a lesbian by choice and brags that she married a man but got divorced when she found out he expected her to cook and clean house. She is about twenty-three years older than me. Yes, a wise, old woman. When I tell her about the Holy Tree of Life layout I use in the tarot readings and for my own studies, her face lights up.

In March 1998, we establish the Santa Barbara Kabbalah Study Group. At first, just we two are the members. We meet once a week and discuss the tarot, the Kabbalah, and the Holy Tree of Life. In our sessions, we also read *Kabbalah: Tradition of Hidden Knowledge,* written by Z'ev ben Shimon Halevi, and the ancient Kabbalistic text, the *Sefer Yetzirah,* translated by Rabbi Aryeh Kaplan. We also examine the origins of numbers to help us understand the tarot's Minor Arcana cards. We pursue other avenues of interest too, such as listening to spiritual music that moves us, and we hold a special workshop on the Nine Muses of Greek mythology. Our study group is a godsend to me in fulfilling my divine directive to learn and master an "occult" metaphysics. When we begin our group, little do we know it will continue for more than twenty years.

Then Gail and her partner Peter join the Kabbalah study group. Peter is a blond-haired, blue-eyed attorney. When I first moved to Santa Barbara, people who told me about Gail also mentioned that Peter was a good and honest lawyer. Now, years later, it makes sense that they are a couple.

Late in 1998, I finally locate the supervisor for the Ninth Circuit's court-appointed, criminal appellate panel. She is in charge of admissions. As with most legal jobs, and even appointed positions, a written sample of work is required. I submit an appellate brief I worked on for one of the Los Angeles immigration attorneys. My request for appointment is declined.

Through Chris, I meet a sea captain who is a retired pro tem judge and who acts as a defense attorney in death penalty cases in California. The retired judge asks me to assist him in a case concerning a crime that occurred in the city of Compton in Los Angeles County. The stories one hears coming out of that area are heartbreaking. Kids arrive late for grade school, because they have to dodge a knife-wielding drug addict or bullets flying from a gang feud. The whirl of the police helicopters is commonplace as they survey the neighborhood for suspects.

The facts of the Compton case are in the public record. Two boys were charged with murder while in the process of a daytime break-in and robbery. One of them is our client. Before the break-in, they watched the house and assumed no one was home. Once inside, they came upon the owner, an elderly woman, and killed her. The defendants were eighteen and nineteen years old at the time of the incident. The Los Angeles district attorney asks for the death penalty and a joint trial. My tasks for the retired judge are to draft a legal motion and accompanying legal memorandum to request separate trials.

The prosecutors have a strong, clear-cut case, and the boys are found guilty. With no chance for an acquittal, the best the defense can do is to get our client a sentence of life without the possibility of parole.

Undaunted by the initial rejection, when I complete the severance-of-trials memorandum, I know it will be perfect for resubmission to the Ninth Circuit's court-appointed, criminal appellate panel. In late summer, a letter arrives from the panel's supervisor in which she encourages me to resubmit. I do so.

Meanwhile, Chris and I become engaged to be married. It feels like I'm being moved along by a strong wind, but I know intuitively that it is not going to work. At the same time, however, I also know we will remain friends forever, just like with my first teenage boyfriend who was named Chris. We break up at the end of 1999, when I also receive notice of my appointment to a three-year term on the Ninth Circuit's Central District of California Criminal Justice Act Appellate Panel. This includes Los Angeles, an area in which major crimes occur. My appointment will begin in March 2000.

Wow, I made it. As the door to marriage plans closed, another door opened to a new and important professional opportunity.

After my meditation in the ruins of the Santa Barbara jail house near the mission, and thanks to years of studying the Nazis' mass incarcerations of Jews and other people deemed subversive or subhuman, I am eager to work on criminal appeals. As long as the defendant was fairly and properly convicted under the law, he or she should do the time for the crime. But whether by trial or guilty plea, I do not want anyone to spend any more time than necessary in prison.

❃

As the new year starts, I come home in the early morning on January 1, 2000. I have just completed a fabulous gig as the guest tarot reader at the San Ysidro Ranch New Millennium Party in Montecito. The one-room adobe building at this five-star hotel was transformed for me. Dozens and dozens of candles were lit and set on side tables around the room and in the overhanging chandelier. I did the readings at a large, round, wooden table surrounded by high-backed chairs for the San Ysidro Ranch patrons. I was scheduled to read for only three hours, but the demand for readings was high, and at midnight, I spoke to the hotel manager, who extended my contract an additional hour because a family of eight still wanted a tarot reading.

This event leads to a private client who is a Las Vegas casino owner. Judging by his pacing, the constant interruptions of cell phone calls and the thuggish conversations I overhear, I am sure he is Mafia connected. During the reading, I become convinced of it when the cards indicate he is embroiled in lawsuits and fears going to prison. As is my standard practice, when the spread reveals that my tarot client is involved in legal matters, I inform him (or her) that I am a lawyer but cannot advise him concerning the case or any pertinent laws. However, I can discuss the querent's emotional state surrounding his legal concerns.

In March, my first Ninth Circuit criminal appellate case arrives. It comes in the form of a letter that designates me as appointed counsel and gives the name of the defendant and the case's Court of Appeals for the Ninth Circuit docket number. Because I am just starting out, the supervisor has sent me an appeal that arises from a guilty plea. It is an extended and complex case.

The first thing I do is online research of the case via the Public Access to Court Electronic Records (PACER) site, which provides the docket of the district court record and the name of the attorney or attorneys who handled the district court case. At this time, I am not able to review any of the filed documents in the district court record, but from the docket, I learn this is a guilty plea for conspiracy to manufacture and distribute, and the distribution and possession of methamphetamine. In my phone call to the trial attorney, most of our discussion is covered by attorney-client privilege. However, I learn some facts that are in the public record.

This case, *United States v. Chavez*, commenced from a multidefendant indictment. My client, Mr. Chavez, was determined to be a high-level supervisor in the Mexican Mafia. At this time, it was the biggest international conspiracy to distribute methamphetamine in American history. My client was sentenced to twenty years of incarceration and five years of supervised release.

The trial attorney agrees to give me copies of the district court documents filed in the case. Appeals courts will only review documents that are in the record. Thanks to my clerkship at Goodman, Eden, I know I must read everything from cover to cover, like it's a novel, and take notes while I read.

A few days later, I drive down to the attorney's office in Los Angeles to pick up the copies of the documents. Once I'm home, a friend helps me lug the large, cardboard box up to my second-floor studio apartment. It takes up a fifth of the bed-sitting-room.

My makeshift office is a small, computer table set up in my tiny kitchen. The smell of fresh-cut garlic, which just went into my homemade salad dressing, wafts over me while I am researching federal case law from FindLaw, an online resource used to access legal information. From time to time, I also use the local courthouse's law library. My work involves federal law, so I do not practice out of that building. Instead, my cases are filed in the federal courthouse in San Francisco and oral arguments are usually held in Pasadena.

Situated above a breakfast and lunch diner called Judge for Yourself, my home is kitty-corner across from the Santa Barbara County Superior Court. A two-story structure, the courthouse is a magnificent example of the city's Spanish Colonial Revival architecture. The city of Santa Barbara hosts a number of civic events on its outdoor, stone-slab stage.

The good news about my apartment is that it has a lot of windows. My back kitchen faces west, so I can see a bit of the mountain range, and the south side windows face the El Mirador, the turreted clock tower, and the palm and evergreen trees on the grounds of the courthouse. The studio has a small, walk-in closet. With the door closed, it is dark and quiet and the perfect place to do my daily, twenty-minute meditation while sitting on a folding chair. Besides mine, there are three more studios on the second floor of the apartment building. Another great thing about my place is that the other studios are each rented to a professional woman, all of whom have become my good friends. They are beautiful and bring wonderful things to my life. Liz cuts and colors my hair, Andra is my aesthetician, and Valarie is into management and is our social planner. She holds fantastic, themed parties in her small place.

Sitting on my couch, I read through the district court record and the transcripts of the lower court hearings in *United States v. Chavez*. I break the documents into bite-sized summaries and write these summaries on a yellow legal pad. I also jot down the page numbers, which will allow me to locate precise passages for references and to later assemble the excerpts of records.

After much research, I eventually write and file the appellant's opening brief. In it, I challenge the validity of Mr. Chavez's guilty plea and also argue the ineffective assistance of his trial counsel, a Sixth Amendment issue. The government files an answering brief. I file a reply. Many months later, the justices on the Ninth Circuit's three-judge panel grant an oral argument hearing.

Under the US Constitution, everyone has a right to a direct appeal from a criminal conviction, unless this right is legally waived. However, not all appeals are granted oral arguments. Perhaps fewer than a quarter of all cases go to oral argument, and probably fewer than that in the area of criminal law. In the court of appeals, the justices are nominated by the president of the United States and approved under the advice and consent of the US Senate.

If I want a reappointment to the court-appointed appellate panel three years from now, the Ninth Circuit justices will be asked to evaluate my work. So will the attorneys at the US Department of Justice, in particular the Los Angeles office.

Although the supervisor administers the court-appointed appellate panel, she does not oversee our work.

❋

Before the April 2, 2001, oral argument hearing in *United States v. Chavez* at the courthouse in Pasadena, I deal with my lack of confidence by starting to prepare weeks in advance. You can't wing it in legal work. This means a review of all relevant materials, after which I make arrangements for mooting sessions with fellow attorneys and lay people. In a mooting session, after they read the government's brief, my opening brief, and a reply brief, if I chose to file one, they ask me questions as if they are the justices who will hear the appeal. Including people who are bright but not lawyers helps me to clearly explain the issues and legal matters. Marla is really good at mooting, so we set up a number of sessions to do over the phone.

When we were young kids, she was the one who stood up to everyone. The family thought she was going to be the lawyer.

The day of the oral argument hearing in *United States v. Chavez* has finally arrived. Last week, the three Ninth Circuit justices overseeing the appeal had the option to cancel it, but they didn't do so. This means the panel still has questions about the validity of Mr. Chavez's guilty plea and the competency of his lower-court attorney. Last night, I wrote out summary answers to anticipated questions the three judges could ask on two sheets of paper and included them in my oral argument binder, which holds copies of relevant case law for easy reference. The Mark Cross briefcase Jamie gave me is now stuffed with all the briefs and the excerpts of record filed in this appeal. At the oral argument hearing, my time will be limited to ten minutes. This includes the opening statement and the rebuttal unless the justices grant me more time.

I stay with Marla in Venice Beach for two days before the hearing, and she drives into Pasadena with me. Even so, butterflies fluttered around in my stomach all last night and are still busy this morning. As we walk toward the Richard H. Chambers United States Court of Appeals Building, I take in the beauty of the gorgeous, pink Spanish Colonial Revival courthouse situated in a rich, residential area a few streets from downtown Pasadena. At the turn of the twentieth century, it was the Vista del Arroyo Hotel and bungalows; during the Second World War it served as a hospital; and in the early 1950s, federal agencies took up residence. By the mid-1980s, it was fully converted to the federal courthouse.

First, I check in with the court clerk. Then my sister and I go have coffee in a private attorneys' room while I look through my summary notes. A few minutes later, we enter the designated courtroom and sit in the public area, along with other attorneys whose cases are on this morning's docket. When the case before ours is finished, the assistant US attorney and I move to the front of the courtroom and take our places at the appropriate tables on opposite sides of the lectern, which has a microphone and a timer that clocks down the minutes. (When the red light comes on, you are going over your designated time.)

The presiding justice calls, "United States v. Chavez."

I take my binder and move to the lectern. "Good morning, Your Honors," I begin. "May it please the court, my name is Myra Mossman, and I am the court-appointed appellate attorney for the defendant. Mr. Chavez pleaded guilty to the charges." Then I list the crimes and the issues I want to raise. "Unless the court has any objections, I would like to discuss the methodology the district judge used in the plea hearing to determine Mr. Chavez knew that nature of the charges. The district court started his colloquy with an example in which he claimed the defendants in his courtroom were only answering yes to his questions not because they understood but because they thought it was a test. Despite this assertion, the judge only asked Mr. Chavez questions to which there was a single response. This was yes. I submit, Your Honors, by the court's own admission, this is unresponsive and not indicative of understanding. We cannot be sure that Mr. Chavez understood the nature of charges against him or that he knowingly and willingly pleaded guilty."

One justice asks, "How can you say this, counselor?"

"Well, if I will be permitted to go outside of the plea record," I reply, "for sure, we know that Mr. Chavez did not understand the charges because of his claims of innocence at his sentencing hearing." I reiterate some facts for the Ninth Circuit panel and then say, "Now, the district court judge at the change of plea should have required Mr. Chavez to give an explanation of the charges in his own words. He did not do this. Mr. Chavez only said yes. Perhaps when he responded with yes, he also shrugged his shoulders or raised his hands up in the air. We cannot tell from the transcript. Nor did I have the privilege or the advantage of being the trial attorney. However, I took it upon myself to look up the definition of 'yes' in *Merriam-Webster's Collegiate Dictionary*." I cite the edition and then add, "It states the word yes can function as or mean 'uncertainty or polite attentiveness or interest.' I submit that Mr. Chavez was uncertain."

"Counselor," one of the justices says, "that is a creative argument. But don't you think we should give the district court great deference? Why, he has probably heard sixty to a hundred changes of pleas."

A few months later, the three justices deny the appeal. Due deference ruled the day. You do not become an appellate attorney if you only care about winning. I promise my clients to do the best for them. My professional integrity is pitted against their loss of liberty, because with every case, the Ninth Circuit justices and the prosecutors at the US Attorneys' Office assess my legal work, and ultimately my career and reputation.

As it turns out, my decision to focus on business and economics while in law school proves exceedingly useful to my ability to handle my appointed cases. The nature of the convictions can be for anything in the large array of federal crimes, like securities fraud, bank fraud, money laundering, or federal kidnapping and drug crimes. In all instances, I carry on a lively inner conversation with the Divine, now my law partner. Because it is important to know the case against my client, God plays the role of the devil's advocate. My ability to debate and have a ruthlessly honest, ongoing internal dialogue about legal matters proves to be one of my greatest assets.

Chapter 41

"THE HALLMARK OF EVIL AND unholiness is an attitude of 'it just happened.' Nothing is coincidental to the Jew; every event is purposeful and significant." This old Hassidic saying reminds me of an incident that occurred about six years ago, just before my fortieth birthday. The lessons I learned then are still helpful today.

Back in early January 1995, I was in Vail, Colorado, with my sister and brother and his family. After a few days on the slopes, I tried to ski the famous Back Bowls. On the gondola ride up to the peak, my brother, sister-in-law, and I passed over an evergreen forest. We couldn't help but remark on the beauty of the day and the spirituality of the area.

Jamie and his wife are much better skiers than I am and more suited to the expert slopes. Soon, I was over my head at the black-diamond level of difficulty of the ski runs. I fell down and could not stand up. As my sister-in-law knelt by my side to give me comfort, Jamie hailed a medic on skis, and they loaded me onto a toboggan. The medic then skied down the mountain, pulling me behind him. Because I'd fallen at the top, it took more than fifteen minutes for us to arrive at the hospital in Vail. It was a gorgeous ride.

Orderlies promptly moved me from the toboggan onto a gurney and wheeled me into a private examination room and then left me alone there.

Soon Jamie walked in. "How do you feel?"

"Great. I'm not in any pain."

He sat down in a chair and picked up a brochure from the table next to him. He looked it over, and then looked at me. "It's about the Steadman Clinic. Geez, Juan Carlos, the king of Spain, is an honoree trustee. Kind of pretentious, eh?"

I didn't know what he meant, but I could hear the hushed talk of people in the hallway whispering, "Dr. Steadman. . . Dr. Steadman." Then I heard footsteps coming closer to my room. A nurse rushed in and announced, "Dr. Steadman will be here shortly to talk to you."

I had no idea what to expect and kept my eyes on the door. Soon I saw a nose and a hand and a foot, and then in walked this tall, god-like man. Dr. Steadman, I presumed. His golden hair shone under the hospital lights with a halo effect.

He introduced himself. "I am Dr. Steadman. Do you mind? I am just going to examine your knee. Usually, I am not on call. You got lucky." He smiled and gently pressed, poked, and bent my injured knee. "Yes, you seem to have ligament issues. We'll have you take an MRI to be sure. It would be best if you came up to my clinic. We can take a closer look there. It's just a few floors up."

Jamie nodded his head, and I said, "Okay."

The doctor left and an orderly wheeled me to the elevator, with Jamie right behind us. On the way to the clinic, we pass down a hallway lined with autographed pictures of sports greats. I recognized skiers and football and basketball players. All of a sudden, I got excited.

The orderly placed me in a private examination room across the hall from a room full of people standing around a bed. I noticed someone sitting on the edge of it, though from my angle all I could see were huge legs. When the people around him moved away, I looked up from the legs to the patient's face.

Oh my goodness! It was Jim Kelly! The long-time quarterback for the Buffalo Bills.

Dr. Steadman uses a revolutionary procedure to make a contact point in the bone to introduce torn ligaments. The hope is that the bone and ligaments will realign and reconnect through the buildup of scar tissue. A successful reattachment can thus come without the aid of metal pins. That is how I understand it. Many pro athletes are in sports that involve the knees doing "cutting" actions that require them to suddenly change directions. Injuries to the knees can be career-ending. Dr. Steadman's procedure is done with arthroscopic surgery followed by a lot of physiotherapy.

My therapy started the day before surgery was scheduled. I used a stationary bike and did other exercises to keep the full range of motion in my knee, so it would not stiffen. When Dr. Steadman found me in the exercise room, he pulled me aside. We sat side by side on a bench.

"Myra," he said, "your martial arts days are over. I am concerned with the snapping of the knee when you are kicking. It will be adverse to a successful recovery."

"And I had plans to join a club." I tried to smile. "Okay. I'll find something else to do."

On the day of the surgery, I was placed on a gurney, wheeled into a "prep and recovery" room, and then placed in a cubicle with the curtains drawn on all sides. There was only a small opening through which I could see the doorway when Marla came into the room.

All at once, the curtain to my left swung wide open. It was Jim Kelly! He was lying in bed in the cubicle next to mine. He looked at me and then at Marla. He looked at us again.

"Yeah," I told him. "We're twins."

A man who seemed to be the quarterback's handler apologized. "Jim just had surgery."

"Did it hurt?" I ask. What a dumb question to ask a pro football player.

Jim and the guy just laughed.

Marla walked over and introduced us to them. Then she turned to me and whispered, "You're really not going to wear that pink lipstick into surgery, are you?"

I giggled and asked her for a tissue and then rubbed it off.

After the surgery, I had a bit of a rough night. The nurses hooked up a machine under my knee that kept it bent and in motion. The next day and the day after that, I went back to the physiotherapy room. By then, I was fairly adept at using crutches. One afternoon, Jim Kelly and his handler were waiting at the elevator. When he saw me, Jim's face lit up. "Want to have a race?" he asked. "What do you say?"

"Okay. Let's see who's the best on crutches."

Jim and I hobbled along the hallway, both of us giggling, and I almost fell in love with him. At least until I found out he was married.

I was released from the hospital the next morning, and that afternoon, Marla and I got a flight back to Santa Barbara. When we boarded the airplane and found our seats, I looked around and spotted a man who had once asked me out for dinner. I had turned him down, probably because he was too "normal." Today, he was seated behind me and next to him was a petite, pretty woman. He introduced her as his girlfriend. She looked about my age.

"I noticed the crutches and the brace on your knee," she said. "What happened?"

As I explained about blowing out my knee in the Back Bowls of Vail, she looked concerned and said, "I tore my ACL and ML too. Now I have an eighty-year-old knee."

"You don't look eighty," I said. "I am so sorry to hear about your knee." I made a silent vow to never let that happen to me.

Healing my knee was like training in martial arts. No excuses. Just do it. For the first week, Marla nursed me at her townhouse in Montecito. From there, I went to my downtown Santa Barbara studio apartment and was surprised to find a large box waiting for me. Jamie had sent me a stationary bike, a Lifecycle fitness machine, so I could do my own "physio." I also found a doctor in San Luis Obispo who had trained with Dr. Steadman. I was confident I would heal and have an age-appropriate knee.

While I was recuperating at Marla's place, she gave me a collection of cassette tapes titled *"The Mystical Kabbalah"* narrated by Rabbi David A. Cooper. The series is almost eighteen hours long and includes a number of guided meditations. I listened to those tapes over and over again, maybe more than a hundred hours. They made my idle time purposeful. I also gained a deeper understanding of the Tree of Life and the tarot, which aided my professional readings.

The crutches were gone after a month. I wore the brace for six months more. I even met Chris, the sea captain, while I was still wearing it. My knee healed perfectly, thanks to my diligence in my physiotherapy and the care and help from my sister and brother. After a year of using the stationary Lifecycle bike, I sold it and replaced it with a computer stand and a computer chair. Now what was once my physiotherapy area in my tiny kitchen became my law office again.

My spiritual deepening in the mystical Kabbalah and the lesson of maintaining a positive attitude toward healing my knee translate six years later into trying my best in my federal criminal appellate practice. While I cannot promise my clients they will win and their convictions will get reversed, I can promise I will give their appeals 100 percent of my effort.

In 2000, I get my second court-appointed appeal. *United States v. Calvin Thomas* turns out to be a doozy on the facts.

As a matter of public record, it involves a daytime robbery a number of years earlier, when the three male defendants exited a UPS shipping facility, entered a jeep, and took off.

One problem with their scheme was that they looked suspicious: three grown men carrying women's purses. Another problem was that the UPS building was located across the street from an FBI field office. A number of the agents were driving back to work from lunch when they spotted the three men. When the robbers took off in the jeep, the FBI followed. A shoot-out ensued. No one was hurt, but the robbers ran into an apartment building, where they holed up for a number of hours. A stand-off followed until the police used tear gas to enter the building and the three were arrested.

My appellate case is limited to an appeal from a remand. The Ninth Circuit sent the case back to the district court for a resentencing hearing. The defendant is a young man in his early twenties who was sentenced to fifty years. He was convicted not only for the robbery, but also for being the shooter who fired on the FBI agents during the chase.

In my opening brief, I argue the ineffectiveness of counsel because no evidence was offered on remand to bring the resentencing judge current on the defendant's efforts at rehabilitation. The substandard advocacy of the resentencing attorney left my client totally exposed to inferences that he had no mitigating factors relevant to resentencing, and that he was a danger not only to the general society but also to the prison population. This posture could be interpreted as a tacit admission that my client had no redeeming qualities or considerations. Counsel had failed to do anything but offer arguments that the sentencing judge had clearly rejected the first time.

I try, but I do not prevail in this case. It is difficult to win an appeal, and it is almost impossible in an appeal from a resentencing hearing if nothing new happened during the proceeding.

My third court-appointed case arrives in early October 2000. *United States v. Dominguez Benitez* concerns a federal drug conviction following a guilty plea. The defendant signed a plea agreement and waived his right to appeal. He was sentenced to the mandatory minimum of ten years of incarceration plus five years of supervised release.

I know there is no such thing as a small case, even if the court record runs to only a few hundred pages. By now, I also know to pay attention to my intuition, even when it involves the law. While reading over the transcript of Mr. Benitez's guilty plea hearing, I feel a quickening in my body. This sense of knowing brings my mind into an extra sharp focus. Something was wrong in the hearing, but the error was not brought to the district court's attention.

Despite the appeal waiver in the plea agreement, I file an opening brief in February 2001 and raise an issue in the case for the first time. On appeal before the Ninth Circuit, I assert that the district court erred in the guilty plea hearing when the judge failed to warn the defendant that the court was not bound by the sentencing recommendation expressed in the plea agreement. The judge had a duty to tell my client that any agreement about the length of his sentence was not binding on the court and Mr. Benitez could not withdraw his guilty plea if he did not get the sentence he anticipated. Neither the defense counsel nor the prosecutor informed the judge of this omission, which could have helped to correct the error.

Because I am raising this issue on appeal, there is a much higher "burden of persuasion." I have to show the appeals court the error was plain, or obvious and clear, and prejudicial to my client, and that because this was not a harmless error, the guilty plea must be invalidated, and the conviction reversed.

In addition to the opening brief, I file a number of motions and a request to file a supplemental brief based on recent decisions in the Ninth Circuit that are favorable to my client. However, the Ninth Circuit withdraws those cases. Because they are no longer authoritative, my request for more briefing is denied.

In early December 2001, the Ninth Circuit hears oral argument in *United States v. Dominguez Benitez*. As usual, after a thorough review of the record and the case law and participating in a number of mooting sessions, I am prepared. The night before, I write out my answers to anticipated questions in my oral argument binder. At the hearing, the three-judge panel is active and asks lots of questions. Afterwards, I feel upbeat.

At the same time, the US Supreme Court grants certiorari, or agrees to review, in a relevant case, *United States v. Vonn*. This leads me to request the Ninth Circuit to grant supplemental briefing and to stay its proceedings pending the Supreme Court's decision in that case. The Ninth Circuit agrees. When the Supreme Court issues its decision, I file a supplemental brief, as does the assistant US Attorney handling the case for the government.

Now we are in a "wait and see" period. It will last until the Ninth Circuit panel renders a decision.

Chapter 42

ON THE WAY HOME FROM a Christmas in Connecticut at Jamie's and then New Year's Eve in New York City with Marla, I dash through the terminal at John F. Kennedy International Airport to make a flight. There is little time to spare before the boarding starts on the plane headed to Los Angeles, where I will catch a connecting flight to Santa Barbara. While I'm scurrying along, I catch a broadcast coming from a TV in one of the JFK airport lounges. The announcer says something that causes me to stop dead in my tracks. "The Sexually Dangerous Facility at Bridgewater is where the psychiatrists were having sex with the inmates. A documentary was made about the institute, in the late 1960s."

Wow. That's where Lasinski was held in custody. That's where the doctors determined Lasinski was fit to stand trial. A likely inference is that a doctor, a psychiatrist, or someone else on the staff found my assailant attractive, and attraction led to sex. Lasinski was fit, tall, dark haired, and handsome in a tough-guy way.

Hearing that broadcast feels like a punch in my stomach, and anger wells up in me. It is early January 2002 now, and

I felt the same anger when I read the *Vineyard Gazette*'s reports. The first one was back in 1978, while I was in Falmouth Hospital just after the attack. The article mentioned Lasinski's arrest. It made me angry because it also revealed my name and where I lived without my permission. Decades later, when I read two more articles about Lasinski doing his prison time on Martha's Vineyard, I felt even angrier because those reports made it seem more like he had a vacation than a period of incarceration. Now this TV broadcast leads me to think Lasinski was involved in a torrid, sexual affair while at Bridgewater. It seems to be a rational explanation for why he was kept there for six months instead of the usual two or three weeks it takes to determine if someone is fit to stand trial.

Once I'm settled on the airplane, I try to distract myself from thoughts of Lasinski. I reach into my shoulder bag and take out the latest *New York Times* bestselling murder mystery.

❂

In late January 2002, the Ninth Circuit issues its decision in *United States v. Dominguez Benitez*. In an opinion soon to be published in the *Federal Reporter*, the three-justice panel decides in favor of the appellant on one of my issues. As a result, my client's guilty plea is reversed, and his plea agreement is voided.

I prevailed, which is quite a professional accomplishment. Of course, I feel proud. A published opinion means the outcome will directly apply to my client and will also be authoritative for all similarly situated defendants within the jurisdiction of the Ninth Circuit, which includes nine western states and two Pacific islands. Nevertheless, Mr. Benitez must remain in prison because the government has filed petitions for reconsideration before the three-justice panel who heard the case, and for a rehearing en banc, or "before the entire bench" of eleven Ninth Circuit justices at a new hearing. I file answers that ask the original panel and the other judges to deny the government's petitions. The Court of Appeals for the Ninth Circuit agrees with me and turns down the government's requests.

In August 2003, Ted Olsen, the solicitor general of the United States, and his assistants file a petition for certiorari in the US Supreme Court in this case. I quickly get admitted to practice before the Supreme Court and file a response, asking the court to deny their petition. Almost a year and a half has passed since the Ninth Circuit reversed the guilty plea of my client. During all this time, Mr. Benitez has remained in prison.

The Supreme Court grants certiorari, more briefs are filed, and the oral argument hearing is set for April 21, 2004, in Washington, DC. I am more than thrilled. The pursuit of the divine directive to become a lawyer has brought me to this most prestigious place. It is a great honor . . . but I have a lot of work ahead of me.

A few weeks after the Supreme Court's announcement, I receive a telephone call from a lawyer in Texas. He is wondering why the Supreme Court decided to take my case rather than a similar one his firm is handling. The Supreme Court has abated, or held back from making, a decision in his case until one is reached in mine. I have no idea why the court would do that. The Texas lawyer and I talk some more, and it turns out we get along quite well. About a week later, I get an email informing me his law firm will file an amicus curia, or "friend of the court" brief. They also want to send this lawyer to Washington, DC, to help me prepare for the upcoming oral argument hearing. They will allow me to use their office in Washington too.

Chapter 43

ONE DAY THE PHONE RINGS in my Santa Barbara apartment. I answer, and the conversation goes something like this.

"Hello, Ms. Mossman. My name is David Savage. I'm a reporter from the *Los Angeles Times*. I understand you are representing the defendant in an upcoming Supreme Court case. I am writing an article. Can I ask you a few questions?"

"Yes, I am the attorney of record in the Supreme Court. I'm sorry. No comments."

"Ohhhh. Okay. All right. Goodbye, then."

On December 9, 2003, Savage's piece is published in the *Los Angeles Times*. It fills almost half a page and gives a good layman's account of the technical legal issue that is before the Supreme Court in *United States v. Dominguez Benitez*. But the reporter fails to mention that I was the attorney who represented the defendant in the Ninth Circuit appeal and prevailed.

The other court-appointed criminal appellant cases I handle have become more extensive and more complicated. Generally, a single case can include a voluminous record, with thousands of pages of documents and transcripts from numerous preliminary hearings, a jury trial that lasts several weeks, and a number of post-trial and sentencing hearings. To focus just on Mr. Benitez's case, I go off rotation in the Ninth Circuit court-appointed appellate panel and do not take any new cases while I prepare for the oral arguments before the Supreme Court. The hearing is expected to last an hour, with thirty minutes per side.

On a Saturday night in early March, my friend Valerie throws me an elegant "Supreme Court Champagne and Dessert" party in her studio apartment. The mood is set with low lights and tall, bar tables with candles in our hallway. Lots of my friends come to wish me well and eat a delicious coconut cake.

The day after the party, it is back to reviewing the *Benitez* briefs and pertinent case law. During the month, my friend Gail hosts two mooting sessions for me at her house. A number of Santa Barbara lawyers and laypeople participate. Also, the Los Angeles office of the federal public defender provides a mooting session with its stafflawyers. A week before the oral argument hearing, I head to Washington, DC, and book into a hotel just a few blocks from the US Supreme Court. A branch of the amicus brief's law firm is located on Pennsylvania Avenue, not far from the Capitol and the White House. When I arrive at the law office the next day, the place is almost empty. It is large and looks vaguely familiar. My lawyer friend tells me it was used in the Julia Roberts–Mel Gibson movie, *Conspiracy Theory*.

My first appointment is a mooting session at Georgetown University with prominent lawyers from Washington-area law firms, like Jones Day. The attorney from that firm points out the difficulty with the government's position, which tries to prove something that is counterfactual. I like the phrase and hope to use it before the Supreme Court. I am wearing a pale blue suit coat with a matching dress underneath that has a little flare and disguises my nervousness. After the Georgetown mooting is finished, the coordinator of the event, who is the person I've been in communication with, grabs me by both hands and twirls me around. "You did great," she says. "You did great."

But I don't feel so good about my performance. Perhaps, this is why I wear my baseball cap the next day when I go to the Supreme Court's law library to find an obscure case. I tell the clerk that my oral argument hearing before the court is in a few days. He introduces me to the law librarian, who is seated at her desk. I notice a slight smirk on her face. Perhaps this is because I'm still wearing the baseball cap. I walk past her into the main library room. No one else is here. I feel a strong sense of history.

The place drips with history. Even when I first entered the building, I could imagine lawyers arriving in their horse-drawn carriages. In the law library, I imagine the stacks filled with leather-bound books and the court records office filled with parchment scrolls. I imagine documents written with quill pens. I have read some of those old cases. I have also dreamed about appearing before the Supreme Court. I feel excited and prepared . . . but not quite ready.

Chapter 44

IT IS NOW APRIL 20, 2004, the night before my oral argument hearing. Marla has come in from New York City, and I meet her at the train station in downtown Washington. The building is modern and inviting, not like the old-fashioned Amtrak station in Santa Barbara. We have dinner at a Chinese bistro on the second floor. I like their barbeque pork fried rice. Afterwards, we take a slow walk back to my hotel, which is a few blocks away. Marla pulls her small, rolling suitcase behind her. We are staying in separate rooms tonight, because I need to be alone to prepare my oral argument binder. Sitting at my hotel room desk, I write out answers to anticipated questions and add Post-it notes to the two open pages, so I have more writing space. Before going to bed, I meditate and feel myself snug in the hands of the Divine. I'm surprised that sleep comes easily.

The next morning, there is a knock on my door. I open it to find my sister.

"Oooh!" she says. "You look just like Condoleezza Rice."

"Good!" I modeled myself after the current national security advisor for President George W. Bush, because the Supreme

Court requires attorneys to wear professional business attire. I'm wearing a midnight blue suit jacket with a white knit top underneath and a pencil skirt that hits just below my knees. The pearl earrings, a pearl necklace, and my hair flip further mimic Condi's style. "How did you sleep?" I ask my sister.

Marla shakes her head. "You won't believe it. The hotel wanted Douglas to stay in my room, but I told the guy in the office that he is an Orthodox Jew and cannot stay with a woman who is not his wife. I am not his wife."

Marla and Douglas are two of my guests at the oral argument hearing. He is our first cousin, on my father's side. "So what did the hotel do with him?" I ask.

Marla yawns and says, "They sent him to another hotel altogether." She sits down on the edge of the bed. "It seems some group came in last night, and the management had to rearrange the guest rooms. Then later that night, the heater came on and I was baking. It was way too hot and hard to get to sleep."

"Well, whatever happened, you look great," I tell her. "I love your black, pleated skirt suit. I'm ready. Let's go downstairs and get something from the continental breakfast. Maybe Douglas and Jamie are here too."

The guys have arrived and are waiting for us in the lobby. Douglas looks handsome and professorial with his bow tie. A forensic psychiatrist and teacher at a university, he flew in from Cincinnati. Jamie came in from Connecticut. My brother looks relaxed and debonair. I give my brother a hug, but not my cousin. An Orthodox Jew cannot touch or even shake hands with a woman who is not his wife.

My case before the Supreme Court is not a sexy one. It involves the question of the proper standard of review an appellate court should use, which is probably not interesting to the general public, whereas the whole world is eager for the oral argument hearing next week in *Hamdi v. Rumsfeld*, a case stemming from the September 11, 2001, terrorist attacks at the

World Trade Center and the Pentagon. Everyone remembers where he or she was on that horrible day. I was huddled with a friend in front of the TV set in my Santa Barbara studio. For hours, we watched the tragedy that took so many lives. We were forever changed that day.

Even though *Benitez* is not a landmark case like *Hamdi* will be, I am proud to walk to the courthouse with my sister, brother, and cousin. Instead of using the famous front stairs, the three of us go through a side door reserved for attorneys appearing before the court and their guests. On our way into the Supreme Court building, we meet up with Gail and Peter and I give them big hugs. They drove to Washington from Santa Barbara and are also my guests for this morning's oral argument. Special seats have been reserved for my family and friends. It took a lot for me to coordinate all this, plus prepare for the hearing, but I am glad to have them here with me.

We part ways as I go to a special chamber for the attorneys appearing before the court. The amicus curiae attorney from Texas, who is already there, greets me. Although he is not arguing today, he will sit next to me in the well of the courtroom. Also present are a few other lawyers whose case will be called after mine. The clerk I met the other day at the law library talks to us about court procedure. He reminds us that before responding to a question we should address the justices by their names. Then he hands out cards with the justices' names printed according to their seating arrangements on the bench. Supreme Court Chief Justice William Rehnquist sits in the middle and is flanked by the associate justices: from left to right, Ruth Bader Ginsberg, David Souter, Antonin Scalia, John Paul Stevens, Chief Justice Rehnquist, Sandra Day O'Connor, Anthony Kennedy, Clarence Thomas, and Stephen Breyer. Of course, I know who's who, but in the middle of a heated colloquy, this card surely will be helpful.

To our surprise, the clerk announces that Justice Thomas will read from his decision today. Thomas is notorious for not asking questions during oral arguments. Most people never hear his voice. The clerk also mentions that Chief Justice Rehnquist will have to stand during the hearing and walk around for health reasons. Rumor is, he has irritable bowel syndrome.

Now the clerk leads us behind the bar and into the well of the famous courtroom. I have made personal history just by being here, and now a lump forms in my throat. The walls and pillars are white marble and offset by the blood-red drapes. The attorney and public gallery sections are full. The seats are dark wooden pews with handrails. I see my family and friends seated in the guest area. The sides of the courtroom have seats reserved for guests of the court and the press. These are not quite full, as no one expects the court to issue an opinion today.

Waiting at the attorneys' tables are pure white quill pens, mementos for those who appear before the court. I take my seat. To my right is a table with a small, wooden lectern. The attorneys from the Office of the Solicitor General sit at a table on the other side of the lectern, and behind us is another set of tables. These are for the attorneys in the case that follows ours on today's docket. Just a few feet in front of my table stands the long dais where the nine Supreme Court justices sit. At the moment, the black leather swivel chairs are unoccupied.

I move the quill to a corner of the table, arrange my binder, and place the card with the justices' names where I can easily see it. The amicus curiae lawyer takes a seat to the left of mine. At the same time, two men are pressing against the back of my chair as they carry on a conversation. One is the assistant solicitor general, the prosecutor on my case. As required, he is dressed in the traditional morning suit of gray-striped trousers, a waistcoat, and a dark jacket with tails. The other man is an attorney for the next case up. It seems they knew each other in the past.

The closeness of these two men annoys me and seems sexist, in that they're crowding my space. In response, and to try to dislodge them, I inch my chair closer to the table. They take a step back and continue their discussion. Instead of further expressing my frustration, I reach for my briefcase and take out my mystical tools. One is a copy of the Holy Tree of Life glyph. It shows the sacred Hebrew letters and tarot cards associated with the pathways connecting the ten *sephirot*. Meditating on this image helps me stay balanced. I also silently utter a prayer to Polyhymnia, one of the nine Greek muses. She is the muse of eloquence. I ask her to help me listen to the justices' questions and better communicate with them.

When I am finished with my brief meditation and prayer, I leave the courtroom and go find the ladies' room. On the way, I bump into another of my guests, Todd, who works in the city as an important lawyer for the US Securities and Exchange Commission and is my first cousin on my mother's side. We hug, and I admire how tall and handsome he looks.

When I get back into courtroom, US Solicitor General Ted Olson walks in. First, he shakes hands with the two men still standing behind my chair, then comes over to say hello to me, and finally takes a front-row seat. He personally wrote the reply brief.

"Oyez! Oyez!"

The US Supreme Court clerk gives the traditional call for the crowd to be silent and come to attention. All at once, the long, red curtains part in numerous places. Steven Spielberg could have directed the drama as the nine justices wearing long, black robes enter the courtroom and take their seats. It takes my breath away.

The first order of business is a swearing-in ceremony conducted by Chief Justice Rehnquist for a number of attorneys. When this is completed, the chief justice states the Supreme Court docket number and calls out, "United States v. Dominguez Benitez."

After the assistant solicitor general addresses the court, I pick up my oral argument binder and walk over to the table with the lectern. "Good morning, Your Honors," I say, "and may it please the court, my name is Myra Mossman, and I represent the respondent, Mr. Benitez." Next, I lay out the premise of our position.

Justice Breyer interrupts and starts talking. The more he talks, the smaller I feel. As my self-confidence shrinks into the floorboards, my inner voice shouts, *You're going in the wrong direction.* Like a prizefighter coming up from the mat, I muscle up some courage and imagine myself getting bigger. The justices on the bench are active, and sometimes it seems the nine-member US Supreme Court panel are mostly talking among themselves. At other times, they have a lot of questions for me.

At one point in the oral argument hearing, Justice Ginsberg asks me to cite directly from the record. My stomach starts to ache. I have not looked at those actual documents for many months. The seconds tick by. I cannot let fear consume me. I silently say the *Ana Be'Koach*, an old Kabbalistic prayer that relates to the Tree of Life, while I pick up the *Joint Appendix* from the pile I placed on the table before the hearing started. It contains relevant documents from the court records and was compiled by the prosecution and me, then filed in the Supreme Court a few months ago. The volume includes dozens and dozens of exhibits.

Call it luck or the power of the *Ana Be'Koach* prayer—I open the appendix to the precise page. My heart stops pounding, and my stomach relaxes, while I read the relevant portions into the Supreme Court record. After answering a few more questions, and making my summation, I take my seat. The assistant solicitor general walks over to the lectern and addresses a few points on rebuttal. Then he sits down.

Chief Justice Rehnquist says, "The case is submitted."

This signals the end of the Supreme Court's oral argument hearing in *United States v. Dominguez Benitez.* The attorneys for the next case are ready to take their places at the front table, so I quickly stuff the merits briefs and other documents, the *Joint Appendix,* and my oral argument binder into my briefcase. It won't close, so I have to carry it under my arm. I feel like a running back holding a football as I exit the center aisle of a packed courtroom.

In the hallway, the amicus curiae attorney grabs me by the shoulders. "You did really well, Myra."

"Thanks," I say. But I know this case is lost. Even though I tried my best, I know it is hard to win in the Supreme Court on the facts of this case, plus a conviction by a guilty plea along with a signed plea agreement.

The amicus curiae attorney and I walk out of the courthouse together. My sister and brother, who are already at the bottom of the Supreme Court's famous front steps, shout up at us to wait while they take photographs. More shots are taken when Gail, Peter, Todd, and Douglas come through the doors, and then there are more photographs of the whole group at the bottom of the steps. Our group includes another lawyer from the amicus curiae's law firm and his girlfriend. This other lawyer came into town a couple of days ago to help prep me for oral arguments. He appeared before the Supreme Court several years ago.

My cousin Todd made lunch reservations for our group at the historic Willard Hotel. Only two blocks from the White House, the Willard has been the center of political hobnobbing since 1818. Gail and Peter agree to meet us there and take off to find a taxi. The rest of us, minus the out-of-town lawyer and his girlfriend, decide to walk down the National Mall to get there. The weight of the day is off my shoulders now. Spring is in the air and in my step. As we wait outside the restaurant to be seated, we all look elegant in our professional business attire. So it is funny to see Gail bum a cigarette from a stranger on the street. (She's cute that way.)

Once we're seated, I order a salad and mashed potatoes with lobster. I'd never heard of this combination before, but it tastes yummy. Drained from the months of almost nonstop preparation for the oral argument hearing, I remain quiet during lunch, while Jamie is happy and carries on a lively conversation with everyone at our table. When we are done with lunch, Todd goes back to work at the Securities and Exchange Commission, and Gail and Peter go sightseeing. After the amicus curiae attorney bids me farewell, Marla, Douglas, Jamie, and I go back to my hotel room, which I now share with my sister. The guys talk, the girls relax.

Later, after my brother and cousin have left to catch their flights home, I change into blue jeans and a jacket but keep on the white top from this morning. Marla and I head out to roam the streets of Washington, DC. First, we walk back to the Supreme Court building, and she takes more photographs of me standing in front of the tall brass doors. Afterwards, we wander the streets and sightsee and window-shop for hours. Finally, exhausted and hungry, we find a seafood restaurant with an outside terrace that overlooks a waterway. It seems appealing. Neither of us knows where we are.

Just as we sit at a table, my cell phone rings. It's Gail. "I've been trying to call you all afternoon," she says. "Peter and I are in a horse-drawn carriage tour of Washington and we're famished. Have you eaten yet? Where are you?"

"Sorry," I tell her. "I forgot and turned my cell off while we were in the hotel room and just turned it on now. Marla and I just got to this restaurant. We haven't ordered yet. What a minute. I'll ask someone where we are."

I look around for a waiter and notice that everyone on the restaurant's patio is African American. Maybe my Condi Rice impersonation somehow guided Marla and me here. I spot a waiter, then relay the address he gives me to Gail. She gives it to the driver, then says, "I can't believe it! We're just two blocks away. Don't order. We'll be there in five minutes."

The meal is delicious. And fun, even though I am fairly quiet the whole evening.

The next day, Marla boards a train back to New York City. Gail and Peter leave town too. My destination today is

Washington's International Spy Museum, where I meander through the installations, which include a replica of a cobblestone street and storefronts in Germany during the Second World War. One shop attracts me. Through its windows, I can see shelves filled with rows of dozens and dozens of clear glass jars, each one holding a single piece of white cloth. I read the information plaque. That store was not selling perfumes. The jars were used to preserve the scents taken clandestinely from people of interest. Using dogs, the Gestapo could later track down these individuals. Years of research, watching movies, and reading books about the Nazis bring the museum exhibit alive for me. The profound fear of the millions of victims, and the stench of a traumatized humanity seem to accompany me out of the building. I take in the fresh air and walk silently back to my hotel room.

The next morning, before catching my flight back to Santa Barbara, I visit the US Botanic Garden. As I walk through the lush greenery, I find the varied fragrances a pleasant counterbalance to yesterday's tour of the lives of spies, traitors, and secret police.

Chapter 45

SINCE THE *BENITEZ* WIN IN the Ninth Circuit a few years back, my court-appointed appellate cases have become exceedingly complicated and involve major crimes committed in the United States. In 2003, I was reappointed to a second, three-year term. Some of my cases concern convictions for drug crimes, while another case involves an international conspiracy to distribute child pornography that includes foreign videos of the rapes of children. The defendant, a man in his thirties, was also convicted of the possession of child pornography and the sexual assault of a child under the age of eight. What makes that a federal crime? He crossed state lines to get closer to the kid. The defendant got thirty years. Because the appeal is sealed, I cannot discuss this case any further.

In other appeals, my law school background in financial and corporate law give me some insight into complex money laundering, securities fraud, banking fraud, wire and mail frauds, and tax evasion schemes. These cases concern fraudulent dealings, including a $400 million, check-kiting conspiracy, a $600 million, illegal, tax-preparation enterprise, and a securities fraud that siphoned hundreds of millions of dollars through unlawful corporations from people who thought they were buying interests in oil wells. What they really got was one thousandth of 1 percent of just the bore head and not the well or any land. Such frauds add up to billions of dollars of ill-gotten gains. Many of my clients have prior state and federal convictions, which end up increasing their current terms of incarceration.

Any notion of a compassionate God seems contrary to the acts of some of the criminals I encounter in my legal work. An interesting character pattern has emerged, for example, in the fraud cases. I've noticed how charismatic executives can willingly lead unsuspecting employees into criminal conduct. People want to connect to the energy of their leaders and don't ask too many questions, or they rationalize their suspicions away.

A goal in an FBI investigation is to get someone high on the corporate or criminal ladder to plead guilty. With a recommendation for a lower sentence, such a charismatic person agrees to become a cooperating witness for the government. In exchange for a possible light sentence, they will dish dirt and not file an appeal. The executive thus helps to convict as many people as he or she can.

Yes, I've seen CEOs on the dark side turn on their staffs, employees, and others. People get caught up in the charm of a con artist and end up in prison. Charges are often brought against these low-level followers, now termed coconspirators, because they had blind faith in their leader's word. They failed to do their own due diligence and instead are "doing time." Some people also go to the dark side because they have lost their connection to their soul. They act only in their own self-interest, regardless of who it hurts and what harm it does.

Some crimes are particularly odious. To properly defend people on appeal, I must apply the Golden Rule as articulated by Jesus of Nazareth when he summarized the teaching of the

Torah: "So in everything, do to others what you would have them do to you, for this sums up the Law and the Prophets" (Matthew 7:12, NIV).

Many defendants come to their appeals ill-informed about their own cases and ill-advised about their chances. They often confuse me with a magician. After I set them straight, many want to toil away in their prison law library, which is fine by me. My rule is that if they want to be my "co-counsel," I am the leader. Don't waste my time with frivolous issues. A clear, concise, proper, and persuasive argument is my plan of attack.

Contrary to many attorneys, I keep my clients fully informed.

In almost every case, there is something new to learn. Many hours of research are thus required. This learning curve also includes mastering the Ninth Circuit's mandatory electronic filing requirements for most motions, briefs, and excerpts of record. The good news is that I don't have to schlep boxes of documents to the post office to file via the US mail. Now cutting and pasting from the electronic documents makes the work much faster and more accessible then handwritten notes and page numbers on yellow legal pads.

Several months after my oral argument hearing, the Supreme Court ruled against my client, and his conviction by a guilty plea is affirmed in *United States v. Dominguez Benitez,* 542 US 74 (2004). The Supreme Court held that a reversal of a conviction is warranted from a district court error raised for the first time on appeal, when the defendant shows there is a reasonable probability that, but for the error, he would not have entered the guilty plea. This is a hard burden to meet. Justice Scalia wrote a separate opinion in which he disagreed with the standard used by the court's majority, though he did agree with their conclusion. He noted, in an oft-cited phrase, that "these ineffable gradations of probability" can confuse judicial reasoning.

Consequently, the Ninth Circuit withdraws its previously published opinion, which renders it not authoritative. In its place, the court issues a published decision in concert with the Supreme Court's ruling. Mr. Benitez must remain in prison.

In 2005, I move to an elegant, spacious, second-floor, two-bedroom, two-bath apartment on Santa Barbara Street. I convert one of the bedrooms to my home office, which also has a couch that pulls out into a double bed for stay-over guests. (Because all my legal clients are convicted and incarcerated when I get their appeals, I do not expect them to come and visit me here.) Tarot clients who book ahead for appointments do come, and the readings are done at my dining room table. Made of brass and iron by acclaimed furniture designer, Mark Brazier-Jones, the base is a twisted tree trunk of a tree whose branches hold the thick, round, glass top, which is set on a bent, iron rail from a train track. There is even an iron beetle nestled among the leaves, whose tips are tinged with a bluish green patina. Marla gave it to me when she moved from Venice Beach to New York City.

Along with my office, the living room, one of the two balconies, and the dining area overlook the famed Alice Keck Park Memorial Garden. For eleven years, I ambled through the park's themed and landscaped grounds at least three times a week. Now I live right across the street from the duck pond, grassy knoll, and plenty of palm trees. A half a block away is Alameda Park. But I am still an inner-city Santa Barbara girl who prefers the movie theaters, restaurants, and downtown State Street that are only a five-minute walk away.

These days, I don't socialize much. From time to time, I'll go to a party or an art opening, but there is no time for dating. Brian, my sister's former boyfriend, who is like my brother, comes over to my apartment, mostly on the weekends. Beforehand, he'll pick up Thai food. Then we eat and watch old black-and-white, film noir movies together.

I gave up the pursuit of marriage to learn about and master the six divine directives; move to the other side of the continent, learn a metaphysic, learn a martial art, learn about meaningful coincidences, learn how to meditate, and then become a lawyer. Because of the weight of my professional legal responsibilities, I sometimes feel like a captive of my computer. With all the research and legal writing demands, my life is now limited to either working on the federal appeals or thinking about the appeals or both. I've cut my tarot clients down to just a few. My self-styled martial arts fitness training and the Kabbalah Study Group act as a balance to the intense legal work.

A woman named Iris comes to study Kabbalah with us. There is no charge. Everyone is welcome. Then come Cesena, Susan, Annemeike, Jai, and Ira. Each brings light, wisdom, and curiosity. Many others come to study with us, and twice a month my apartment is alive with discussions about the Kabbalah, the Torah, the tarot, and the Tree of Life. On many nights, when our talks, prayers, and practices transform us, we know the *Shekinah*, the feminine consort of God, is present too.

Although I love what I do, there are good days and not-so-good days. When friends ask how I'm feeling, my humorous retort is, "Every day above ground is a good day." As with all good humor, it's partly true. Besides my daily chants and meditations and preparing for and having the study group over, what also helps me stay on top of things is working with a Jungian therapist. We talk about my bouts of sadness and the mundane aspects of my life, but most important, we discuss my recent dreams. A few sessions center on the memory of a powerful dream I had while living in Toronto. Its influence still persists and helps to boost the good days.

In this dream, it is dawn and the sun is just rising over the barren sand hills of a desert valley. All is peaceful. In the distance is a huge T-shaped structure, so large it dwarfs the surrounding hills. The top of the T is a place of worship. The great size of the edifice puts me in awe. I also feel afraid and alone.

And then, in the next instant, my dream-self is in a dark room. One of the walls of the room is the sloping face of a mountain. As I start to walk up the mountain, fireflies light my way. I am a young girl, about eight or nine years old, and am wearing a short dress with a crinoline petticoat. On my way up the mountainside, I pass two young boys coming down. I sense they just left their Torah study lessons.

At one point in my hike up, a narrow alcove appears. It is cut into the mountainside. There is a stone bench nearby, where I sit there a minute and decide to turn my dress with its crinoline petticoat inside out. I now feel like a little princess. The crinoline sparkles just like the fireflies do. Two people (a female and a male) are waiting for me at the end of the alcove. They are dressed in robes. They lay a gold wreath around my neck and tell me I have been chosen to see God. They speak no more but point down a long hallway that runs past the narrow alcove and goes into the mountain. This hallway ends in two huge doors. I know that inside is the presence of God. I open the doors. The dream ends.

A few days after I first had that dream, I called my good friend and mentor Professor Charles Laughlin. He commented on how my dress was turned inside-out in the dream, which he interprets by telling me to reveal my inner spiritual thoughts and feelings and not keep them hidden. He also encouraged me to re-enter the dream and to keep learning from it.

Years later, the dream continues to substantiate my faith that God is close and that the Divine is my partner in both the law and my professional tarot readings. I often meditate and enter that dream chamber to sit at the foot of the Divine, where we talk.

Many years later, while studying the *Zohar,* an important Kabbalistic text, I come across several verses about "the voice of the children engaged in Torah studies who save the world." The *Zohar* notes the gold wreaths worn by these children. Hmm.

Chapter 46

ONE NIGHT, MY MOTHER GOES dancing. A few days later, she is in critical care. For the past year, she has complained of stomachaches, but after scores of tests, the doctors found nothing.

Now it turns out now that she has pancreatic cancer.

When Mother is admitted into a hospital in Windsor, Ontario, my sister and brother fly in from New York to be with her. Jamie is determined to get her the best care and hires an air ambulance to transport her to Memorial Sloan Kettering Cancer Center in New York City.

I've been appointed to a third, three-year term and am currently preparing for oral arguments before the Ninth Circuit in an appeal from a jury trial that lasted twenty-two days. My client, along with seven codefendants, was convicted of conspiracy, securities fraud, and other frauds. He was sentenced to five years in prison, a relatively short time. Because of my mother's grave condition, I file an emergency motion to continue the oral argument hearing.

After the Ninth Circuit promptly grants my request, I take a flight to JFK airport, then a taxi to Memorial Sloan

Kettering. When I arrive, my mother is so thin and old looking, I hardly recognize her. She is sitting in a chair and wearing a drab hospital gown.

"Mommilla, I love you." I rush over to hold her hands.

"Hello, sweetheart," she says.

Her tender words touch my heart. Tears flow down my face. I've never seen my mother look so gaunt or her cheeks so hollow. She is aware, but tired.

Over the next few days, my sister and I walk the thirty blocks to the hospital from Marla's place and meet Jamie, who comes in from Greenwich, Connecticut. Our mother has a stunning, private bedsitting room with dark wood paneling, a couch, and a chair that pulls out into a twin bed. The hospital's restaurant is four-star quality. I eat my way through sadness. My nephews and sister-in-law also visit. We all end up in tears. My mother's second husband (they are now divorced) also comes to see her. They were going to get back together, but he tells us it is too late now. She is near death.

I've been in New York City for about a week. We know Mother's situation is dire, but we still hope to be with her for a few more months. In preparation, my sister, brother, and I visit a highly recommended Jewish hospice facility in Brooklyn, but we come away from the tour feeling gloomy. My brother tells us he will take her to his house and set up special care for her there.

Later that night, Jamie and Marla choose to sleep at the hospital. My brother takes the couch in the floor's lounge, while my sister calls dibs on the twin-bed pullout chair in Mom's room. There is not enough space for me in the hospital, so I stay at my sister's place. It is after midnight when I hear my cell phone ringing.

It is Marla. "Mom is dying," she says. "You better come back to the hospital."

"Okay. I'm leaving now."

I pull on some clothes, grab my purse, and race to the

elevator. I'm waiting on the ninetieth floor of the high rise, and the elevator seems to take forever. Outside, it has begun to rain. I race to the curb and try to hail a cab, but wet weather in Manhattan means it might be impossible to get a taxi. Luckily, a Yellow Cab pulls over. I reach to open the passenger door at the same time two people are trying to get in from the other side.

"My mother is dying," I tell them. "Please, I have to get to Sloan Kettering right now. Please, let me have this taxi."

The couple backs away, and I jump in as the vehicle takes off. At the hospital, the doors to my mother's floor are closed. I press the late visitor's entry button over and over, trying to get someone's attention.

The night nurse finally comes. She looks annoyed. "You are going to wake everyone up with that constant ringing."

"Sorry. My mother is dying."

I race to her room. It is too late. Mother is dead. Jamie, Marla, and I stand at the foot of her bed and hold hands. Through our tears, we say the *Shema*, the cornerstone of Hebrew prayers.

Our mother passed away a few minutes after midnight on Thanksgiving 2007. I miss her terribly almost immediately. At times, she was an extremely wise woman, and I could open up to her. Now I miss her advice and her humor.

Arrangements are made with a rabbi from Detroit to conduct the funeral services. Her body is flown to Canada, in accordance with Jewish burial laws. Because Mother was not a practicing Jew, we arrange for a three-day *shiva* at her apartment. Jamie orders enough food to feed people for the traditional seven days. He also charters a private plane and his family, my sister, and me to fly together to Windsor. Rick, my brother's house manager, comes too. He knew my mother well and loved her. Jamie books rooms for us at the Hilton. Mine has a gorgeous view overlooking the Detroit River. I don't want to sleep in our mother's apartment or in her bed. With both of my parents gone, I am now an orphan.

Although it is late November, the sun is shining, and the air is warm. Some of my favorite people in the whole world are here: Aunt Gladys and Uncle Jay and their daughter, my "older sister" cousin Bonnie from Detroit. Uncle Bobby and his wife Lynn, also from Detroit. My dear cousins Mollie from Dallas and her brother Douglas from Cincinnati, who came to my oral argument hearing at the Supreme Court a couple of years ago. My friend Francine and her mother Elizabeth are here too. I've known them since childhood. My mother was pregnant with Marla and me, and Elizabeth with Fran when we all lived on Virginia Park in Windsor. Other friends we've known since childhood are also here, like Steven, Shelley and Abbee. Over a hundred friends of our mother and ourselves from the Windsor/Detroit area come to attend the funeral services. I am comforted by their presence.

At the cemetery, we bury her next to our father. Following Jewish custom, cousin Douglas heaves dirt to cover her grave.

The weather stays warm during the funeral and through the two remaining days of *shiva*. It is in the low 70s, which is unusual for November in Windsor. When the period of Jewish mourning ends, the next day there is a blizzard. The sky is gray, and the temperature is about two degrees Fahrenheit. The contradictory conditions between one day and the next mirror Mother's bipolar tendencies. When Marla and I clean out her apartment, my dream about the garden in its fallow season and the old babushka lady pulling a garment rack full of new underwear comes to life. In one of our mother's closets, we find a large suitcase. It is full of new bras and panties.

Chapter 47

IT IS MEANING TO OUR lives that we are all looking for. Understanding the circumstances we find ourselves in from moment to moment. The more deeply I dig into myself, the better tarot reader I am.

After doing hundreds and hundreds of tarot readings, I have yet to meet a dull "ordinary" person. Yes, many people have issues. I've read for the poor, for professors at Stanford, and for prison guards. Once people learn through their reading that they can overcome personal blocks, their cards reveal that they are rich with amazing, inner gifts and undiscovered talents.

Shuffling, then randomly choosing tarot cards might seem accidental, or by chance, just like the randomness of my murder on Martha's Vineyard, but the card picked can be highly significant and its meaning might be transformational.

In a reading, we witness an oracle at work. The traditional meaning of the word "oracle" is "seer, revelation, and place." I am the seer, the revelations are the insights my clients receive from the random picking of the cards and the words spoken, and Santa Barbara is a place of the oracle (a bit like the legendary Oracle at Delphi). When my clients work to go beyond their initial tarot reading, this will develop the seer within them too. It entails using their reasoning mind and intuition to comprehend the world defined by numbers and symbols. These symbols can be personal, cultural, and universal.

The tarot reading is the first big step to unravel answers to questions that drive someone to see me. Doing the homework afterward—the research, meditation, and contemplation—is the process that integrates the reading and the cards into one's life. It is the foundation for more revelations to arise from the oracle. The mystical Kabbalah is explained as "received knowledge."

I give lessons and lectures in the tarot and the Kabbalah to aid people in their self-discovery. Sometimes we feel stuck and do not know what the next step to take is. A method to solve this dilemma, without relying on the cards, is to pay attention to the coincidences and the unexpected events in one's life. "Street tarot" means using the signs, symbols, and wonders found in everyday life. Many people notice the occurrence of a favorite number, and they feel good when they see it.

People can move beyond this simple example and become aware of the personal, secret, symbolic language expressed outside themselves in seemingly happenstance ways. Synchronicity, or meaningful coincidence, provides guidance in times of confusion. To enhance personal growth, I encourage people to trust their intuitive powers and be open to receive. In our discernments, we should be ruthlessly honest with ourselves. Street tarot involves a sense of wonder. So does an open mind.

In the Kabbalah, there are a number of ways we can work with the ten *sephirot* to deepen our understanding of the divine mystery between the unknowable, unchanging, everlasting *Ein Sof* and ourselves. First, the Tree of Life glyph shows how essential energy flows through the ten power centers on the tree. The phenomenology of life in creation unfolds along the twenty-two pathways that connect the *sephirot*, which can be associated with the tarot cards and the letters of the Hebrew alphabet.

For study and as mystical practice aids, we can make a line drawing of this glyph. I remember when Charles made a nine-foot image on butcher's paper and laid it on the floor for the meditation group to sit around. It is best to start with a much smaller drawing to learn the proportions and arrangements of the *sephirot* in the four Kabbalistic worlds: the spiritual, intellectual, emotional, and physical realms.

Victoria, from my study group, and I take this to the level of fine art. I draw the tree on a sixty by twenty-inch piece of heavy cardboard. We both paint the tree and the background with acrylics. A few years later, with Victoria as my art consultant, I outline and then paint a Tree of Life glyph onto a seventy-two by thirty-six-inch stretched canvas using the proportions of my body as a measure. It's important to note that our human body, male or female, is directly aligned with the lower seven *sephirot* and the upper three are like an aura that hovers near the right and left ears and above our heads. This aspect of nonlocality shows that the self does not stop at the skin. To properly capture the depth and the mood, I use metallic paint. It takes many months to color the background, enhance the pathways, and display the dynamics of the *sephirot* on the Tree of Life.

My studies in Kabbalah continue as I learn more about myself and my connection to the Divine. I do my own tarot readings and also attend a number of workshops conducted by rabbis. One such class, whose title is about black and white fires, centers on writing the traditional handwritten Torah scroll. Along with a few of the other people in attendance, I lean over the shoulder of the young rabbi as he demonstrates the precision a scribe needs to precisely write the sacred Hebrew letters. One error would disqualify the entire scroll. The scribe would have to start all over again.

An opportunity arises for me to ask the rabbi a question. "From the Babylonian Talmud," I say, "I understand that the dark ink of the sacred Hebrew letters represents the black fire. The white parchment, from the hide of a kosher animal, forms the spaces around the letters and between the words and represents the white fire. But from the title of your workshop, what does 'white fire on black fire' mean?"

The rabbi tugs on his beard for a moment, then says, "I don't know."

I find his answer—or lack of one—astonishing, but I say nothing.

White fire on black fire. Black fire on white fire.

These words are important to me. They describe the electric-like grid of squares that appeared in my mind's eye when I lay dead on Martha's Vineyard. The number of squares reduced in geometric regression until there was only a one. That's when I knew it was time to break back into life.

Subsequent studies on my own bring me to the Jerusalem Talmud, a commentary on the second century *Mishnah*, or Jewish oral tradition, which acknowledges that God first gave Moses the Torah engraved with white fire on black fire. The Torah was given in fiery flashes, letters flying and rising through the air (*Zohar* 2:226b). But because Moses could not understand and discern the words of the Torah, God presented it as black fire on white fire. The Torah is dynamic, and some Kabbalists refer to it as the instrument that brought about creation.

Chapter 48

SINCE MY MOTHER'S DEATH, MY heart has been heavy, but the frequent telephone talks with my Aunt Gladys have been comforting and have helped me to focus on the law and my legal responsibilities.

But now I need a break. A long break. Not only am I teaching a course at a law school in Santa Barbara, but it's also been thirteen years and four terms as a court-appointed federal criminal appeals attorney in the Court of Appeals for the Ninth Circuit. I find it to be a great honor to handle cases of major crimes occurring in the United States, and I am proud of the high degree of professionalism with which I conducted my legal practice, but for now, at least, I am done fighting for justice and fairness in the legal system. So in February 2014, I go back to the university. At California State University, Fullerton, I learn more economic stuff, in particular, how the stock market works and how to understand financial statements.

At the same time, I take the advice of my friend Stephen, a freelance writer from Windsor, Ontario, and begin to develop the craft of creative nonfiction writing. Decades earlier, and without any training, I had written about two hundred pages of a memoir. Rereading the piece now gives me a stomachache. After listening to hours and hours of CDs from the Great Courses on the subject of writing, I decide to start over from scratch. This happens more than once. I also attend many semesters of Shelly Lowenkopf's brilliant memoir-writing course, in which I improve my skills related to narrative voice, and making dialogue not sound like it comes from a trial transcript. I also tried reading passages of my memoir out loud and then editing the drafts according to Shelly's and the other students' critiques.

Meanwhile, I travel east for Christmas in Connecticut in 2016. My brother, who retired from investment banking, went back to school, and earned a master's degree in theoretical physics. He was divorced but is now remarried to a beautiful lady. I love his former wife and his new one too. She is great fun, an aware woman who acts as a psychic bridge between Jamie and his sisters. One of my nephews is studying at Cornell University and is on the school's paintball team. His plan is to go to law school. (He does.) My other nephew is soon headed to Yale to study physics.

On this same trip back east, I also visit New York City to bring in the new year with Marla. As the founder and director of a nonprofit, the Peace Caravan Project, she's been to Afghanistan, China, Egypt, Israel, Syria, and Uganda. The project's mission is to document my sister's cultural and religious solo journey along the Silk Road and other ancient trade routes through photographs and videos, about which she gives educational presentations and lectures. The New York Foundation for the Arts is the nonprofit's fiscal sponsor. I am the organization's legal advisor.

Over the holidays, my sister and I agree to meet Ms. Dark-Haired Beauty at a Greek restaurant. She is the vivacious person I met when I visited Marla in London, England, in the mid-1980s. That was the time I looked forward to a dinner with my sister and her two friends. They had taken courses together at Sotheby's, the fine art auctioneers. Now jump ahead thirty years.

Marla and Ms. Dark-Haired Beauty have reunited in New York City, where they both live. They are good friends. The subject of our dinner conversation eventually turns to the memoir I'm writing and the attack on Martha's Vineyard. "The man was caught," I tell them, "but a legal determination had to be made to see if he was fit to stand trial. The judge ordered a psychiatric evaluation. This usually takes two to three weeks. Instead, the guy who left me for dead, John Lasinski, was held in the Bridgewater State Hospital for six months. Years later, I heard about an ethics investigation of the Treatment Center for Sexually Dangerous Persons at Bridgewater, which found that the psychiatrist and staff were having sexual relations with the inmates."

"That's incredible," says my sister.

"There was a film made about the terrible conditions at Bridgewater in the 1960s," I add. "It was called *Titicut Follies*. Inmates were forced to strip naked and were hardly bathed. But I haven't seen the documentary. And I don't want to."

Ms. Dark-Haired Beauty puts her fork down and pushes her chair back from the table. "You guys won't believe this," she says. "My mother was a therapist at Bridgewater. She used to bring the patients home all the time for dinner. She ended up marrying one of them."

"What a coincidence!" I look at Marla, then at Ms. Dark-Haired Beauty. "Ask your mother if she would be willing to talk to me. The man who left me for dead was a patient there in the fall and winter of 1978–1979. That's the period I'm interested in."

"I'll see. But she's not feeling well." Ms. Dark-Haired Beauty shakes her head and shrugs.

"Well, don't push her."

A few days later, I hear back. Her mother does not want to speak to me. She had left Bridgewater a few years before

Lasinski was under observation there, and it's understandable that she might not want to discuss confidential information about her colleagues. Nevertheless, something else related to Ms. Dark-Haired Beauty's revelations occurs. My heart opens up and fills with even more compassion for her. I get a glimpse of her past. Perhaps when she was a teenager, she might have wanted more of her mother's attention and, instead, her mother heaped her affection onto the current inmate under her care.

I see the mother's behavior as confirmation of the continuing unconventional relationships between the Bridgewater psychiatric staff and their patients. It also begs the questions. Did this pattern persist with Lasinski? Was his doctor's assessment sound? Based on my experience, I can only speculate about why John S. Lasinski killed me.

Chapter 49

ALSO IN 2016, I MEET the future editor of my memoir. Among the dozen or more editors at the writers' conferences I attend this year, Barbara Ardinger stands out, not only because of her spiked, pink-tipped haircut, but also the quality of the markups she did to the five pages of my writing submission. We have ten minutes to chat. When she mentions the mystery writer Raymond Chandler, I know I have to rewrite the whole manuscript. Even though he wrote fiction, I also know I want to work with Barbara. She can help with my true crime story and also the mystical aspects and the subsequent six divine directives.

It takes me a year to do the rewrite. Then in November 2017, she begins to work her editing magic on the metaphorical garden of my memoir. Armed with a PhD in English and brutal honesty, she metaphorically rips out the weeds around the flowers of my writing and expertly prunes my trees to make my writing the best it can be. And all the while, she teaches me with her edits, suggestions, and critiques.

In late December, Santa Barbara and Ventura counties experience the largest fire in the history of California, after which the winter rains turn the barren burn areas of the mountainsides into mud that brings a runoff of death and devastation. Many people are under mandatory evacuations. The whir of helicopter blades can be heard all day and into dusk as first responders rescue people now stranded. Everyone knows someone who has perished in the tragedy of these past few weeks. A lot of smoke and ash and sadness are in the air. To walk outside anywhere in the county, we must wear face masks.

After the torrential rains end, a friend comes to town. This is Ron, the guy from Toronto who introduced me to porn videos and made delicious salads we could eat with bread, not forks. When I lived in Toronto during the 1980s, there were times when I felt low. His friendship saved me.

Now, thirty years later, Ron's timing is perfect. On the surface, he is a wordsmith and a great cook with a great sense of humor, and his presence helps to lift my spirits. He is also one of the most lovable, charming, and nicest sexually deviant persons I've ever known. While his escapades don't stop at porn movies, everything he does is consensual and with age-appropriate women. He is the ideal person to talk to about why Lasinski killed me. The police and the newspaper understood it as a sexual assault. Even with my background in criminal law, I feel it is Ron who can help me understand the Evil Man's perverse nature.

Another reason Ron's timing is perfect is that we both love football. After he prepares homemade pizzas and a salad of fresh dandelion leaves he picked in Alameda Park and washed about a dozen times, we settle in to watch two NFL playoff games held on Saturday, January 13, 2018.

On Sunday, other good friends of mine invite us to watch the Saints and the Vikings play. I know Ron will enjoy them and the game. I first met J'Nelle when she entertained my friend Gary and me at one of Gail's parties with stories about her camel-caravan journey in the deserts of Morocco. J'Nelle has a most youthful spirit, wears her three-foot-long hair tied in back in a braid, and is fun to be around, especially at art gallery shows or just taking long walks in nature. She also introduced me to her husband, Stephen Holland, a down-to-earth, world-renowned portrait and sports action artist. He's been commissioned by famous baseball, football, and basketball players and sports teams to paint their portraits. He tells great stories of his adventures, and misadventures, as a youth in the Bronx.

We have a blast watching the football game. There's lots of talking, and everyone's into the action. Stephen's brother John is up on all the sports stats, and so we are current about who's who and their physical capabilities. The Minnesota Vikings take the playoff win over the New Orleans Saints. J'Nelle is a beautiful Southern belle (born in Louisiana) who doesn't fret over her team's loss.

After the game, when we are back at my house, we discuss Ron's plans to cook up a storm for my birthday dinner next week. He's going to bring a large rack of ribs marinating in a Tupperware bowl and barbeque it at Gail's house. She's hosting the party. He has seven other dishes to cook too. We've invited J'Nelle, Stephen, and Peter.

After we've discussed the food, I change the subject and ask Ron what he thinks could have driven Lasinski to attack me.

"For men, the desire starts in the head," he says. His eyes sparkle as he talks.

"As a fantasy, even to kill someone?" I ask.

"Yes, Myra. Okay, I've never had anywhere near a desire like that, so I have no idea what would make someone get off by killing or maiming or harming anyone. But I do know a lot about what culture might call sexually abnormal behavior. Threesomes, foursomes, watching, swingers' clubs, sex clubs, bondage, and so on." He giggles as he lists some of his activities.

I don't feel at all uncomfortable hearing his words. Quite the opposite: he gives me courage to share something. "Well,"

I begin, "I was once with a lovely married couple and a dear girlfriend. Both times, it was more like mutual foreplay plus a one-time anthropological experience. I was young and curious. It wasn't the result of any driving desire of mine. I have a feeling of genuine love for them all."

Ron laughs. "For me, it's the driving desire."

I chuckle too, then add in a more serious tone, "The difference is that Lasinski's conduct was criminal. He grabbed hold of me without my consent. He was intent on killing me. This accounts for why the Commonwealth of Massachusetts charged him with assault and battery, attempted rape, and attempted murder."

Ron nods his head. "The criminal aspect of Lasinski's act is part of the fuel that drives him to act. It's all in his head. He first imagines the acts. This arouses him too. Maybe even more than actually doing it."

"So anticipation of the moment is when the excitement starts?" I ask.

"The anticipation builds the energy. Sometimes it can be more powerful than the actual act. It's the energy that leads him to make the images in his head real. The thought of doing it stimulates him. He is hooked. He really wants to do it. You know, this feeling can be explosive."

Trying to process what Ron is saying, I ask, "When Lasinski attacked me and left me for dead, he was so calm. How could he appear so calm? He never said a word to me."

"He might appear to be calm. On the outside, he seems calm. But inside, his heart is racing." Ron taps his chest to the beat of his heart. "Ba-boom. Ba-boom. That energy needs to be released. He's thought out and planned every detail. He knows how he's going to do it."

"So he went to Martha's Vineyard to fulfill his desire?"

"Yes." Ron nods again. "He's on the prowl. It's visceral. The energy starts to build. Scoping out the place is the beginning of the buildup. He wants to let the fantasy scenario in his head play out on the island. The bestial nature is on the hunt."

Ron's words are powerful. "When I first saw Lasinski, it was his shiny white van that caught my attention. Victor and I had just purchased a used Toyota mini-pickup to come to the island and then to take me to a job interview in Lawrence, Massachusetts. And there was Lasinski, leaning against a shiny white van. But I only saw the back of him. Even so, his evil penetrated me. At that time, was he was on the prowl?"

"Yes."

"He was standing on the top of a cliff," I add, "and below was a famous nude beach. But it wasn't warm enough that day to be naked."

"Even so," Ron says, "he was definitely there to find his victim. He was already excited."

"Excited with expectancy?"

"Yes. That's part of it. The build-up. Feeling stimulated. Then he has to commit. He has to release to the desire. His inner world takes away any sense of morality and rationality. He needs the action, no matter the consequences. The desire is ruling him, commanding him."

"So," I say, "when Lasinski sees me walking on a narrow country road, he tells himself, 'This is my chance.' He was on his way to the beach to pick up his brother. But within a minute, he turned his van around and drove past me again. I lost sight of him while he was setting his plan to get me in motion."

"He's really charged up now," Ron says. "Obviously, part of his fantasy has to do with ambush and attack. Every detail is plotted out. Now his excitement builds and builds."

"Under the law," I conclude, "that would be premeditated murder. But he wasn't charged with that crime. He was looking under the hood of the van when I next saw him. I couldn't see his face. He'd concealed himself from me. A part of his surprise tactic, eh?" I go quiet for a moment, then add, "His eyes revealed what he was thinking. He didn't want to stare me down while I was walking toward him. But I had no choice because I was on my way back to Victor's place. At first, I thought he might be a neighbor, but when I got a few yards away from him, I knew. He was the Evil Man."

"Myra, while he was under the van's hood, he was probably overcome with excitement. And thinking, 'It's gonna happen. It's gonna happen. It's gonna happen.' This is his moment. This is the time to make his desires real."

It is past midnight when Ron and I finish talking. Our conversation has moved me and stirred my thoughts.

Chapter 50

NEWS ABOUT SPECIAL COUNSEL ROBERT Mueller's counterespionage and criminal investigation into whether US President Donald Trump and members of the Trump campaign conspired with Russian President Vladimir Putin in Russia's sabotage of the 2016 presidential elections to put Trump into the White House, captures my attention and temporarily satisfies my legal appetite. While writing this memoir, I have taken a sabbatical from the practice of law and sublimated my lack of legal work with opining about Trump's criminal exposure, and his possible impeachment, with family and friends. Ron is one of these friends.

After he cleans the fish he just caught at the Santa Barbara pier, I help him cook it and the rest of the meal. As we work, we chat about the status of the federal indictments and the number of Trump's associates who've already pleaded guilty. Although he's a Canadian, my friend has an interest in US affairs and a legal bent too.

This is why I can talk to him about the case against the Evil Man. Ron successfully represented himself in the Ontario provincial courts against wrongful charges. He is not a criminal. He's not dangerous. And he's different from John S. Lasinski in another way too.

Ron's never been married. He's lived with two women, each for more than seven years. A famous rock 'n' roll singer and great girl who is now living in Los Angeles and married to a hip lawyer, was one of them and still his good friend. He had three kids with MK, the other women he lived with, and they also remain close. On his first date with his current girlfriend, when he told her about his unusual sexual proclivities, she said, "Where do I sign up?" They've been together for more than thirteen years.

A couple of days after my conversations with Ron, the film noir ringtone on my iPhone breaks my concentration. It's Chris, the sea captain and my former fiancé. We are still good friends, and we often talk politics and about deep spiritual stuff too. He is also one of the kindest, most wonderful, and most sexually uninhibited people I know. Which is one reason why we broke up. He's too advanced for me. Since we've split, he's been married and divorced and married and divorced. He is the perfect person with whom I can speculate about the Evil Man's married life.

"The greatest sex starts in the head," says Chris. "Desire might come from a perverse sense of curiosity. It's the forbidden fruit. His marriage might be a morality trap. His morality, perhaps his upbringing, won't allow him to kill his wife, so he transposes his desire. In a relationship, especially a marriage, one is dominant in the giving and receiving. This might switch or it might not, depending on the circumstances. Maybe one side feels repressed. Maybe Lasinski needed to be the dominant one. Or his wife might have been too overpowering, so he took the oppression and refocused his anger and his frustration by dominating another person through force and violence."

I think about that for a moment, then say, "I know you were a paratrooper in the military where killing is different."

"Yes," he says. "In war, killing is your job and you want to survive. You don't think about it as the killing someone.

You're removing an obstacle. It's not personal." He goes quiet for a moment.

I let his words sink in, then say, "I just have to ask. You must have been upset with your wife at some time and gotten divorced. But did you ever want to kill her?"

"I had to get a divorce. Of course, I never thought of killing her. I just wanted her out of my life. This Lasinski was different though. He was in a personal ritual where fantasy takes over. His wife or family events might not have triggered his fantasy. Maybe it was just the thought: what would it feel like to put my hands around someone's neck? The basics are not overly complicated. You see something on TV. It starts something in your head. The fantasy builds and builds . . . until the thoughts run you. Then the parameters come together. You have a plan, and then you see an opportunity."

"I think the doctors misdiagnosed him," I say. "He actually was sexually dangerous. I remember when I talked to the district attorney after Lasinski pleaded guilty. As a condition of his release, he had to undergo a psychiatric examination to evaluate if he was sexually dangerous. From my own legal practice, I know criminals. They are highly manipulative people. They can appear charming, but emotionally they can be void of compassion. Maybe Lasinski's wife was tougher than him . . . but I can only speculate about that. Presumably, he told his wife in Syracuse that he needed to go on a fishing vacation. He wanted to be alone, away from her and their kid. He figured he could go off and prowl for a woman while his brother was fishing. He would have been alone on the island for hours and hours. Thinking about his planned conquest. That's why Lasinski wasn't fishing with his brother that fateful day.

"It was late September," I continue. "Maybe his wife stayed home because their kid was in school. Nevertheless, Lasinski was out roaming on Martha's Vineyard. Perhaps he turned his frustration with his wife into taking control over another woman. I think that day, September 23, 1978, he went out to kill. That was the day my life was forever changed."

I remain quiet and think to myself, Victor's life was altered too. Because of what happened, we started taking martial arts together, and when I moved to Ottawa, he stayed behind but continued to train hard and achieved a black belt in karate. Later, he opened a martial arts supply store in Vancouver.

Feelings of fear, doubt, and worry can be my constant companions. This is part of life. But because of my efforts, I've learned how to give them no attention. Some days I am better at it than other days.

Because I can only speculate about his motive to kill me, I have occasionally flirted with the idea of talking to the Evil Man to get his side of the story. Now I have no inclination to try to locate John S. Lasinski. Perhaps someone reading this memoir knows him and can help set something up. Please leave the information on my blog page at www.myrandomdeath.com. You never know what might transpire. Mind you, it must be credible and verifiable information. No scams. No pranks. State nothing but the truth, as you know it. Or if you, John Lasinski, are reading this, please know that you can contact me. I am emotionally stronger now and ready to meet with you. Most important, you are forgiven. The value of the incident coalesced when I came back to life and received the divine directives. My primary task now is to continue to master them.

While I'm reading about the black and white fires in the *Zohar*, which is a seminal text of Kabbalah, an informative but paradoxical phrase jumps out at me: a spark of impenetrable darkness flashed . . .

Perhaps the *Zohar's* poetic and symbolic language describes what we call "miracles," those fortuitous occurrences that come out of the depths of despair. We also think they're happenstance. One of their messages is "Don't let these random events pass you by, like flashes of light that quickly disappear and then are forgotten. Contemplating them may lead to opportunities." Another way of looking at the phrase from the *Zohar* is contained in common sayings like "Every cloud has a silver lining" and "Look for the silver lining." In other words, within the darkness exists indiscernible light that we cannot see with our eyes but which we all can intuit with our inner wisdom.

What have I learned so far? Develop and trust my intuition. Couple this with a rational assessment of my everyday life. Value my dreams. Notice details. Pay attention to the street tarot, or the personal signs, symbols, and wonders within the commonplace. Dig deep, and then layers of meaning will reveal themselves. Stay curious and want to learn more.

My journey into self-discovery isn't over yet. I'm sure there's more to come.

Acknowledgments

MY MEMOIR CAME TO BE WITH the loving help, encouragement, and support of my brother and sister. I was born wealthy because they are in my life. Marla read and reread the drafts, gave me insightful critiques, and persuaded me to dig deeper and express more of myself. She and Jamie both offered critical suggestions at the final draft stage.

My love and gratitude goes to Victor.

My friend from Windsor, Stephen, a freelance writer and a deep-thinking man, advised me to take creative nonfiction writing classes. I started by listening to the Great Courses audios of professors of English and nonfiction writing. This led me to take many semesters, offered through the Santa Barbara City College continuing education programs, with the inspiring instructor of memoir writing, Shelly Lowenkopf.

I was blessed to work with the editor Barbara Ardinger. An author herself, with a PhD in English, she is a living treasure for writers. Equally wonderful is the Insight Institute Press' publishing team who worked on my memoir: the Zen-like Master book producer, Gail Kearns, calmly shepherded us through the book publishing process; and Deborah Perdue, a most creative book designer, graciously collaborated on the cover and interior designs.

Ron Iuliani came up with the book's title.

A special thank you to the *Vineyard Gazette*.

www.ingramcontent.com/pod-product-compliance
Lightning Source LLC
Chambersburg PA
CBHW030302080526
44584CB00012B/404